Alligood writes with a tr   n-
gers and shenanigans that

—Capt. Richard C. Noble
Port Captain
Offshore Towing Division
Seabulk/Seacor Marine Inc.

Experiencing Hurricane Rita and the immediate recovery effort in the good company of Captain Bill Alligood made reading his manuscript all the more enjoyable.

—Captain Jim Robinson
U.S. Coast Guard (Retired)

I am very proud to say I endorse Captain Alligood's book.

—Bebo Smith
Sr. Director of Operations
Port Manatee, Florida

Cap'n Bill's book is a collection of sea yarns, personal recollections, and amusing anecdotes told in a very warm and affable style that makes the reader feel as though they were there, experiencing each event with the author.

—Jim Stone,
Deck Hand (Retired)

I am honored to endorse this well thought out book.

—Capt. David K. Scarborough.
Master Mariner.

My lifetime on the water

Al,
Take care my friend and
May God Bless
Captain William C. Alligood

My lifetime on the water

as told in my own words
about tug boating

Captian William C. Alligood

TATE PUBLISHING & *Enterprises*

TATE PUBLISHING
& Enterprises

Tate Publishing is committed to excellence in the publishing industry. Our staff of highly trained professionals, including editors, graphic designers, and marketing personnel, work together to produce the very finest books available. The company reflects the philosophy established by the founders, based on Psalms 68:11,

"THE LORD GAVE THE WORD AND GREAT WAS THE COMPANY OF THOSE WHO PUBLISHED IT."

If you would like further information, please contact us:
1.888.361.9473 | www.tatepublishing.com
TATE PUBLISHING & Enterprises, LLC | 127 E. Trade Center Terrace
Mustang, Oklahoma 73064 USA

Published in the United States of America

ISBN: 978-1-5988685-4-8

07.03.15

AUTHOR'S NOTE

Have you ever wondered what it's like to work aboard a tugboat? This book will answer some questions that you might have about the tug boater's life. My name is Captain "Bill" Alligood; I have worked aboard tugboats for over twenty-nine years, which is also why I have written *My Lifetime on the Water* to share the experiences that I have actually lived. I started in 1977 as a deckhand; I then obtained my Master of Towing license in 1980 where I worked as a relief Captain until 1987, when I was then given a full time Captain's position. I worked mainly in harbor service until 1996 and then transferred to the newer and larger Tractor tugs that the company had built in 1995 and 1996, those three tugs also worked on offshore jobs.

I have been married for thirty-seven years with four wonderful children and one beautiful granddaughter. I have written this book with the hopes of showing how I have spent most of my adult life. I have worked in different ports throughout the Gulf of Mexico, which includes Mexico, Texas, Louisiana, Mississippi, and most major ports in the state of Florida, the East coast of the United States, as well as Puerto Rico, and Trinidad, doing all types of tugboat work.

This book is also a collection of some of the most memorable jobs I have encountered throughout my Maritime career. While some stories are funny, others are of a more serious content, while still others are related to my home life. I have also tried to write them in a chronological order, to help the readers experience the steps I took from being a deckhand, to a Captain of conventional tugboats, then progressing on to the bigger more powerful Tractor tugs. I have operated some twenty-seven tugboats over the years, and at the start of this book, I was the Captain aboard one of the most powerful, high-tech, state of the art Tractor tugs that was working in the Gulf of Mexico.

I have so many stories to tell that related to working aboard a tugboat, the stormy seas, and even the hurricanes we encountered when on duty. While mainly working in Tampa, Florida, the latter years of my career took me places I never dreamed I would see. I was even in Trinidad in 1999, which is also when I lost my Father while I was working down there. At times, it seems like just yesterday that I was a deckhand chipping and painting, but in reality, I'm glad those days are gone and I can enjoy the wheelhouse view of which I have written stories about in both of those classifications.

This book is about the last three decades of my life, which to me has been a very interesting career. I hope you too will experience them through my writings. There is so much to tell with twenty-nine years behind me; however, I am sure that when this book is read, the readers will yearn for more of what we Seamen call our "Sea Stories."

ACKNOWLEDGMENTS

I have enjoyed writing my first book, of which my hat goes off to anyone who has also written a book, there is an incredible amount of work that goes into it. I thank everyone that I have worked with throughout the years that either gave me guidance, or that trained me in the proper operation of the many tugs that I have operated over twenty-nine years to date. The experience that I acquired was taken with thankful gratitude.

I give thanks foremost to Almighty God, for giving me the opportunity to experience the past twenty-nine years in an industry that is also intoxicating for some. Then for giving me, the will and fortitude to undertake such a challenging project as this book has been. Philippians 4:13 (KJV) says, "I can do all things through Christ which strengtheneth me." I needed him to watch over me with divine guidance from the beginning, which he did.

Secondly, I have to thank Captain Carroll Dale for teaching me the ropes of the trade in the beginning of my career, and for also becoming my lifelong friend. He has also been involved in a large part of my personal life as well, as seen in my writings. Carroll was a natural boatman until he retired, and from the time that I started working on the tugs, he never lost his operational skills that he passed on to me.

Thirdly, Chief Engineer Bob Taylor, he left the company years ago. During the years that I worked with Bob were also the years that I enjoyed the tugboats the most. Bob was a natural engineer who took his job seriously; he also left me with a large selection of material to choose from, of which I used in the book. Having worked with him for so many years, I miss his presence and hope he is doing well.

I also thank the Management from the previously operated companies, Manatee Tug and Barge Lines, St. Philip Towing, Bay Transportation Corporation, Hvide Marine Corporation, and Seabulk Towing of Tampa. Finally, Seacor Holdings, which was the name of the last company from the years of Marine Tugboat Company acquisitions that had taken place since my initial employment, and was also the last company that I worked for, thank you all for allowing me to serve as an employee.

I have mentioned some one hundred and thirteen people throughout this book; most I knew personally, while others were involved within the Maritime Industry. There were those that contributed more than others had, while still others just happened to be involved in some of the stories written. However, the first two people aforementioned also happened to be my first crew aboard a tugboat and had a significant influence in my life, not only as a seaman, but also as close friends.

I also want to acknowledge my wonderful wife Lois, who never wavered from the beginning of this book to its completion, of the huge task that I had undertaken to attempt and ultimately accomplish. My immediate family also helped by giving me the confidence needed with their continual positive critique during the writing. I wish that I had another twenty-nine years to work on the water, but all good things must come to an end.

I thank everyone, and may God Bless you one and all.

Liliana and Paw Paw with the Mighty tug *Hawk*

*I dedicate this book to the brave Seamen that have
died or have been lost at sea over the years.*

TABLE OF CONTENTS

MY LIFETIME ON THE WATER

As told in my own words about tug boating

When I started working in the Marine Industry on tugboats over twenty-eight years ago, the date was March 28, 1977. I never knew what an adventurous roller coaster ride I was about to have. Having a lifetime of events to share, with some being funny, while others are not, they are of times past. With that in mind, I thought I would try my hand at writing a book, since I have been told throughout the years that I expressed things good in print. I will tell some stories that'll be funny, with the hopes of making people laugh.

While some will be sad and bring tears to your eyes, still others might reflect on their own life experiences, and can relate to them in their own past. Most will be job related, but there will be some that I must share, just because of its relationship to my home life. Finally, while not written in a chronological order, they are written in my own words, and are true to the best of my recollection, please enjoy.

This is a list of the tugboats I have worked aboard throughout tʰ years, I either ran them for jobs and eventually became the Captain trained others in their operation.

1. *Palmetto*-3,300 hp single screw tug ~ my first boat assignme
2. *Bradenton*-3,300 hp single screw tug ~ first boat as relief C
3. *Yvonne St. Philip*-3,300 hp single screw tug ~ first boat as
4. *Gloria St. Philip*-3,300 hp single screw tug
5. *A.P. St. Philip*-3,300 hp single screw tug
6. *Canaveral*-3,600 hp single screw tug
7. *Orange*-2,000 hp single screw tug ~ she was built in 19

8. *Laura*-2,400 hp single screw tug
9. *Edna St. Philip*-3,300 hp twin screw tug ~ slow boat
10. *Challenger*-3,600 hp twin-screw tug
11. *Tampa*-6,000 hp twin-screw tug ~ Carroll retired on this tug
12. *Trooper*-1,000 hp twin-screw tug
13. *Harbor Island*-1,000 hp twin-screw tug ~ Panama City trip
14. *Ybor*-1,600 hp twin-screw tug
15. *Ray Hebert*-1,600 hp twin-screw tug
16. *Winslow C. Kelsey*-4,300 hp stern drive Tractor tug
17. *Hawk*-6,700 hp stern drive Tractor tug ~ Captain at start of book
18. *Condor*-6,700 hp stern drive Tractor tug
19. *Eagle II*-6,700 hp stern drive Tractor tug ~ duty in Mexico
20. *Reliant*-4,300 hp stern drive Tractor tug
21. *Kinsman Falcon*-3,000 hp conventional Tractor tug
22. *Escambia*-4,000 hp SDM, (Ship Docking Module)
23. *St. Johns*-4,000 hp SDM, (Ship Docking Module)
24. *Suwannee River*-4,300 hp SDM, (Ship Docking Module)
25. *Seabulk Katie*-4,300 hp stern drive Tractor tug, duty in Trinidad
26. *Seabulk Carolyn*-4,300 hp stern drive Tractor tug, duty in Mexico
27. *Osprey*-4,000 hp stern drive Tractor tug

In the Maritime Industry we also call the propellers, screws, so when a boat is referred to as a twin-screw boat, she has two propellers. Tractor tugs are unique when it comes to their operation; they have what is known as Azimuthing drives, or Z-Drives, where there are no rudders for steering. Instead, the drives rotate 360 degrees, where the propellers are mounted in kort nozzles, which magnify the direction of the thrust. Operating these boats is a tug boater's dream. I believe their maneuverability is unsurpassed by only one other tugboat, which is the SDM.

The first Tractor tugs that the company built (*Eagle* and *Falcon*), have he drives forward of midship. These type boats look like they're running ackwards and use the stern as if it were the bow; that is where their line nch is located. The SDM's are different, yet they have a Z-drive prosion unit on each end of the boat, eleven feet off the centerline, one he port side, and one on the starboard.

hey too have their line winch on the stern, with all of the ship dock-

Captain Bill Alligood aboard the tug *Yvonne St. Philip* in 1988-Courtesy of George Atkins

ings and sailings being done from the stern. I started on a single screw tug, however, at the start of writing this book I was serving as the Captain of one of the most powerful stern drive Tractor tugs working in the Marine Industry today. She was the Tractor tug *Hawk*, working for Seabulk Towing Inc. based in Tampa, Florida.

CHANGING JOBS

This is how it all began for me. I had been working the past six and a half years with the Manatee County Port Authority, which was a new Sea Port in Tampa Bay, Florida. Whenever we as line handlers pulled the lines from the ships during the dockings or sailings of the vessels in Port Manatee, I was able to observe the tugs during the jobs and was very impressed. With their graceful maneuverability, they seemed to have the agility that swans have when they danced on the water.

I was always amazed at the power of the smaller but mighty tugs, which seemed to push and pull on the much larger ships with such ease. I had the opportunity to get to know the crews aboard the tugs very well during my employment with the Port. At this particular point in my life, it seemed like a good decision for me to make a move to the tug company, since a deckhand's job had recently came open, which was a rarity. Although working with the Port Authority would have also been a career job I could have retired from, I did not. After talking with the tug crews, it just seemed that the tugboats would be a more interesting, adventurous career.

My First Day on The Tug

The company those days was called Manatee Tug and Barge Lines Inc., which was a subsidiary of St. Philip Towing, with the main office being based in Tampa, Florida. The day I was put on the payroll was the beginning of my lifelong adventure working on the water, which ironically started with a pair of groundings. It all started with the tug *Tony St. Philip* being tripped and sinking while working on a grounded ship up the bay in "F" cut, just north of Port Manatee geographically.

Apparently when the ship came off the bottom from being grounded, the ship then came ahead to stop the sternway she had from the tugs pulling on her at the time of being freed. This resulted in the *Tony St. Philip* to be towed backwards, causing her to be pulled over sideways, tripping we call it, which resulted in her sinking. Certain boats could not be pulled backwards; single screw boats were in this category.

The tugboats *Palmetto* and *Bradenton* used Port Manatee as their home base at that time. It was a Friday, my last day working for the Port Authority, when we were called at home that night to report to the boat where we were to go assist another ship. The second grounding was one that had drifted aground attempting to avoid the grounding operations up the bay. The ship we were going to assist was the *Chevron Arnheim*, a loaded gasoline tanker that in reality had only drifted against the channel's bank. She just needed a little nudge to be pushed back in the channel, before continuing to her berth in Port Tampa.

My first boat assignment was the tug *Palmetto*, with Captain Carroll Dale and Bob Taylor as the engineer, both of whom I knew from working with the Port Authority. I had been assigned to a good crew. I had not worked with them on the boats, but my best observation was that Carroll was one of the better Captains working with the Company, and Bob was one of the better engineers. Throughout the years, we had numerous work schedules, which also varied between union contracts. This was something I had to adjust to, since the port had a schedule that did not change from week to week.

The schedule that the tugs were on that year was two weeks on, and one week off. When I was first hired on and started working with Carroll, he asked me what I wanted to do on the boats. I told him I wanted his job, since I was going to make tugging my career, I wanted to climb the ladder and go up. I said where the money was at is where I needed to be, and that was at the top, which just happened to be a Captain's position.

There was so much to absorb in learning the operation of the tugs. From learning the correct channels to navigate, to going alongside a moving ship, to the proper placement of the lines we used on the ships and barges that we assisted, and so much more. Carroll let me steer the boat whenever we were underway, going from place to place. After he observed me steering the boat for awhile, passing and overtaking other

The tug *Palmetto* was my first assigned tugboat-Author photo

traffic in the different channels, he said to me, "I do believe you're a natural." Well, that made me feel pretty good about what I had accomplished in the short time we had been working together. Although I already knew them, it's just not the same until you actually spend a lot of time with co-workers.

Carroll, Bob, and I talked a lot about different subjects in the beginning, from different jobs we had held, to their past experiences on the tugs, and even about our family values. These conversations helped bring us closer together not only as a crew, but better than that, it made us valued friends for life, as we are today.

Job Change Party at Home

I was twenty-six years old when I was hired to work on the tug, married to my beautiful wife Lois with two lovely children, William Charles II and Jeanne Marie. I came home one day and found out that my wife had planned a surprise new job party for me. She had made my favorite meal for supper, and afterwards my wife brought out a little cake she had baked that day. It was also decorated to look like the water with fish swimming in it, and it even had a toy tugboat placed on the top of it. This was how my wife viewed my career move; she said she would stand beside me, with whatever decision I made.

With the different work schedule than I was used to working, it wasn't long before I had figured out this might be like having a honeymoon every time I came home from working a tour. Anyone working on the water, or as far as that goes, anyone working away from home on any type job, it can test your relationship with your loved ones. The way I looked at it at the time, this was a great opportunity for me to make a better living for me and my family. I was also lucky to have an understanding wife, she told me, "You're the one having to work this schedule, go for it, we'll just deal with it." Whenever I started this book, we had been happily married for over thirty-six years.

Monkey's Fist Throw
Over The House

A monkey's fist is a seaman's aid in the transfer of lines from one vessel to another. They are usually made from a quarter inch to a three eighths inch line. It is formed into a ball lapping and weaving through itself at least four times, making it workable. Something round and heavy, like a ball of metal, is then inserted into the middle of what looks like a bird's nest. Then the lines are tightened one tuck at a time, until all the lines are tightened enough to not let the metal ball fall out. The *Palmetto* had a large chunk of lead; we would cut off a chunk about an inch squared, pound it round, and then insert it into our monkey's fist.

After being made, they are then spliced into the same size line to be used as a heaving line. That is tied to a tag line, usually a three quarter inch line, which is tied to our ship docking line, a nine to ten inch line. I had thrown these heaving lines before while being a line handler for the port. The heaving line was also used anytime we went alongside a high ship; I was also very proficient in this little task, thinking this is where it all went terribly wrong. Carroll had shown me how to make a monkey's fist using a butter knife for tightening the line, and all the little tricks. After making my first one, I asked him if I could take it home to show my young children what their Daddy had made. Saying yes, I put it away and could hardly wait to get home.

It was a sunny Saturday morning when I was finally heading home, but expected to be called back to work when a ship had ordered. I pulled in front of my house, parked my truck, and greeted my family inside the house. At the time, Will was seven years old and Jeanne Marie was five. After a little while and expecting a phone call anytime, it was time for the big show. I herded up my children with the neighbor kids; we were also the Kool-Aid house on our street.

I lined up my little audience and explained to them what the little rope ball was that Daddy was holding, and how it was actually used. I showed them how heavy it was; I even let each one of them hold it. Then I said, "Come on kids, let's all go to the back yard and I'll show y'all how it's thrown up in the air." If I had the ability to look into the future, the show and tell would have been enough for my little audience.

However, not having that ability, I put my little ducks in a row and made this bold statement, "Watch, this is how Daddy throws the monkey's fist when I'm on the boat." Having just the monkey's fist without the usual sixty feet of line spliced into it, I threw it as hard as I could. Now I'm standing in my backyard, probably one hundred and fifty feet from my front yard, facing the backside of my house.

The ideal throw would have been almost straight up into the air, coming down just a few feet away. When that monkey's fist left my hand, it made a perfect arch all the way over my house. Remembering where I had parked my truck when I came home, that monkey had put his fist right through the driver's side window of my truck. Hearing glass shatter, we all took off running towards the front of the house.

When I turned the corner and saw what had happened, I could have died. All the children were jumping up and down screeching and saying wheeee, my son said, "Do it again Daddy." I looked inside my truck and saw what looked to be ten thousand little pieces of glass, from on top of the dash to all over my seat and floor. My wife could only laugh hysterically and say, "I think the children enjoyed the show you put on for them." A broken window on a Saturday morning and with me expecting to be called back to work, I thought to myself what next, and then the phone rang.

I heard my wife say; "Hon, you have a phone call, it's the dispatcher." Yep, I had to go back to work; he said to get back to the boat ASAP. There was now only one thing to do, sweep the glass off the seat and hope it didn't rain until I could have the window replaced a couple of days later. Those kids' laughter was nothing in comparison to how Carroll and Bob laughed when I told them my monkey's fist story. It is also one of those things that we look back on and laugh at. Just like they say in Texas, "Oil well." (Oh well).

DIVING ON THE TUG

Tony St. Philip

My first work week, we were instructed to go to the tug *Tony St. Philips'* location where she had sank a few days earlier for line retrieval. When we arrived on site, one of us had to dive down to the tugs' bow and come back up with the tag line that was tied to the ship docking line. With me being the new man aboard the boat, I was elected to hit the water, so to speak. After diving down and retrieving the tag line, I threw the end of it up to Bob, who was still dry, and climbed back aboard the tug.

We then pulled the bow line from the sunken tugs deck out of the water by hand, and back then that's how it was done, because we didn't have a capstan on the boats. After showering and putting some dry clothes on, I went up to the wheelhouse, which was my new favorite place to be. I made the comment to Carroll that this is going to be a job I could get used to very quick.

I then asked Carroll, "Is this a normal activity that happens often, or is it something we did because of the sunk tug?" He tells me, "We do this kind of work all the time," but as time went on, I discovered Carroll was a big kidder. Carroll, Bob, and I also became known as the crew that got along with each other better than any other crew did. There were actually crews that were envious at the way we worked so well together and tried to break us up. We did our job and we did it well, so we just let our performance speak for itself, which kept us together until 1980. That was when I had gone to Sea School, then sat for my Captains license and got it.

The Lash Barge Shuffle

I can remember one time when we were putting lash barges under the phosphate-loading chute in Port Manatee to be loaded. These lash barges were small barges that were put aboard a very large ship, usually loaded from the stern of the ship two barges at a time. The phosphate terminal would load the barges, and then we would take them and make them up in a tow. Three barges wide and five barges long, with two barges split in the middle on the bow end. We would usually have multiple tows made up, and on location before the ship came into their loading site.

At this particular time, we had worked for over thirty-four hours straight. This was also a time when there wasn't as many safety concerns or mandatory drug testing, which is totally opposite of today's rules and regulations. With working the hours we were asked to work, sometimes we needed all the help we could get, just so we could do our job. One of us had some "West Coast Turn Around" pills, as we called them, sort of like No-Doze. I do not condone this practice nowadays, but after taking them, we were able to keep going for as long as need be, and I can say, "Without incident." After the particular long run we had just pulled, we were dispatched back to the dock, told to shut down with this job being over. Bob and I had told Carroll to ask the dispatcher, wasn't there something, anything that we could do; we were still ready to work?

He said no, "Go home," so we went home and drank some milk, killed the pills, and then slept like a baby for some well-needed rest. The reason we made the tows up in this way was to transport the seventeen-barge tows to a predetermined place, where the tows could then be broken back down. With more tugboats assisting in the operation, they were then loaded aboard the ship. Some of these ships were usually too large to come into a berth for the loading operation.

I can remember one ship that had to anchor out at the Egmont Key anchorage, because of her height. She could not clear the old Sunshine Skyway Bridge, which had a vertical clearance of 151 feet back then. The newer Sunshine Skyway Bridge was constructed after the older bridge had been hit by a ship called the *Summit Venture*, back in 1980. The older bridge was replaced with a newer designed higher bridge, which now has a vertical clearance of 175 feet today.

THE SUNSHINE SKYWAY
BRIDGE COLLISION

We were coming on duty that fatal Friday morning, May 9 1980, when the ship *M/V Summit Venture* had a collision with the Sunshine Skyway Bridge. I had started to leave for work and actually waited on the weather to calm down some before leaving my home; the wind and rain seemed to be blowing extremely hard that particular morning.

I only live about six minutes from Port Manatee and had always left around 07:30 for work. I was now experiencing the weather that just minutes earlier had just entered Tampa Bay. We all had CB radios back then and kept hearing people talk about a bridge that was struck by a ship on the way into work. Then someone actually said it was the Skyway Bridge. When I heard that I wondered to myself, how much damage could a ship do to a bridge, not really knowing the whole story until later that day. When we arrived at Port Manatee where the boats were moored, we were immediately dispatched to the bridge, to give assistance where needed. When we arrived on the accident location, we were shocked at what we saw, even worse, what we didn't see.

We were instructed by the Pilot, Captain John Lerro, to assist the tug *Dixie Avenger*, which was another boat that had came to help. We were told to monitor the surrounding area for survivors that might be in the water. The site we were looking at was terrifying; the ship had hit one of the main bridge pilings, in turn knocking a large part of the upper span into the water, on the southbound bridge. We heard on the VHF radio that there were cars in the water, which was on the span at the time of the collision, or had just driven off of it for lack of visibility. We also heard that a Greyhound bus with some people on it had went into the water. A total of thirty-five souls were lost to a watery grave that fatal stormy morning.

We later put up a line on the ship and assisted in pulling her from under the bridge, she also had a large section of the bridge still on her bow, rendering her unable to drop her anchor. We had heard there was a man that had rode that section of the bridge down, still in his 1974 Ford Courier pickup truck, and survived. We stayed made up to the ship all that day and all that night, just holding her in the main ship channel while a decision was made as to what to do next.

While alongside the ship, we all reflected in a somber mood on the recent events, with what had just happened, no one was in a playful mood. This was especially disturbing after we were told to pick up anything we saw floating along in the water to help with identification purposes. With respect to the people still in the water, this was something we had eerily heard before.

We had plucked an assortment of things out of the water that day using a dip net we had on the boat. I suppose the most disturbing items were what appeared to be a picture of a family on vacation, and we also picked up a child's flip-flop shoe out of the water, which made us three grown men cry like little babies with sorrow and sadness. After we had picked up those items, we didn't talk much for a while. We just sat and stared at the damaged bridge, and cried for the poor families that had lost their loved ones this tragic stormy day.

This was the worst accident ever attributed to this bridge that anyone could remember in recent times. The next day, several tugs took the *Summit Venture* back out to the Egmont Key anchorage. Since the bow winch machinery had a bridge section on it, a crane barge was used to retrieve the anchor that was dropped just moments before the accident, the ships crew had also rigged some cable on it to be used for anchoring the vessel.

Holding the ship still in the anchorage, that same crane barge was then used to remove the anchor off the ship after connecting it to a cable. Using the crane, the anchor and cable was then attached to the *Palmetto's* quarter bitts with a nine-inch line. We used it as a strap, as used for hipping up to barges, this time it held the anchor secure while we backed away from the ship.

We discovered something that day that we had always been told for the truth, to be very false. When we were in position to drop the anchor, Carroll gave the signal by blowing the air horn. Bob had the fire axe honed sharp as a knife-edge, and with the axe over head, he was ready to cut the line. When he heard the horn, Bob came down on it with some force. The axe bounced back up and almost hit him in his face, actually curling the edge of the axe on the very first hit.

Not believing what we had just witnessed, we both said, "What was that, how is that possible?" We had always heard the tighter a line was, the easier it was to cut, and had been told with a tight line, all you really have to do was rub a sharp knife across it and the line would split apart. The anchor had the tug leaned over from its weight, we knew that line was tight. We ended up breaking out the infamous machete and chopping on the line like chopping on a tree limb.

It took several minutes to chop the line enough to eventually let gravity do its thing and put the anchor on the bottom. It was quite a while before things got back to normal, having to remove all the debris and the eight vehicles that had crashed into the water. Almost seven years passed before the replaced newer bridge was opened on April 30, 1987. The new bridge was constructed in sections, all of which was made at Port Manatee and taken out to the bridge site on barges.

The *USS Blackthorn* Disaster

Before the Sunshine Skyway Bridge catastrophe, there was another accident we were dispatched to assist with at the same location. We were waiting on the tanker *Capricorn* where we were to assist her into a berth at the Weedon Island power plant. We were waiting up the bay from the Skyway when we heard over the VHF radio that two ships had collided with a reported explosion. All vessels in the vicinity were to proceed to the Skyway bridge location and render assistance, so we immediately proceeded to the location of the accident.

When we were getting close, we were advised to retrieve anything floating, to aid in identification, something we would hear again in the near future. We learned the Coast Guard vessel *USS Blackthorn* had collided with the tanker *Capricorn*, and had sank almost directly under the bridge. Bob and I were taking turns picking up items of interest out of the water.

Well, it happened to be my turn and wouldn't you know it, there was something that looked like a human head floating about six inches under the water. Carroll and Bob kept saying they were glad they didn't have to dip that head out of the water; they probably already knew what it was, this just wasn't the time. All I kept thinking about was the reported explosion which was on my mind; I was also not looking forward to plucking this object out of the water. After Carroll pulled up close enough to get the dip net under it, you will never know the relief I had to discover it was only a large pink colored jellyfish instead of what I thought it was, I just yelled with a big relief.

That was the last laugh we had that we were able to enjoy for quite a while, especially after we had learned about the Coast Guard crewmembers that had just lost their lives. The *Blackthorn* had just departed from the shipyard from an extended period of time having work done to her. They were outbound approaching the bridge that every vessel has to go under when departing Tampa Bay, when tragedy struck. The smaller *Blackthorn* was no match to the much larger, and loaded oil tanker *Capricorn*. When they collided, the result was that the Coast Guard buoy tender *USS Blackthorn* capsizing.

The sinking of the *Blackthorn* literally shut down ship traffic in Tampa Bay, since it sank right in the channel close to the bridge. Needless to say, the commerce in the Tampa Bay area was in jeopardy, so there was some scrambling going on to come up with a plan to keep traffic coming and going. A plan was devised that would allow ships with shallower drafts to pass under the bridge through what was called the alternate channel.

This chosen channel was between the two pilings just north of the main channel pilings, it was not near as wide, but was accessible to Tampa Bay with limited beam width. The vessels were also to have tug escorts in both directions when transiting this channel. This procedure went on for a long period of time until preparations were made to remove the Blackthorn from the channel and was removed from the area. This was also something that we were involved in when it came time to bring the crane barge out to the *Blackthorn* location to lift her out of the channel. This was a necessary task that needed to be done in order to clear the channel for the safe movement of vessel traffic.

Escorting Vessels In

Alternate Channel

I can remember one inbound ship with Captain John Lerro aboard her that would become infamous for another incident, a little more than three months later. This vessel was a large ship but with shallow draft and was attempting to navigate close around the *Blackthorn* location. The current at that time was coming in strong (a flood tide) and for some reason the ship tried to stop before going under the bridge.

We could only assume Captain Lerro had his doubts about making the transit under the bridge safely. She dropped her anchors trying to stop, but when the ship backed down, the current set her sideways to the bridge striking the north main piling with the port quarter of the ship, knocking a big chunk of concrete off.

The tug *Palmetto* along with a survey boat that was summoned to help was unable to push the ship off of the bridge up into the tide, and had to back out from under the bridge. The ship had to just drive ahead to come around the bridge piling with her anchor down from where she had dropped it earlier trying to avoid hitting the bridge. The next time Captain Lerro came in contact with the bridge, it would have a monumental consequence.

The day came that we were dispatched to get a barge known as *Little David*, from the Hendry Dredge Company yard in Port Tampa. This was an "A" frame-lifting barge with exceptional lifting capacity that we took to the *Blackthorn* location. There was also some Navy divers aboard that had dove down to assess the situation aboard the buoy tender *Blackthorn*.

We heard them report that there were crewmembers still in their bunks with some gruesome scenes down there. of which I will not repeat out of respect for the lost souls. It was not long before business was back to normal with ship traffic resuming. After this tragedy, there were plenty of times that we were thankful to God that he was always with us and watching over us, keeping us safe when we were on the waterways.

KNIVES ON THE DECK

To a lighter note, we as a close-knit crew tried to make our job enjoyable and fun whenever we were working, especially since we spent more time together than we did with our families. We were alongside and working an inbound job one day going into Port Manatee. After putting up our line, Bob and I went into the galley to play a hand of cards, which is something we did often; cards and tugboats just seem to go together. We were always thinking of pranks and often played jokes on one another, this particular time was no different. Bob pulled his knife out, laid it on the table, and made a comment about what he might have to do with it if the card game did not go his way.

I stood up and picked up a kitchen knife out of the sink, laughing I said, "And now what?" He in turn picked up a bigger knife from the silverware drawer, he said, "That's what." I said, "I'll be right back," in turn I went to the crew room and got the machete we had on the boat, the same one used to cut the strap used in the *Summit Venture* saga. By this time we were out on deck, with Bob having the fire axe with him.

We also hadn't noticed the Asian crew members up on the ship that had congregated during our little skit. After seeing them talking, laughing, and pointing at us, we did put on a show for them. We hadn't even noticed we were approaching the dock. Carroll yelled down at us and said the pilot had called him and said, he didn't know what was going on back aft, but they needed the crew to tend lines. He said for us to go back in the galley so the crew would stop watching and they could tie the ship up.

If you don't enjoy being at your workplace it would usually make what you do for a living unpleasant to be there. You really had to know Bob to appreciate what Carroll and I did to him on another occasion. Bob was one of those fellows that kept himself groomed and clean almost to the point of obsession, which made our next practical joke that much funnier.

BOB AND THE SARAN WRAP

There was this one day when Bob had eaten something that had his stomach upset in a bad way. We thought for a while about what could

Chief engineer Bob Taylor-Author photo

we do with this information, so before we were dispatched for our next job, and without Bobs' knowledge, Carroll and me went to the head where we stretched saran wrap over the toilet bowl, but under the seat. With that task behind us and done so well it was very undetectable, Carroll and I high fived each other for the fine job of wrapping the bowl. We could only wait for Bob to play King and go sit on the throne. While underway to our next job, Bob and me was sitting in the galley talking when, you guessed it, Bob got the incredible urge to go to the toilet. Bob jumped up and took off towards the head; I could only think, boy this is going to be a good one.

When he shut the door to the head, I called Carroll on the PA system and said, "He's in there, I'm on the way up." I didn't even get to the bottom of the stairway to the wheelhouse when I could hear Bob screaming and swearing up a storm. I knew I better clear the area, so I hot footed on up the stairs to be where I was sitting with Carroll with faces of innocence.

When Bob shot up the stairs after cleaning up the mess he made, he had come to the wheelhouse to ask us some pretty messy questions. He wanted to know which one of us had put the saran wrap on the toilet, well me and Carroll without cracking a smile just looked at each other and said at the same time, "What's he talking about?" He told us when he sat down there was some pressure built up, and when it was released something just didn't feel right. He put his hand back there to see what in the world it was that he was feeling push up on him, need I say more.

Bob could really get along with anyone; he just seemed to have a prank magnet on him that drew the pranks to him the way metal is drawn to a real magnet. I used to call Bob on the loud hailer just to get him to come to the wheelhouse. When he got there, I would say things like; "I just wanted to know how you're doing today Buddy, or is everything going okay with you?" Most of the time he would just laugh and say I'll get you; well, he never did, let's get back to Bob's mess.

There were marine type spring loaded faucets installed on the sinks, which had to be physically held open to get water to come out. They could not be turned on and left open, so this water conservation devise made Bob's clean up process that much harder to do. Bob was still steaming as he told us about the almost impossible mission it was to wash his hand and backside off at the same time, with those dratted faucets.

Me and Carroll busted out with laughter, which made him turn redder, and it finally made Bob laugh too. Neither one of us ever admitted to the prank, which was what also set us apart from every other crew: after the pranks we pulled on each other, we just went on with our business at hand, which was doing our job.

Barney Fife the Park Ranger

We were sent to Egmont Key anchorage one time to pick up a crew-member that was getting off his boat; the tug was at anchor awaiting us. We arrived there and went alongside the tug to pick up our package. We had on many occasions crew changed at the Mullet Key dock; this day should have been no different. We approached the dock when a park ranger that looked just like Barney Fife came strolling towards us, only this Barney was about seven feet tall.

As we got close to the dock, oh Barney went to yelling, get away from here. From the wheelhouse window Carroll said, "Excuse me officer, I just have to put this man on the dock, and we'll be gone." He told him, "I won't even touch the dock; I'll pull up close and let him jump off." Barney put his hand on his gun and yelled emphatically, "Do not touch this dock with that tug, or there will be repercussions you will not like." I looked up to the wheelhouse and hollered, "Carroll, Barney Fife's going to shoot us!"

Some of the people fishing were talking trash too, which must have been all that old Barney needed to build his courage up so he could strut his stuff with his demands. Barney was ranting on, and said, "I have the whole Pinellas County Commission behind me, now get away from this dock, now." Carroll yelled back to him and said, "Hold on old-timer, we're leaving."

Carroll backed away from the dock, and then turned the boat to where the stern was facing towards the dock. When he had a little sternway, he shot her ahead, the wheel wash took some of the fishing lines that the people had in the water, and washed them under the dock. Carroll said, "I hope Barney Fife and his cronies are happy now."

We now had to find another way to put this crewmember on the dock, where the taxi driver was waiting on him. There are sometimes when plan "A" doesn't work, you have to improvise. This was one of those times, and short of taking him all the way back to Port Manatee, we had to find another way. Lo and behold there it was, our plan "B," a pipe dock, a long piece of an old dredge pipeline sticking out in the water.

Carroll pulled the boat close enough to stick the bow on the bank. We then took our sixteen-foot extension ladder and placed it off the bow, down to the pipeline where the seaman could climb down and not get wet. We pitched him his gear and bid him farewell. I can only hope not all of the Pinellas County Park rangers acted this way, which would be a Chamber of Commerce nightmare.

CHIPPING GUN FELL

OVERBOARD

Us three guys on the boat figured as long as we got along and had fun while still doing our jobs; it couldn't get any better than this. While the pranks came and went, there's one that comes to mind that was pulled on me. One job that a deckhand has is to chip rust on the boat and cover it with primer and paint. I was doing that very thing one day on the stern of the *Palmetto*, chipping rust with a pneumatic rust chipper. Carroll and Lee Rogers, an engineer off the tug *Bradenton*, came back aft to see how the job was going. Carroll suggested I go to the galley and get some water to cool off; well it was summer time, and it was also very hot. So I said, "Good idea Zeke," and laid my chipping gun on top of the bulwarks with the air hose disconnected.

When I returned back aft, they had hid the chipping gun on the top deck behind the fishplate, where it couldn't be seen. Carroll and Lee were both looking over the stern, asking each other, "What was it that hit the water, it sounded like a fish had flipped?"

I looked to where just minutes before, I had laid the chipping gun atop of the bulwarks, it wasn't there. I asked them, "Where is the chipping gun that I had left back there?" They both looked at me, and then started questioning me as to where I had left it. I said, "On top of the bulwarks, where I have left it many times before." They said that must have been what they had heard make a splash in the water. Carroll said, "Dick Pepper was on his way down to the dock, and he would probably fire me when he found out I had lost that chipping gun," Dick was the Manager.

He said they cost over three hundred dollars, and Dick might overlook it, if I made like I had fell in the water while chipping. He said, "We could say the gun must have disconnected itself when it hit the water, you should jump in the water with your clothes on, to make it look real." I didn't want to get fired, so I started taking things out of my pants so they wouldn't get wet. Carroll said, "No, don't do that, it would be more convincing if all my things along with my wallet were wet when Dick arrived."

I said, "Okay," and started to jump in the water, when Lee said, "No, go get in the shower instead of jumping in the water," that way they wouldn't have to help me back on the boat. That was fine with me, and I headed for the shower. I guess they felt bad for me and stopped me just before stepping into the running water of the shower. Carroll said, "I'll bet you'll remember this, and to never leave the chipping gun where it could fall overboard," which was something I never did again, lesson learned.

THE PAPER TOWEL SEAGULL

Since I had learned the different channels, Carroll felt safe with me on the wheel. We were on our way to Port Tampa one night while Carroll was getting some needed rest, and I was running the boat. I had the windows open in the wheelhouse letting some fresh air in, since the *Palmetto* was not equipped with air conditioning. Nevertheless, the weather that particular night was just glorious anyway. It was about two o'clock in the morning, so I was sitting back enjoying the view.

With the wind blowing in my face and not having a care in the world, something was afoot. The only sounds I heard was the boat plowing through the water, except an occasional whistle. I would stand up and look around on deck, thinking Bob was trying to get my attention.

I was not expecting what happened to me next. I had just sat back down when an ice cold, soaking wet wad of paper towels came flying through the window, and plastered me right in the face. That scared the bageebers out of me, I screamed at first, because I thought a seagull had flown through the window on me. I got up and looked down on deck, where I saw Bob looking up at me laughing. I said, "You got me Buddy, that was a good one," I thought to myself, I'll get you back.

First New Year's Eve

in The Fog

My first New Year's Eve was celebrated with Carroll and Bob anchored in the Point Pinellas channel because of fog, we didn't have a radar unit on the boat at that time. What we did was during clear weather, we would run a course right on the ranges and write down what we read off the compass, crude but that's how we found our way when foggy. This night was a fog so thick we had trouble seeing the bow of the boat. With safety being a concern to Captain Carroll, he told Bob and me to get the anchor ready to put out.

We finally saw a channel marker and knew exactly where we were. After anchoring the boat, we were on the stern looking in the water and noticed small sea snakes, by the thousands. That night I found out that Carroll was deathly scared of snakes; naturally, I filed that bit of information for later. Since no one had cell phones yet, we made phone calls through the Marine operator to our respective homes, to wish our wives Happy New Years, and then we pulled our wheelhouse watches.

We had pulled straws earlier to see which watch we each had. Carroll said we would each stand a two-hour watch, that way we could all get some sleep. The next morning we were still fog bound with no traffic encountered the whole night. The last man on watch had breakfast ready for the crew when the sun came up. We ate breakfast, washed the dishes, and noticed the channel marker we had been close to all night, had disappeared.

After a few hours of dragging anchor, we came up on a marker we weren't familiar with. After locating it from the chart, it showed we were heading towards Port Manatee. We picked up the anchor and proceeded towards the entrance to Point Pinellas channel giving security calls as we went with caution. Captain Max Pate on the *Admiral Leffler*, a tug that made a steady run hauling oil to the Crystal River power plant from Port Manatee, was anchored on "B" cut flats off the entrance of Port Manatee. He heard one of the security calls Carroll made and offered to guide us down the channel with his radar. I learned something that day about the importance of having the right equipment, radar, which was installed later on all the boats.

Max did a wonderful job getting us to the flats, but there was an inbound sea going tug/barge unit that was coming our direction. The inbound tug called us and said we should have enough time to clear before he got to our location, so we stayed our course and proceeded across the flats. Wrong, looking up through the fog there she was, and had we kept going we would have collided with the barge. Carroll came full astern on the *Palmetto*, smoking the clutches and avoiding what could have been a disaster. The Captain on the inbound tug said, "Sorry about that *Palmetto*, I guess you were closer than I thought." It was a near miss for sure. We made it on in to the dock, secured the boat, went home, and gave hugs and kisses to our families.

Second New Year's Day
in The Fog

Another fog story, once again on New Year's Day a few years later, I had been transferred to the tug *Bradenton*. I was at home about to enjoy a feast prepared by my wife when the phone rang; it was the dispatcher letting me know we had to go to Port Tampa for a job. I left home in the fog thinking, on the water, visibility was going to be worse than this. It was so bad when I turned off the highway into Port Manatee I turned off my engine to see if I could hear any oncoming traffic before crossing the road safely. I started my engine, put it in gear, braced for an impact just in case, and shot across the road.

My Captain on the *Bradenton* was Denny Cooper and the engineer was Allen Voss. When I arrived to the dock, I could hardly see across the slip, which is only about eight hundred feet. Allen started the boat up and I questioned Denny if we should even leave the dock with the visibility being what it was. He said, "When you are a Captain you have to make every attempt to get to a job using your knowledge and experience." We let go and started out the channel using the compasses courses Denny had previously written down. We made it out of Port Manatee channel, and without incident, so far I was impressed. Denny turned the boat on a course towards Point Pinellas channel which had our next set of markers that we should see.

After a few minutes of running full ahead, we started getting into shallow water with the boat sucking down, that's what they do when running in shallower water. Denny pulled the throttle back, turned to me, and said, "Well Willie," that's what he called me, "what do we do now?" I said Denny, "I wouldn't have left the dock in this fog, you're on your own." He said, "We had attempted to go to the job, we could not make it, so we'll just run a reciprocal course back to Manatee channel, find our way in, tie the boat up, and go back home."

That was a good plan, if had it worked. We ran longer than we should have, and you guessed it, we missed Port Manatee entrance altogether. We did however come up on some pilings that were close to a range tower, so Denny said, "Let's put a line over the top of the pilings and shut down until the fog clears." The office ended up sending the tug *Montclair*, the only boat at the time with radar to do the job that we were supposed to have done.

We played cards for the rest of the day and into the evening. After the tug *Montclair* finished the job in Port Tampa, they were dispatched to our location to guide us back to the dock so we could go home. Wouldn't you know it, just minutes before they got to our location, the fog lifted where we could see clear as a bell.

We went back to the dock on our own with the *Montclair* coming to Port Manatee and tying up with us. The *Montclair's* crew had to stay aboard their tug, where we were able to go back home, that's where we should have been the whole day. The one thing about being in the fog on water is you definitely lose your sense of direction, and it doesn't take very long to do either.

TIED UP IN THE BUNK

Before I had been transferred from the *Palmetto*, I can recall something that was a classic in prank Ville. We had come back to the dock from a job one day to get some sleep, but earlier in the day I had painted the bunk in the Captains' quarters. Carroll made a beeline to the crew's quarters and jumped

Bob and Carroll in 1977-Author photo

into my bunk after securing the boat. He told me to go in the galley and lay on the bench. I said to myself "Okay, just wait until you go to sleep." I waited for a while to let both Carroll and Bob go to sleep. When I was sure they both were in La La Land, I took a heaving line in there where I then proceeded to tie their feet to the bed rail, being very careful as not to wake them. I made half hitches over both of their feet, snugging the line up tight as I dared to, and was amazed that neither one of them even so much as tried to turn over. So see, there was a reason to sleep, we were all tired, and that was why I needed my bunk. After I had done the deed, I went and got Captain Denny to show him what I had done; after all, I was proud to show off my knot tying skills.

When he looked through the porthole he said, "You had better untie them two before they try to get up and get hurt." I said, "No, I don't think so, I have to get them to get up real fast, just to see the look on their sleepy little faces." Bob was one of those guys that got up from a sound asleep and was in gear when he went to start the boat, I used this knowledge well. Knowing this, I ran through the door yelling at them saying, "Carroll get up, the office called, we have a job ASAP, Bob start the engine we have to go!" I then went back through the door for about fifteen seconds, to give them time to notice they were tied up.

When I opened the door, I couldn't have imagined what I would see sprawled out on the floor. Carroll had come off the top bunk and was holding himself off the floor with his hands, with my boy Bob on the floor right underneath him. They were both hollering at me to untie their feet, but all I could do was stand there and laugh. I said, "Now ain't you two just precious, that'll teach you to take my bunk!" Bob wiggled around and was able to untie his feet, and then untied Carroll's feet yelling the whole time. Afterwards we all had a big laugh, that was one of the better pranks that had been pulled with us three, so far.

COLD WATER IN THE SHOWER

I guess payback was inevitable after that stunt; it came one night when I was in the shower. While we were running down the bay to a job, I told Carroll I was going to take a shower. The door lock was broken, and had been since I'd been on the boat. You just didn't think anyone would come in there while you were taking a shower, right? I suppose the water monster waited until my head and face was soaped up, rendering me without the ability to see, or even need to see.

With no shower curtain and a door that couldn't lock, I was an open target to the five gallon bucket of cold water that hit me broadside. That was something I never would have expected, after catching my breath I wiped my eyes and looked real fast to see where that skin tightening water had came from.

Only seeing a closed door I hurried and dried off, got dressed, and took off to the wheelhouse, where I found the two canary eating cats just sitting there like nothing had happened. After a little grilling as to which one was to blame for that little stunt, all I got was a lot of finger pointing. To this day, they have both blamed each other, and have never admitted to me who the culprit really was. I do know that Carroll told Bob to fix the door lock so the same thing couldn't happen to him, which Bob did, as fast as he could get to it. Now to me, that would make both of them look suspicious, Carroll for telling him to fix it, and Bob for fixing it as fast as he did.

Collision With The
Gulf Deer

There was so much that happened throughout the years it's hard to know what to say next. Here's one, we hit the loaded gasoline tanker *Gulf Deer* one time when the *Palmetto's* steering went out. After the first contact was made, we started sliding down the ship banging into it several more times. It seemed to us that the Mate must have thought that this guy can't run a boat.

He started running down the deck keeping up with us, every time we hit the ship he would yell, "You want the line here Captain!" Carroll yelled back to him, "No, I don't, I'm just trying get away from the ship!" After we had initially hit the ship, I noticed I had lost the heel to one of my boots; we must have hit her pretty hard to knock the heel off my boot. Dick Pepper was the Manager of Manatee Tug and Barge Lines and was also one of the Captains on the tug *Bradenton*. he was aboard her that day for that job. He told Carroll to have Bob take the hand held radio to the steering room where he could steer the boat by pushing the steering contacts with a hammer handle.

He said that way we could at least finish the job, Carroll would get the commands from the Pilot and could work the engine controls, relaying to Bob which way to steer the boat, while doing the steering from the steering room below. Carroll told him, "That's not a good idea, and he wasn't even going to attempt something like that." Not really knowing exactly what had happened, it could be electrical, or even maybe the steel cable that pulled the rudder around could have broke. It turned out to be an intermittent electric problem with the steering, the hardest type problem to find. It was looked at with no definite fix, since it seemed to be okay after that particular incident.

Collision With a

British Navy Ship

The mystery steering problem we had discovered one day was back in the neighborhood looking to visit someone. This time we were dispatched to dock a British Navy ship over in Bay Boro at the St. Petersburg Harbor. I was running as relief engineer that day, with Joe Duncan who was a new deckhand aboard the tug *Palmetto*. I was standing on the bow with the tag line in my hand ready for the toss. As we were approaching the ship and just before going alongside, Joe was in the galley getting our bill bag to send an acknowledgement ticket up with our line.

When we hit this time, unlike the tanker we had hit just days earlier, these sailors were in uniforms. Several of the crewmembers even had their dress whites on and were lined up standing at attention, looking just like a white picket fence. We hit so hard it made some of the crew lose their footing and stumble a bit, but went right back to attention without missing a beat, now that's concentration.

I crouched down on the deck trying not to be thrown overboard upon impact, and was awarded with a wet surprise. When we hit the side of the ship, some water shot up like Old Faithful from between the ship and the tug, it had also came right down on top of my head leaving me drenched. This time we only hit once, and was able to back away from the ship. I immediately took off running to the steering room to see if the same problem that had plagued us recently, had come back.

Seeing the steering motor working, I had no idea what had happened. I went back towards the bow, when I passed the galley I saw Joe lying on the galley table with blood coming out of his head. His head had hit the porthole when we hit the ship, the same instant that he was getting the bill bag, he was okay since it was just a little cut. After we went back alongside, we were able to finish the job without further incident; we then tied up in Bay Boro to see if we could ascertain what the problem was, again.

George Atkins had come to the boat to see what he could find out about this incident. We had been told that the point of contact where the tug had hit was probably the worst place on the ship to bend a plate. They said it would also be very expensive to straighten the hull, because of all the electronics that would have to be removed in that area before any welding could be done, and then reinstalled after the work was done.

An electrician was also called, and it took him a while to find this little intermittent problem. It turned out that when the engine was running at a certain RPM, it caused a vibration in the follow up steering, where a loose lug on a wire was discovered. This caused the steering motor to go hard over to the right, which then caused our problem, not having steering when we needed it most. You can bet that every lug on every wire was looked at and tightened before the electrician left the boat that time.

SMALL BOAT ENCOUNTERS

We had gone into the Florida Power Corporation power plant slip one night where we had tied up to a barge moored in the slip to wait for a job. Had we known there was a small fiberglass boat between the barge and the dock, we would not have tied there. However, we did, and you guessed it, the little fiberglass boat sank. It turned out someone had tied it there to go for some gas. The company had to replace the boat for the person; you would think someone would have enough sense to leave it in the open to be seen. The weight of a tugboat and a fiberglass boat just does not go together, especially with the tug on the outside.

We had several encounters with smaller boats over the years. We saw some fellows waving frantically one day, as if they needed some help close to a capsized boat, which was a pretty good sign. Luckily, their boat was in deep enough water for our thirteen feet of draft, so we eased over to see if we could help them. We also found out through our initial contact that only one of them could swim. If you are on a boat, being a non-swimmer makes for a disaster waiting to happen. These two were just holding onto their little capsized boat, hoping to be rescued.

When we hauled them from the water, they were two happy fellows. We then took them to a dock where they could call someone to help them retrieve their sunken boat. Just like a Boy Scout you should always be prepared for anything, the first on the list as a boater should be swimming lessons. It really makes you feel good when you can give people assistance, and just might have saved a life.

Man Treading Water

With a Gun

That's what we did for a man that we found treading water near the channel, about two o'clock in the morning on our way back to Port Manatee coming from East Tampa. I was Captain on the tug *Yvonne St. Philip* with Bob as my engineer and Carlo Juncal my deckhand. We were running ahead of the ship that we had just sailed. The pilot on the ship called to me on the radio and said, "*Yvonne*, come back to me quick, hurry." I immediately turned around and headed towards him, thinking something was wrong with the ship. He said, "The bow watch radioed back to the bridge and said he heard someone yell." They ran out on the bridge wing and also heard someone yelling, so he called me back to try to give assistance to whoever was yelling for help.

When we got to where he said he had heard the yelling, we looked with the searchlight for someone in the water. We found a man floating just outside the channel, where we immediately helped him aboard the boat. When Bob and Carlo got him aboard, they noticed he was holding a pistol in one of his hands. Carlo took it from him and slid it down the deck away from them. He asked him, "What in the world are you doing with a gun?" The gun also had his hand stained with rust. He said he'd seen on the news where sharks had eaten people swimming before.

He said that if he would have felt a brush against him, or something had hit his legs, he was going to shoot himself instead of being eaten alive. Going down on the deck with them and hearing this, I told him that we had probably just saved your life, almost in tears, he agreed, thanking us for coming back for him. After he had showered and got some dry clothes on that Bob and Carlo gave him, he told us how he had gotten into this predicament. He had just purchased a new boat and had an argument with his girlfriend. He said he had been drinking and had taken off in his new boat to cool off for a while, and had not told anyone which direction he was heading. He said he had been treading water since the previous evening, which had to be several hours since it was around 02:00 at that time. He didn't say how the boat had sank, but judging from what he told us with him drinking, he probably shot a hole in the bottom of his boat.

His girlfriend had reported him missing earlier; we found that out when I called the Coast Guard at his request to come pick him up. He later sent us a thank you note for what we had done for him; Bob kept it posted on the wall in his room as a reminder. If he wasn't insured with that new boat, I'll bet he'll remember to get it on his next purchase.

WATERSPOUTS WE SAW

Some weather stories now, we have seen some good and bad weather out on the waterways throughout the years. We were coming back from Big Bend on the *Yvonne* one night, where we had spotted eight waterspouts in Tampa Bay, all at the same time. We were even close enough to one that I stopped the boat and shined the spotlight on the base of it while it crossed the channel right in front of us. The lightning was so fierce that night it almost kept the horizon visible to a constant state. I wish I could have taken a picture of what had to have been a weather phenomenon, because I've never seen anything like it before or since.

Although, when I was still a deckhand aboard the tug *Palmetto* with Carroll and Bob, we came upon a waterspout near "G" cut one day. Carroll says to us, "I wonder what'll happen if we let that waterspout go over us." I think he was just trying to get a rise out of us because he knew it would probably clear the deck of all our lines if we got close to it. However, we had to react just to make him feel good, so we jumped up and started begging him. We said, "Please don't do it Carroll, we'll be killed," we acted all scared and such. We carried on for a few more minutes like that, and then when we started laughing, he knew we turned it around on him.

Lightning on The Barges

Once when I was working on the *Bradenton* as engineer with Captain Denny Cooper and Phil Eubanks, or Snake as we called him, we were once again doing the lash barge shuffle. The weather had been bad all day and was getting increasingly worse, with high winds and fierce lightning strikes, keeping the sky lit up as the day went on. Dressed for the rain, Snake and I had our foul weather gear on when we were about to go back out on deck from a short break.

As we opened the hatch, we saw lightning dance across the tops of the barges, then heard a deafening clap of thunder. Slamming the hatch closed, we knew this was not a good idea to be out there on those electrifying barges, especially when safety comes first. We looked at each other and both told Denny at the same time, "We're not going back on deck until this lightning stops."

Denny went to the wheelhouse to call the dispatcher on the company radio to advise them of a delay due to the weather. He couldn't raise them on the radio, so after checking out our radio we had found that lightning had hit the antenna splitting it into a thousand pieces. That was probably what we had been witness to just a few minutes earlier. It was quite a while before the weather calmed down enough for us to complete the job, so we made the best of it and got a few games of cards in. Lightning is nothing to play with, and that day was not the time to start taking chances with a million volts of electricity running around the decks of those barges.

Dead Ship *Azteca*

We had a job come up one time when I was still a deckhand on the *Palmetto*, which was different for me. There was a Mexican ship, the *MV Azteca* loaded with coal that someone tried to sink by blowing it up. They failed in their attempt to sink her because when the explosion went off, it went up, instead of down. It was actually powerful enough to blow a hole from the engine room, straight up to where it left a hole about forty feet across destroying a major section of the deckhouse.

They sent four harbor tugs to assist the big offshore tug that was towing the crippled ship to Port Manatee. A sister ship to the *Azteca* was scheduled to come into Port Manatee and be moored outside of her to take the cargo from. After the *Azteca* had been unloaded, she was transported to a shipyard in Mobile, Alabama for repairs.

We were made up on the starboard quarter with three lines out to act as power and rudder with the *Bradenton* made up the same way on the port side way, for the transit up the bay. There was a pilot's ladder hanging down to have access to the ship, Bob and I climbed up on the ship just to look around.

The ship appeared to have a lot of damage due to the explosion; most of the windows in the wheelhouse were blown out. While we were trying to look into a window a crewmember jerked the curtain back, we presumed to look out at the same time we were looking in. We jumped like we had been hit with an electric cattle prod. I told Bob, "I'm out of here," that scared me. We both went back to the tug and couldn't believe that only one man was killed during the explosion.

WENT CRAZY ON THE BOAT

Around that period of time, there was a deckhand on the *Bradenton* named Mike Coleman. I had knee surgery prior to working on the tugs that left me with a scar about a foot long on my right knee. I had taken some gear out to my car at the end of a workday. When I got back on the boat, I found out Carroll had told Mike he had to hit me in the knee with a pry bar one time.

I picked up on what he was doing and just played along to see where it would go. Carroll said to me, "Show Mike where I had to hit your knee that time," so I showed him my scar. Carroll told him that I had gone berserk and had completely lost it one time. When I came on the boat that day, and after a while had gone by, I had a reaction from some medication I was taken. He said, "Bill was like a wild man possessed, so I got a pry bar and hit him in the knee to take him off his feet, I then had to call the Coast Guard to take him off the boat for medical attention."

Carroll said, "It was a few years ago, but sometimes whenever he gets upset he'll have a relapse from the damage it did to his brain." It just so happened we started playing cards about this time. When cards didn't go my way, I would jerk my shoulder and make repeated "*grrrrrrr*" sounds, like I was having a flashback. I sat on the bench close to Mike, and when I made that sound, he would start sliding away from me, a little bit at the time; this one was going better than we had thought it would.

Carroll would jump to his feet and say, "All right WC, you know what happened before, don't you make me get that pry bar." I would make some grunting noises and calm down a bit, while Mike stared at me to see what was next. We left work that day not telling Mike any different from what he had been told, and seen.

It just so happened Carroll, Mike and I were working together on the *Palmetto* not long after this. I noticed Mike was very cautious around me, I knew what was on his mind, so here we go again. We were going out the channel that day and were both on deck. I walked towards the stern but stopped at an open porthole to the crew's quarters. I started talking into the porthole and carrying on a conversation as if there was somebody talking back to me. I kept watching Mike out of the corner of my eye as I walked back aft to the stern of the boat. He eased towards the porthole and looked all around inside, as if to see someone in there I was talking to.

He took off to the wheelhouse where he asked Carroll what it meant when Bill talked to an imaginary person. Carroll told him to stay away from me because that means I'm about to lose it again. "Stay clear of him and I'll deal with him," he said. "He knew right where to hit me to take me down," he added. At the time, I didn't know what Carroll had told him. After a while, he came back down to the galley where I was waiting to talk with him.

I thought something was up when I said, "Come here Mike, I want to ask you something," and out the hatch he went. I went to the galley hatch to see where he had gone to; he was climbing over the bulwarks onto the tire fenders that were on the outside of the boat. He said, "Stay away from me or I'll jump," I said, "Mike, come back on deck, I just want to talk to you." He was adamant about jumping and kept saying, "Stay back, don't you come any closer or I'll jump, I will, I mean it." We heard Carroll laughing from the wheelhouse window, he told Mike, "We were just kidding, he really ain't crazy, now get back on deck." We had a good laugh at how gullible Mike was; I was ready for the next one to take place, but this time it was Carroll's turn to be on the so-called hot seat, and yes, Mike was that gullible.

A BISEXUAL STORY

Carroll had a Ford conversion van that he was trying to sell one time. He had told me there was a gay man that he knew who was interested in buying his van. I knew someone else had to hear this, just to see what would happen. Well wouldn't you know it, I happen to mention to Mike that Carroll was bisexual. He said, "No way," I said, "Yes way, I know he's married and has kids, but he likes women and men."

I said, "We all know he's like this, so far he has never been forward with anyone trying to come on to them, but you never know." Sharing this story with Mike I said, "Come go with me to the wheelhouse and I'll prove it." We took off up the stairs and sat down, Mike sat behind Carroll to where he could just sit and observe. With Carroll looking straight ahead while steering the boat, I then started asking him some funny questions about his gay friend. I said, "Carroll ain't you trying to sell your van to a gay buddy of yours?" He said, "Yeah, I think he's going to buy it."

I winked at Mike and nodded my head. I asked him, "You hang out with him at the bar?" He answered, "Yeah!" I said, "He's a good friend of yours, and you like him right?" He said, "Yeah, why all these questions?" I winked and nodded at Mike again and said, "No reason, I was just won-dering," and with that Mike and I went back down to the galley where I could see his reaction and what he had to say. Mike said, "I would never have believed it but I heard it with my own ears." He said, "I guess that proves what I've heard all my life, you can't judge a book by its cover, I'm a straight man and don't want to hurt Carroll's feelings, I'll just do my job and stay clear."

Mike had a head full of red hair and had it shaped like an afro. I told him, "You know Mike, Carroll's never messed with anyone, but he has also never worked with a red head either, be careful." Later Carroll asked me what I had told Mike. I said, "Why, what do you mean, what's he doing?" He said, "Usually when he brings me up a cup of coffee he sits down and talks a while, but the last few times he hands me my coffee at arms length and down the stairs he goes, it's just like something's bothering him."

I said, "I don't know, I might have mentioned you were bisexual," which he wasn't, "that might have something to do with it." He said, "You told him what?" I said, "Now you know what all the questions about the gay guy that you know was all about." I said, "You could not have answered my questions any better, they just fell right into place." There are some things in life that you just hate to straighten out, especially when they have gone so well. This was one of those times, but it had to be done for peace of mind for Mike, who was already traumatized from working with a crazy man. Carroll laughed and said, "That explains it," he couldn't figure out why the change, he was beginning to think he had body odor and needed to take a shower.

Grabbed Lee in The ER

As it happened about the same time every year the shipping business slowed down to the point where the Company laid a boat up until business picked up. The *Bradenton* was chosen as the sacrificial lamb, which meant some crew members transferred to other boats. At that time, I had made engineer aboard the *Bradenton* and was bumped for lack of seniority in that position.

I was back to the *Palmetto* as deckhand with Captain Reggie Atkins and Lee Rogers as engineer. The schedule we were on then allowed us to go home at night, subject to call back for jobs after hours. We would secure the boats with locks on the hatches and plug the refrigerator into a shore power cord since the generators were shut down when we left. By leaving the boat with no power, it was total darkness, especially in the engine room. We came back one night for a job, and I started planning how I would greet Lee when he came aboard and went to the engine room to start the generator.

Lee had been an engineer for a long time; he had a flashlight placed below in a hanger to use before starting the generator. I hid my car and boarded the boat, then leaving all the hatches locked, I went through the back hatch shutting it behind me to make Lee think he was the first to get there. I figured I would stand behind the stairway, not making a sound, then bear hug him when he got close to me screaming like I was in a house of horror the whole time.

I myself was by no means a little fellow at six feet tall and weighing around 260 pounds, but I knew Lee's strength, he was a pretty stout fellow and strong as a bull. I knew I had better hold on tight when I did grab him, because it was going to be me and him until I could calm him down.

I finally heard him coming; he was easing down the stairs whistling, like he didn't have a care in the world. When he turned the corner at the bottom of the stairs, I grabbed him and screamed as loud as I could. I do believe you could hear Lee screaming louder than I was. As I suspected, I had my hands full until I finally convinced him it was only me. I said, "Okay Lee, calm down, I'm going to turn you loose now just don't hit me." When it was all over, he said when I grabbed him and yelled, he had no idea what had a hold of him and that it scared the mess out of him. After that night when Lee came aboard the boat, he had his own flashlight shining all over the place before going down into the engine room. The only thing I regret is not catching this one on film.

THE BIRTH OF OUR TWINS

In April of 1982, my lovely wife was due to give birth to our twins. Our union at the time was the Master Mates and Pilots, who was also in contract negotiations with the company. They did not seem to be going good at the time, and we had even heard talk of a walkout. I think everyone loses when you have a labor strike, with this one going to be no different, since all Benefits are frozen at the time of a strike. This was a big concern to me with the upcoming delivery, and as luck would have it, my wife went into labor. I took her to the hospital in Manatee County where we lived, only to find out it was determined the babies were trying to come breech. They were also coming five weeks early, which made them premature babies. The Manatee Memorial Hospital staff said they were not set up to care for babies being so small, so another hospital had to be found. After numerous phone calls to most of the local hospitals, one was found.

My lovely wife Lois-Author photo

My wife, along with her Doctor, was transported by ambulance to the Tampa General Hospital in Hillsborough County, about forty miles north from where we were. I had gone by my house to drop off my wife's belongings, and to get some cash for snacks. My Dad knew we had gone to the hospital and came over to see how it had gone, and after telling him the short version of what was going on, I took off like a rocket. With

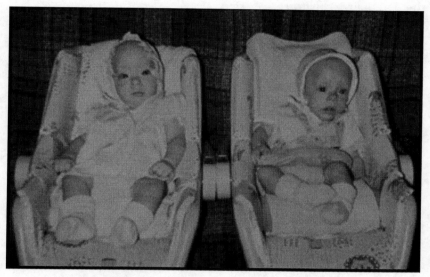

Mary Amber and Joshua Levi five 5 months old-Author photo

the welfare of my wife and babies on my mind, I was also thinking about what would happen if a strike was called, freezing our benefits. I drove my personal car to meet them up in Tampa, with the ambulance beating me there by only a few minutes. I had made the drive in just twenty-two minutes, realizing later at the speed I had driven, I was very thankful that the Lord rode with me, keeping me safe. There were so many things to think about, with the thoughts of my other two children, and my responsibility to provide for them, this was fixing to get more hectic than it already was. We had found out we were having twins only two days earlier. We had one crib, one basinet, and a car that I knew wasn't going to haul the entire bunch that we already had, plus the two new additions that were oh so close.

When I arrived, the ambulance drivers were just coming downstairs with the gurney from the delivery room. I just prayed everything was going okay with not knowing their status. God was definitely in the delivery room the morning of March 6 1982, because my wife gave birth by caesarian section to a 3 lb. 2 oz. girl and a 2 lb. 7 oz. boy. They weren't plump like normal babies; they just looked like little naked people lying there in their incubators.

They both had numerous problems at first with them being prematu re, but both pulled through okay with lots of prayers, and some very smart Doctors and Nurses. We named them Mary Amber and Joshua Levi, names from the Holy Bible. They both stayed in the hospital until they weighed at least four and a half pounds before the Doctors would send them home.

I know there are obstacles in everyone's lives, and sometimes you don't know which way to turn next, but being blessed as we were, everything worked out for us. Having a renewed contract being signed with the company, and the Lord keeping vigilance over the twins, who are now twenty-four years old, it has been a wonderful blessed life. They are both still living with Mom and Dad at home, and have good jobs.

THE SALE OF THE COMPANY

Around noontime on December 31 1986, we heard some very bad news, or so we thought. The boats back then had company radios that all of the boats crews could hear transmissions simultaneous. Our Manager at the time was George Atkins, he said he had a message to tell all crewmembers. There had been a new company, Taurus Marine, which was trying to get established in the Tampa Bay tug market for some time.

We as members of the Masters Mates and Pilots Union had walked on a picket line against them for a few weeks. We thought that it might be about the competition leaving town, especially since that was the company's goal, or so we had been told. In reality, we were now told the company known as St. Philip Towing had been bought out by Bay Transportation Corporation. We later learned that they were the same people who owned Taurus Marine, was it coincidence, I think not. We were all told to remove our personal belongings from the boats and depart the property. Anyone wanting to apply for a job, go to Bay Harbor Inn on Courtney Campbell Causeway in Tampa. This is something no one wants to hear from their employer, especially on New Year's Eve.

I had been working as a relief Captain whenever one was needed for that position, ever since I had gotten my license back in 1980. This particular day I was working on the tug *Yvonne* for Captain Denny Cooper, the only difference was, we had just been fired. Fired is what I kept repeating to the engineer, Bob Taylor, who was listening to the radio message with me. We just looked at each other almost in shock, not even knowing where this place was at, or even how to get there. Reggie Atkins was the Captain on the tug *Palmetto* that New Year's Eve day that we had received the bad news. As we started gathering our gear, he came over

73

and told us we could follow him because he knew the way up there. Since we were in Port Manatee, we had to drive to North Tampa with our belongings in our own vehicles; I rode with Bob to save gas.

We followed Reggie to the Bay Harbor Inn, where we found a crowd of people already waiting to apply for the forty-two jobs, that's the amount needed for the seven boats that were crewed at that time. When we arrived, we added our names to the signup sheet with mine being 71 and Bob's 72.

We saw faces we had never seen before, while others we recognized from other tugs. There were people in suits with briefcases standing around waiting for their turn. We looked at each other and wondered, where did all these people hear about this from? We learned from talking to some of them that it had been posted in the newspaper. We also waited for what seemed to be an eternity to be called for an interview. We saw Carroll there and started quizzing him about what he knew and if he had heard anything new. The Port was literally shut down for lack of tug service, so a decision was made to call applicants out of sequence to get the ship traffic moving again. This made us to believe the new company had been advised who to hire first in order to get the boats crewed.

Bob was called before Carroll or me, and after his interview he was told to report to George Atkins for his boat assignment. He told us he didn't have time to talk, he had to go. With me having rode there with him, I asked him, "What about me, how am I supposed to get back?" He said, "Sorry, you're on your own," and out the door he went. I just stood there dumbfounded not having a clue how to get back, let alone how I even got there.

It turned out that I was called before Carroll, which was good for me because he was to be my ride back later. When I was interviewed, I was asked what I would do if a crewmember came aboard drinking. I wondered, where in the world did that one come from, and then I remembered back with what had happened not too long ago, it was the same scenario that I had just heard.

I was working as a relief Captain recently where we had went home after the workday, but was called back for a job about five hours later. When we came back to the boat that night, I honestly never noticed the deckhand had been drinking. With him acting normal and not staggering when he walked down the deck, I had no reason to think otherwise. The next day I received a phone call from George Atkins asking me if I had something I needed to tell him about the previous night. My mind went into light speed trying to remember if anything had happened that I needed to tell him about.

After checking my computer banks, I couldn't come up with anything to tell him out of the ordinary. I said, "The job went well, the pilot never said anything went wrong," so I was puzzled at what he was wanting. He told me he received a phone call from the Manatee Port Authority, and that a security guard had reported seeing a crewmember going aboard the tug intoxicated.

I, to this day, do not know what he thought he saw, but George said he was going to do what I should have done that night, which was let the deckhand go. This happened the next day, confronting him about it, he admitted to having a few beers before returning to the boat after leaving it. George asked me what I would do if this ever happened again. I said, "I would fire him on the spot, and would definitely not let him aboard the boat." He said with that, he would see about getting me into a tan suit, which was the Captain's uniform color.

When asked what I would do by the interviewer, I remembered the words George had filled my ears with and replied with a strong voice, repeating what I had told George earlier, which must have been the correct response because I was told to go home and stand by the phone. I left the interview room where Carroll was standing just outside asking what they had said. I told him what was said, and then wondered how I was going to get home. Since it was already after 19:00 (7 pm), and my wife was not familiar with the roads in Tampa, I was in a dilemma.

It worked out when Carroll was called a few minutes later for his interview, and was told to do the same thing. When he came out, he said he would give me a lift back to the office. I asked him, "Can't you take me to Port Manatee where I left my truck?" He said, "That man told me to go home and stand by the phone, and that's just what I'm going to do when I leave the office." He did however agree to take me as far as Gibsonton, which was almost halfway. We had been told earlier to come by the office and pick up our paycheck, so, when we got to the office I called my wife to come to Gibsonton to pick me up.

We had agreed on a place that my wife knew the location of, which turned out to be a bar, the Bull Frog Creek Lounge. After being dropped off I stood out of the parking lot up towards the front of the building to wait for my wife. Looking like I was hanging around like a bum, I noticed people looking at me funny when going inside, like, why is this guy just standing there. Then remembering what day it was and not being dressed like the party goers, I just smiled and said Happy New Year, all the while hoping my wife would just hurry up and get there to get me away from the front of that bar.

When she drove up, it looked like a school bus with all the heads I saw moving around in there. I ran up to the car and told my wife to move over, I'll drive. I jumped in the driver's seat and shot out of the parking lot of that bar like Mario Andretti, making a speedy get away. My wife was shooting questions at me so fast I thought there was two of her, no wonder the car was so crowded. All I wanted to know was, where did all these people come from. Our neighbor lady and her kids were at my house when I called, so my wife asked her if she wanted to take a ride. With her and her two children, my wife and three of our four children, that was one packed automobile, especially when I packed my big body in there too. I drove straight to Port Manatee to get my pickup truck; my wife then drove the wild bunch back home.

When I drove into the yard, my oldest son Will who had stayed home came out in the yard and said, "Someone called Dad, and said for you to report to the St. Philip office." I got back on the road in record time, heading right back to Tampa where I had just been minutes before. When I finally arrived at the office, I was told some words that I had prayed to hear, we need you to fill out your tax form for employment, praise God. Captain Denny was there filling out the same form and was told we were going to be each other's relief's as Captains aboard the tug *Yvonne*. I felt like I was on top of the world, after getting my license six and a half years earlier, I had finally gotten a full time Captain's position on my own boat, and better than that, I still had a job, I said, "Thank you Lord for watching over me."

We started working a new schedule too, which was different from the past schedules. The boats now were to be manned twenty-four hours a day, which meant we stayed aboard the boats for three days on and three days off. This would be changed within a few months after the dust had settled. At first we worked three days on duty and three days off duty, with 12:00 noon time being crew change time, nobody liked that schedule.

We were finally changed to a schedule we could get used to, we were on duty for forty-eight hours straight, starting at 09:00 Monday morning until 09:00 Wednesday morning. We were then off for forty-eight hours until 09:00 Friday morning where we were on duty until 09:00 Monday morning. The next week was opposite from the previous week.

I was assigned to the tug *Yvonne* with Bob Taylor as engineer but had a new man, Steve Duffy, as a deckhand. As time went on there was a big turn over, especially with the deckhands. Bob however stayed with me as my engineer until I was transferred to Tampa almost a decade later. We finally got a deckhand, Carlo Juncal, who I had for almost five years until he also transferred to Tampa on another boat, being replaced by Ed Harris. Ed was a man that set the standard for deckhands to follow; of which I have yet to see his work habits duplicated by anyone. Some think they are the best deckhands ever; they couldn't carry Ed Harris's pocket watch when it comes to deckhands.

When he first came aboard, I noticed he was very athletic looking with a muscular body. Ed looked like a black Mr. Clean, with one earring and a shiny head. When we sat down for our first meal, I noticed he gave thanks to the Lord for his meal; I like to see that in a man before they break bread. I said to him jokingly, "Ed, I don't mean to pry, but with a ring in your right ear, doesn't that mean you're gay?" He said, "No way man, I'm right, everyone else is wrong."

We laughed about what I had asked him, and I found out right quick, Ed was going to fit in around here with us real good. When he came back to work on our next tour, he made it a point to show us what he had done, he now had a ring in both ears. He told me and Bob, this way there wouldn't be any questions about it, he'd have all his bases covered. That was one man I hated to lose when a few years later, he too transferred up to Tampa to work on the big boats.

TUGBOAT ANNIE

We were on duty one night and had assisted in docking a tug/barge unit into Port Manatee. The weather was pretty nasty that night with rough seas and high winds, which made what we found the next morning that much more unbelievable. When Carlo started the deck work for the day, he started painting on the mast where he had left off the day before. When he climbed the mast, he heard what sounded like a kitten meowing. That's exactly what we found when we traced where the sound was coming from.

There was a very small, and I mean a very tiny kitten in one of the side tires hung on the boat. Bob crawled down and got the kitten from the tire, where him and Carlo took inside and washed with dish soap to clean it up. While cleaning the kitten they discovered it was a girl cat. She had a lot of cuts and scratches on her from the barnacles inside the tire used as a fender.

We discussed what to do with her and decided to split the cost of having a veterinarian check her out. Bob called his wife to come get the cat and take her to the vet. When she got there, she said the vet would need a name for the record; we came up with "Tugboat Annie," which seemed appropriate to us. Bob's wife brought her back bandaged up with ointment for her scratches. She asked us what we were going to do with a cat aboard the boat. We said we'd play it by ear; she was a pretty little kitten and thought it'd be cool to have her aboard the boat.

As time went on Annie grew to be quite a large cat with the help and care of both crews. Every time she was taken to the vet both crews split the cost evenly, which made her the boats cat. We had told the office we had her aboard the boat, we were told just keep the boat clean and watch out for her. We bought her a pan to hold kitty litter in, and when we bought groceries each week we would also buy her cat food, toys, scratch pole, and kitty litter. Annie stayed with us as our feline crewmember until right after she went into season her first time. One morning she started meowing louder than we had ever heard before, sounding like she was hurting, it scared us. After checking on her and seeing she was okay, we had to make a decision as what to do with her.

A cat in heat that sounded like a mountain lion when she squalled, on a tug boat where crews were trying to sleep, was not going to get it any longer. We had her spade, but she still became a handful to take care of, so Buddy Watts, a deckhand on Reggie's shift agreed to take her home with him, where she is to today some ten years later living the life luxury.

BEGGIN STRIPS FOR BOB

I was getting Annie's food one day with our grocery order, just before she went to live at Buddy Watts' mansion. I had spotted something called Beggin Strips; they're little chewing strips for your dog. I wondered to myself; what could be done with a product that looked like real bacon. I thought for a minute, and decided to buy a bag for my Ole Buddy Bob Taylor, who loved bacon. I kept it hid from him when I got back to the boat with our groceries, for use later when he least expected it. The next evening I cooked a pack of real bacon to make some BLT sandwiches for our supper.

Making sure that he hadn't seen what I was doing, after cooking the bacon I got the Beggin Strips and laid them in the bacon grease to make them smell and look fresh cooked. After me and Carlo, who knew what I was doing had made our sandwiches, I took the extra bacon and hid it in the dish cupboard. With the stage set, I went to his room and called Bob to come eat.

He came bouncing in the galley like a school kid, saying he was starving and it was about time I got his supper ready. I said, "Have at it big boy, the rest of the bacon is yours, me and Carlo have our sandwiches already made." The Beggin Strips were there on the table smelling good and looking real. Bob toasted his bread, spread his mayonnaise on it, and then started building what he thought was going to be the most delicious mouth watering BLT he had ever eaten.

After he got it made he went to work on it, and work on it he did. He liked to have pulled his teeth out of his head on the very first bite. He said, "This has to be the toughest bacon I have ever eaten." I told him it must be that new turkey bacon I bought; me and Carlo had noticed it was pretty tough too," so every time we took a bite of our real bacon, we would act like ours was tough to bite too. He fought with it until he had eaten about half of the sandwich, and then Carlo got to laughing at him. By this time, Carlo says, "Cap, you better tell him, he's going to get mad at us," and with that Bob knew something was up.

He asks, "Tell me, what have y'all done?" I said to Bob, "All I can say to you is this, when I call you from now on, I'll just whistle first, and say come on Bob, here boy." With that said, I showed him the bag that the Beggin Strips came in and I started laughing, Carlo was laughing too. Bob acted like he was mad, then said, "That's okay, I'll get you guys back" and started laughing right along with us after a while, he was just mad because he then had to make another sandwich. When I gave him his real bacon he smiled, but bit a piece of it before putting it on the bread. For a long time if we wanted to get a rise out of Bob, all we had to do was call his name, snap our fingers, and whistle, that would do it.

Paint Spill and Firing

It wasn't long after the Beggin Strips, that Carlo was bringing supplies aboard the boat. Among them were some new cans of white paint without the bail wires on them. Not wanting to make too many trips down the stairs, he would grab as many cans as he could carry in his arms to go downstairs where we kept the paint. You could see it coming, you just didn't know when, and then it happened. From downstairs a crash, followed by some loud swearing, then Carlo came up the stairs with white paint dripping from him like he had been white washed. One of the gallon paint cans had slipped from his hands and had absolutely exploded.

It had everything downstairs covered with white paint including a TV that was stored below. Carlo says, "I quit, I can't believe this happened to me; I'm going home and never want to see another tug boat as long as I live." I said, "No you ain't, you can't quit, at least not until you get that mess cleaned up." Bob stood in the hatch and didn't have much to say, except he was glad he didn't have to clean the mess up.

Carlo had tracked paint every place he put his feet from down below to the outer deck. He had finally calmed down after a while and we all laughed about it, then he cleaned up the best he could, mumbling to himself the whole time. When the paint hit the deck, it was in no way discriminating at what it splashed on, it covered everything, even half way up the walls and lockers.

Later that day at supper, I thought it was time for Bob to get wound up like a clock again. I had told Carlo earlier, I was going to tell him something when we ate supper, just go along with me to see if we could get Bob's goat. Many times we came up with ideas as we went along, and since this was a fresh incident, yes, it was that time. After we had eaten,

I looked at Carlo and said, "I can't believe how clumsy you were." I continued saying how utterly stupid it was trying to carry so much stuff, and not being careful enough not to drop anything. Carlo said, "Okay, it was an accident, just drop it." I said, "Yeah drop it, just like you did with the paint which made a complete mess." Carlo jumped up and said, "All right I messed up, just let it go, I've heard enough about it."

With me hurling smart remarks at Carlo, and him trying to get me to stop, Bob finally got into the act. He said, "It was an accident, he didn't do it on purpose, get off his case." I said, "You stay out of it, this does not concern you." We kept looking at Bob who wanted to say something, but every time he started to I would say, "Stay out of it." It looked like Bob was going to melt under the table the longer we went. Me and Carlo kept our exchange going for several more minutes.

When I told him I should have let him quit, just so I wouldn't have to put up with his sorry ways anymore, that was a good one, it hit home. Carlo got back up to leave the table and said in a loud voice, "Okay then I quit, there, are you happy now?" Just as he opened the door to leave the galley, I said, "Good, get out of here, better than that, you're fired, that way you can't change your feeble mind again." With that said, he slammed the door behind him. Bob went to talking then, "Come on man don't let him leave, you know he needs a job, don't fire him and don't let him quit either," pleading with me like it was for real. I said, "Bob if you don't like it, you can go with him, I'm not going to put up with him anymore."

Bob seemed to be crushed, not knowing how to respond with what I had just said to him, and about that time Carlo came bouncing back through the door and asked me, "How was that Cap, did we get him?" I said, "Carlo, you should have seen his face when you slammed the door when you stomped out of here." Bob asked us, "You mean all this was a put up, and you two didn't mean what you said about quitting or being fired?" When we started laughing at Bob, he was some kind of bent out of shape and said, "Okay boys, the gloves are off, I'll get you both back, and you won't know when it's coming either." I said, "That'll sort be like, well, what we just did to you, right Bob?" We laughed about it, as we always did after a good joke had been pulled off.

Palmetto on Fire,

Both Times

Most times we ran to Port Tampa from Port Manatee where we preferred the main shipping channel. We had just finished a job and were on our way back to Port Manatee for another job, we had some time to kill, so I thought I'd follow the *Palmetto* who was running the Point Pinellas channel. With only about a quarter of a mile between us, I had a good view of her running ahead of us just a short distance.

Me, Bob, and Carlo was laid back enjoying the ride, running half throttle. We were talking and shooting the breeze when I looked at what appeared to be smoke coming out of the *Palmetto*. I said, "Look up there guys and tell me what you see." They both confirmed at what I thought I was looking at, it was definitely smoke. I then called Carroll on the radio and said, "Hey Carroll, it looks like smoke coming out of your engine room, you might want to check it out and see where it's coming from."

He called back out of breath and said, "We're on fire, get up here and get us off the boat, you call the Coast Guard." I put the throttle full ahead and got there just minutes later. Carroll and his crew was back aft, so I got close enough to get them aboard the *Yvonne* with them scurrying as fast as they could to get away from their fire. It just so happened that the *Palmetto's* deckhand was Carlo's brother, Mike Juncal, the engineer was Greg Brown, both were very happy to see us. The Coast Guard came and put out the fire, a very gutsy and brave thing to do, especially since the procedure they did was in an unfamiliar vessel, and a virtual inferno.

The fire caused a lot of damage, even buckling the deck from the heat. The cause of the fire was investigated and a definite cause was never found. It took quite a while to get her repaired and back on line, but the *Palmetto* was worth the money spent on her. There was a lot of work to do even when she came out of the shipyard. After she was running again they started doing jobs, all the while getting her back in shape a little at a time. A few months later, the *Yvonne* and the *Palmetto* were both on our way to Port Tampa, we were to meet an inbound job in "G" cut, and both chose to run the main channel. Carroll had left a few minutes before I did which gave him some distance between us. He was running with his throttle pulled back, so it wasn't long before I caught up with him.

When we come up alongside her, I could not believe what we were seeing. Carroll looked over at us and waved, I called him on the radio and said, "You are not going to believe it, but you appear to be on fire again." He said, "The engineer and deckhand just went back aft to the crews quarters, they went to replace the AC unit that was damaged in the fire, let me call them on the PA to see what it is."

He once again called and said, "You might want to come over and take us off of here." After all the repairs that were made before, how could this be happening again? This fire seemed to be coming from the same area of the engine room, just as before. We once again got Carroll and his crew off the floating inferno, and just as before, the Coast Guard was again called for the second time, to put a fire out aboard the same tugboat.

We called the office to inform them to what had happened, again, and told them neither boat was going to be able to catch the inbound job. We couldn't just leave the boat adrift, so we stayed close to the *Palmetto's* inferno as we had the first time. We wanted to make sure the boat didn't drift into the channel and get in the way of traffic.

When the Coast Guard arrived on scene, they did another wonderful job of extinguishing the fire. Afterwards, we were talking to them about the fire this time, and the first time. As it turned out, they were the same bunch of guys that had come to our rescue before. Just before they left us, one of them said, "Well, I guess we'll see you fellows in a couple of months." That was something we all hoped would never happen again. We didn't know it at the time, but there was more with larger fires to come in the near future.

CARROLL'S TRANSFER LETTER

It was summer time, and several months after the company had been bought out by Bay Transportation Corporation, but quite a while before the two *Palmetto* fires; I had a prank pulled on me that made me mad, and was one that kept me fired up for quite a while. The tug *Yvonne's* keel was laid in 1938 when her construction began, but was not completed until 1939, where she was commissioned as a U.S. Navy sea tug. The *Palmetto* however wasn't built until some years later in 1957, built and owned by the Erie Lackawanna Railroad Company in the State of New York. Although

the tug *Yvonne* was almost twenty years older, she was equipped with air-conditioning, where the *Palmetto* was not. The tug *Yvonne* overall, just seemed to be a more comfortable boat to work on than the tug

Tugs *Yvonne St. Philip* and *Palmetto*-Author photo

P a l m e t t o,

which is why the sting from this was so painful. Carroll had gotten his hands on some stationary with the company's letter head printed on it. He took it to a secretary that we all knew who also worked with one of the companies at Port Manatee. In this letter, he told her to type an

86

official looking document, stating his intent to transfer over to the tug *Yvonne*.

He told her what he needed and to word it the way it would read had the office typed it out. She put in the letter that since Carroll was senior to me, he deserved to be Captain on the better of the two boats, the *Yvonne*, especially since she was equipped with air conditioning. After getting the letter finished, he waited for the time to be just right to get this thing off the ground, and then it happened. Carroll had somehow conned George Atkins, the Operations Manager at the time, to come to the boat and present me with the letter. The reason the air conditioning played such a big part in this prank was that I was, and still am, one of the hottest natured people there is. Carroll knew if I were transferred to the *Palmetto*, it would be a move that would make me mad. I had run the *Yvonne* for months even before the sale of the company. I had also been assigned to her since the sale, I just considered the *Yvonne* as my boat, period.

This never once crossed my mind, which is why when George Atkins came down to the boat that day and presented me with "The Letter," I believed it to be true. George had told Carroll and me to come into the galley; we have to talk about something. We went in and sat down; I was wondering what all this was about. He said, "Bill, I have a very difficult decision to make, here is a letter explaining why I have decided the move." It literally took the wind out of my sails, after reading the letter. I looked at Carroll and said, "I can't believe you'd do this to me, I thought we were closer than that."

George explained; Carroll had asked for this move to take place a few weeks earlier, but he had been taking his time trying to make a decision that wouldn't hurt anyone so they wouldn't have any hard feelings. He said Carroll had a valid point, seeing he had been on the boats a lot longer than I had, and said he had earned the right to choose which boat he wanted to work on. "We'll make the move on the next tour, which will be a Captains transfer only," he said. That too was a slap in the face; Carroll was fixing to take not only my boat, but my crew too.

I said, "George, you know how I am with the heat, being used to the AC like I am now will be something I don't know if I can deal with on the *Palmetto*." They both kept trying to convince me it would be okay, and I would just have to adjust to the heat. Without being convinced on my part, I got up from where I was sitting, threw the letter on the table, looked right at Carroll and said, "If you want to do me this way after all we've been through, I'm not going to like it a bit," and out the door I went.

I left the galley in a pretty bad state of mind; all puffed up with my lip pooched out, like a little kid on the playground that was picked on. I learned later, that when I had walked out of the galley, George had told Carroll, "We had better tell Bill this is just a joke, I don't think this was a good idea, he's taking this pretty hard." Carroll told him, don't worry about it, he'd tell me in a few minutes, he wanted me to stew a while, he said this had went better than he had anticipated. George left the boats and went back to Tampa, and then they started pouring it on thicker and thicker as the day went on. My own crew, Bob and Carlo knew about this little plot to get my goat, and went right along with it.

Bob said, "I don't think it's right what Carroll's doing to you, we'll miss working with you." Then Carlo said, "Cap, I'll tell George I'll transfer to the *Palmetto* too. He also said, "Cap, I'll go to the gates of hell with you." My reply to Carlo was, "That's real good Carlo, you'll go to the gate, but you won't go all the way in, thanks Buddy." This prank carried on through almost the rest of the tour, when I was finally told it wasn't true.

My own crew was the ones that took the monkey off my back with the breaking news. When I found out they knew about it, and were in on it, I was natural born mad. I told them that this one was not funny a bit, while also inquiring as to how long they knew about what Carroll was up to, they said, "We knew for a few days now." I told them, "That's okay, you Guys should have told me, you both had better sleep with one eye open, because I will definitely put my brain into gear thinking up one for each and everyone that took part in it."

Water Hose on Carroll

It wasn't long before I came up with a prank for Carroll. Sometimes Carroll would fish at night, if he was lucky and caught some he would bring them to the boat to clean them. Back then we would tie the boats up alongside each other, side by side. We had a water hose on the starboard side of the *Yvonne* about mid ships, which we hung on a bracket chest high, this would come into play a little later. When we were next to the dock that meant Carroll would tie outboard of us on our starboard side. Carroll caught a mess of fish one night and cleaned them on the bulwarks of his boat, which is like a solid guardrail with a cap on top, using my water hose. The next morning I went out on deck and saw fish scales all over the place, even on my bulwarks.

With his transfer letter still fresh on my mind I went over to his boat with an attitude, I told him he needed to get out there right now, and clean up his mess before the sun baked those stinking fish scales into the paint. He said, "Man, you need to go back to bed and get up again with a different attitude." I wasn't really mad any longer, but it sure felt good to make them think I was. Carroll came outside, and came over to my boat, got my water hose and washed the boat clean. He said, "There, I hope this meets to your cleaning standards." I said, "Thank you, and how about not using all my water up cleaning your fish either."

When Carroll was back aboard his boat, I went to where the water hose was hanging. I positioned the nozzle where it was pointing right at your chest so when you turned it on, it would blast you. I went back across to the other boat and told Carroll, "You broke the water hose valve; I can't even turn it on now." He said, "No way, there wasn't anything wrong with it when I turned it off a couple of minutes ago."

And with that, he shot out the hatch saying, "I'll show you there's nothing wrong with it." When he got to the valve he grabbed it and twisted the handle, just like it was going to be hard. Well it wasn't, the water came shooting out of that nozzle like it was on a mission and wet my boy like he had fallen overboard. We both started laughing at this little set up, and while wiping his face off he said, "That was a good one Buddy, I guess we're even now huh," I said, "Yeah I guess so, until next time."

Rusty Won The Lottery

This is one that is still talked about even to today. We had been dispatched to assist a tug/barge unit from Port Tampa, to out past the Sky Way Bridge one Saturday night. After getting the barge off the dock, the tug made up with a tow wire to tow the barge, so we made up to the stern of the barge with a bow line and took a ride. We were just enjoying the ride since I had the *Yvonne* pulled out of gear, and were just being pulled along by the other tug. With it being Saturday night, this also meant the drawing of the numbers for the Florida lottery was taking place only hours away.

On this particular week, the lottery was over one hundred and twenty million dollars. Chatter over the radio from the tugs up in Tampa was getting to me. They were taking turns bragging about winning the lottery; some were leaving right after the drawing. While some were going to finish their shift and then leave, still others bragged about what they were going to spend their winnings on when they had won.

I had listened to enough of this chatter, and was preparing to launch a transmission of my own over the radio that I hoped would shut them up. After being released from the job we had been on, we headed back into Port Manatee. After securing the boat it was just after 23:00 (11 PM), which also happened to be the time of the lottery drawing. This is some good timing, I was thinking to myself as I walked out to the phone booth to call the dispatcher Russell, on a landline.

When I reached him on the phone I said, "Russell, I have to somehow shut these guys up talking about the lottery, so give me a few minutes to get back to the boat then call me on the company radio so everyone can hear. When I answer, tell me my wife called and wants me to call home, say she sounded excited, but said it wasn't an emergency, just to call when I can. I said, "I'll thank you, then say I'll call her now before I go to bed to see what's up."

After you call me, I'll take it from there, maybe it'll work. He said, "Okay, I hope it does work; it is getting to be annoying to listen to." I went back to the boat and waited for the call. Everything went as planned with our pre-staged verbal exchanges. I just sat down in the wheelhouse chair for about ten minutes. When I figured I had had enough time to go to the phone booth and back, it was time to make the call of all calls. I picked up the radios microphone, and talked just like I was completely out of breath from running.

With an excited voice, I said, " Russell, you're not going to believe this, get in touch with Norman and tell him I have to get off the boat, man this can't be real, it has really happened, I'll give you a land line to let you know what it is, I have to go." With that being done, I went to my room, went to bed, and slept like a baby. Remarkably, there was no more talk about the lottery. What I didn't know was, with Carroll tied up in East Tampa waiting on his next job, he had heard the conversation exchanged between me and Russell.

He called him asking what was up with me, and that he heard what I had told him. He told Russell that if I had to get off the boat, he could run the *Yvonne* and someone else could run his boat, the *Edna*, the boat he was now assigned to operate. I never knew what Carroll heard, or thought he had heard, until later the next day. Carroll not only swallowed the hook, line, and sinker, but he had swallowed the tackle box too.

Early the next morning we were dispatched to shift a tug/barge unit out of Port Manatee over to the Florida Power Corp. power plant in Saint Petersburg. We were to meet the tug *Edna* up in "G" cut where there were two tugs ordered for the docking. After being released from the sailing end of the shift, I took off and ran ahead to get where I knew the *Edna* would be waiting for us. I told Bob what I had done the previous night; we had a good laugh and really didn't give it too much thought.

When I arrived in "G" cut to wait on our job, I stopped about three hundred feet away from the *Edna*. Seeing Carroll and his engineer, Charlie Fernandez, looking like a pair of windmills waving me over closer. I eased over right up to them, stopped the boat, and stepped out on the upper deck so we could talk. Carroll said, "Come on man, tell us what your wife wanted last night, you didn't have to go home, what's going on?" There were questions shooting at me like they were coming out of a gantline gun. I asked them, "What are ya'll talking about?" Carroll said, "I heard what you and Russell said last night, what was all that about?" I had to think quick and come up with something, and said, "The only thing I can think of is that my brother Rusty must have hit the lottery." He turned to Charlie and said, "I told you that's what it was, I knew it, and especially after you told Russell you'd call him."

Carroll knew my brother played the lottery every week, especially when the payout was super high like it was that night. I thought to myself; Hmmmmm, I just might be on to something here. I started out spreading it thin, but it got thicker as I went on. I told them my Mother had called Lois and said that Rusty had called her and said to call the boys and let them know their troubles are over. I said, "The only thing I can think he meant by that was that he must have hit the lottery."

Carroll jumped for joy and said, "Man, we're happy for your whole family, at least someone we know has finally hit the lottery." He said, "Ya'll want to use my Lincoln Town car to go to Tallahassee, you want us to wash your truck?" That was a good one, since my old 1970 Chevy pick up truck was so rusted it would tear the wash rags used to wash it. About the time we had finished talking, the pilot was calling for us. After we finished that job, we headed back to Port Manatee. As soon as we were secured we all got together to talk some more about how rich my Father and brothers had just been made.

We had crew change the next morning with neither Bob, Carlo, nor myself telling anyone any different. The next two days we were off duty, and things I had no control of couldn't have fallen into place any better if I had been directing them myself. Charlie's wife worked for the Sheriff's office, she told some of her coworkers about her husband working with the brother of one of the lottery winners.

Carroll was going into a place he frequented with a bounce in his step, when he stopped at one of the patrons. He told the man, "Life is good, my Buddy's brother was one of the people that hit the lottery." It turns out two people drew the same numbers and had to split the purse. This man told Carroll, "There was one of the families just on TV up in Tallahassee." Carroll said, "Aw man, I missed it, what did they look like?" He said, "It was a big family, one of them was a big guy with a beard." Carroll said, "That was him, the one with the beard, he's my Buddy."

When we came back to work Wednesday morning, I learned about the events of the last two days from Carroll and Charlie. When they asked me when did we get back from Tallahassee and what I was doing at work, especially after coming into such a large amount of money from the lottery? To keep it going I started throwing numbers at them. I said, "Well, you know with two people winning the lottery, and the money being split by two people, that cuts it in half, and after Rusty splits his winnings by five between Daddy and us four brothers being spread over twenty years, that really cuts the yearly payoff quite a bit after taxes." I continued, "It's not going to be enough money to just up and quit my job right now." As luck would have it, just as before, they bought my explanation as to why I had came back to work.

This went on for almost the two full days after we were back on duty. Finally, with me not being able to come up with any more reasons, or wanting to go any longer with them thinking they were working with a millionaire, it was time. I had to give in and break the bad news; I was really going to have to keep on working because my brother Rusty had not won the lottery, he had in reality, missed it by several numbers.

It was all done to get those guys up town to get quiet Saturday night. I said, "Who knew you two were setting there listening to what was said when I called Russell?" I said, "When I pulled up there and seen you two waving like you were trying to throw your arms out of joint, I knew something was on your mind, with what I had said and what you thought was up, I just had to run with it to see where it would go." Needless to say, there were two mad men on that boat that day. Charlie said, "What am I supposed to tell my wife to tell her coworkers, I'm just not going to tell her any different." Carroll said, "I never thought you'd do me this way, I thought we were closer than that, this really pisses me off, I'm truly hurt and don't know if I will ever believe anything you tell me again." I said, "Come on Carroll, that little water hose prank was just to get you primed for the big one."

I said, "This one is payback for your transfer letter, this makes us even." He was mad at Bob, Carlo, and me, not wanting to hear anything we said. When I said, "Come on Buddy, let's kiss and make up," we all started laughing and kept laughing for a while. After a good prank had finally come to an end, laughter was always good for healing wounded feelings, Carroll said, "Okay, but I'll get you." This is something I could count on, with just the way all of our minds worked; pulling jokes on each other was almost mandatory.

Otopan RESCUE

George Atkins called us one day around noon and said we were going to make a run offshore to take a ship some water. He gave me the approximate location that the sulphur tanker *Otopan* would be at around 17:00 (5PM), which was the time she could possibly run out of water for her boilers. He said, "Make sure we had our potable water tank and ballast tanks filled with fresh water, and then plot a course to that position." He told me the ships boiler condenser was trying to shut down and without a fresh supply of water; they might not be able to make it to the Tampa sea buoy. He said, "If we didn't get there in time we would probably have to tow the ship on in." He also needed a time we would be able to get underway so he could tell the agent.

I plotted her estimated position that she should be at around 17:00 from the information given to me on her noon position, from her heading and speed. I advised him, "She'll be one hundred fifty miles south west of the Tampa sea buoy, how are we supposed to find this ship without a Loran to show our location?"

A Loran is an electronic navigation devise that shows your location with readouts on a small screen on the unit. He said, "You have the Loran we had installed on the boat before we sent her to Key West a few weeks ago." I informed him the Loran had been put on another boat and was no longer on the *Yvonne*. He said, "Just go to the sea buoy and head by compass course to where you think the ship will be at 17:00, the ship has forty-eight mile radar capabilities aboard; he can talk you to him."

Knowing the height of eye for the *Yvonne* was approximately 4.5 miles to the horizon, although loaded, the *Otopan* would have a height of eye higher than us. After hearing all this, I knew right then we were going to need Lady Luck along with us for this venture. He told me to take Carroll as an extra wheelhouse man, and depart ASAP.

We got underway not long after we had received the first call, with our charts marked where we could only guess the ship would be at the time she thought she would be, if she didn't run out of water. We departed the Tampa sea buoy a couple of hours later with the best compass course we could come up with using Noah's compass. We were all talking about what if this and that happened. Carroll asked me, "What if we can't find the ship, how are we going to find our way back?" I told him we would just run east until we could see land on the radar, set it on a twelve mile range, and run the coast back to Tampa Bay. We ran until almost 19:00 (7 PM) at a speed of around twelve knots without coming up on the ship, or even being able to contact her by VHF radio.

This was becoming a big concern to us because we had already gone past the time by two hours that we were supposed to come into contact with the *Otopan*. Finally, after repeated tries we were able to raise her on VHF radio. I told him, "I think I know where I am, but have no idea if we have passed the ships location or have gotten to her position, since I was not equipped with a Loran. I suggested for him to alter his course, and turn due east and I would alter my course and run due west. With it being summer time, and although it was 19:00 with the sun about to set, it still gave enough light to see the horizon. After a few minutes had gone by we saw something coming over the horizon, Bob jumped up and pointed forward saying, "Look, there's a sailboat, straight ahead of us."

The more we ran west the bigger Bob's sailboat got. I said, "I believe that's the ship we're looking for, look how big that sailboat's getting Bob, Praise the Lord," I believe his intervention brought us together. I called the *Otopan* and said, "Okay Captain, I'm in visual contact with you now, you can now alter your course back to the Tampa sea buoy."

After her course change, he told me to come alongside mid ship on her starboard side to transfer the water we had brought. After being made secure to the ship, we started transferring what water we had. After finishing, we were told to head back in and bring more water. We turned loose and ran up ahead of the ship using her mast lights, fore and aft, as ranges to get a course heading. By now, it was early the next morning and heard some more of the company tugs talking on the radio. I called them and told them we were just released, and was using the ship for ranges. We learned the agent had ordered more tugs to bring water to the ship, using the *Gloria St. Philip* and the *A.P. St. Philip*.

We passed them after a couple of hours and advised them of the transfer procedure. After getting close enough to have communication with the office, I told the dispatcher to call our relief's in to work. It was after all crew change morning in a few short hours, and we had already had all the fun we could handle for this tour. When we made it back to Port Manatee, we started filling the ballast tanks so there wouldn't be any delay when a fresh crew arrived. We weren't going back, we were going home.

Drowned Man on Raft

There were more happy times throughout the years than there were sad times. A sad time comes to mind that stuck with me for a long time, even years after it had happened. We were assisting a loaded ship docking at Port Manatee berth seven one day. We were on the starboard bow approaching the dock and were told by the pilot to come full ahead.

The *Ouro Do Brasil*, which is an orange juice concentrate ship, was at berth eight on our immediate starboard side, almost directly behind us. Not noticing the crew members working on a small raft positioned on the side of the ship where they were painting, a tragic accident occurred. As we approached the dock, the wheel-wash that was coming from the *Yvonne* went right down the side of the *Ouro Do Brasil*. The little raft flipped over when the wheel water hit it, resulting in the two men to be washed off the raft. One of the men was lucky and drifted away; the other poor soul was tangled up in the lines from the raft and was drowned.

Oblivious as to what was happening behind us, we were alerted by the line handlers at what had happened. I then told the pilot that I had to stop my engine, alerting him to what was going on. We found out later this poor man had several children back home in his South American country. The Port Authority made a policy after this tragic accident, there would not be any rafts in the water with crewmembers on them from moored ships during dockings or sailings.

I had four children of my own at the time of this accident, and really felt bad for what this man's family would be going through. I think you wouldn't have any feelings at all for your fellow man, if something like this didn't affect you the way it did me. This incident stayed with me for a long time, and was very glad to see the new port policy that was now in place. I could only hope it will avert the same thing from happening again.

BOB STAYING DRY

During the years I worked as a deckhand on the tug *Palmetto* alongside Bob Taylor, were the years I discovered the difference between line handling and working deck. There were many times, especially during the cold winter months that I wondered how they could take it. Those were the months that really gave us a cold wet experience, and were also the months that Mother Nature pitched some pretty nasty fits.

Me being larger than Bob, many times he would crouch down behind me while going alongside ships, this so I could shield the water from coming over the bow on him. After I had thrown the heaving line up to the ship, he would then come from behind the human water shield and help me make up the line on the bow bitt.

After I had made Captain on the *Yvonne*, with Bob as my engineer, I was no longer there for him to use me as a shield as he had in the past. Whenever the water was rough, we had a ritual that Bob and I went through almost each, and every time we had a job. He would come to the wheelhouse and look to see if we had water breaking over the bow.

He would turn to me and ask, "Are we going to get wet?" And every time I would answer him the same way, "No Bob we're not, you are, unless this wheelhouse starts leaking, I think I'll stay dry." I said, "You ask me the same thing every time it gets rough, you miss using me as a water break to stand behind, don't you?" I was glad not having to be back out on the deck getting wet, after all, that was what I had set my goal from the get go for, get to the inside of a dry wheelhouse. The night that I was told I had made Captain, yeah, I was one happy man.

Bob The Cook

We really liked working with each other, we also considered us as a team, which Carlo had joined. It was like a carry over from when we were on the *Palmetto* together. Either Carlo or I would do most of the cooking, since Bob's thing was putting a turkey roast in the oven, mashed potatoes, canned gravy, and canned green beans. I remember Snake telling me one time that Bob had asked him if he knew how to prepare a can of clam chowder. Snake told him, "I don't know Bob, let's read the directions on the can here and see if we can figure it out."

We were running up the bay one-day going to a job, with me steering the boat and Carlo busy with a project, that only left Bob to cook. He said he was going to try his hand at cooking some chicken thighs, if I would show him what to do. I laughed and said, "This ought to be good, how am I supposed to help you from the wheelhouse?" He said, "I got it figured out, you tell me what to do, and I'll do it." So with his plan in motion, he started by asking me, should he put aluminum foil in the pan. With each time as he completed a step in his process, he would bring it to the bottom of the wheelhouse stairs to get my approval, and also to be told the next step to do in his cooking class.

He even brought the chicken to the bottom of the stairs between every step, so I could even see how much of each of the different spices he was using. I finally told him to just put it in the oven at 350 degrees, and do not open the oven door until I tell you to. It really turned out pretty good, along with Bob's famous mashed potatoes and green beans. Bob was no cook, but he sure tried sometimes, bless his heart.

DUMPSTER DIVING FOR CANS

When Port Manatee put on a celebration for their twenty-five years as being a seaport, it was before the 9/11 disaster. They were able to have an open house without the fear of terrorism, those times we all miss. They showcased how the port had grown, and with all that had been achieved in the past twenty-five years. During those times, Carroll and I were always going around the different docks picking up aluminum cans for recycling.

I usually took the cans and sold them, put the money in a fair fund jar, then gave it to my kids to share when they went to the county fair every year. The day of the celebration was no different except with the huge crowds that showed up, it seemed everyone there knew we collected cans, so they drank canned sodas like they were going out of style. There were food venders with booths set up for the celebration, and most sold can sodas.

After the day's events had come to a close it was time to get busy can collecting. After the crowds had left port property, we were amazed at what we saw. We would pick up some cans off the ground that were just thrown there. From past experience, we knew we would find the mother load in the large dumpsters that had been brought in for this event. We always went through the trashcans, but these large dumpsters were just begging to be rummaged through.

We also knew we were going to need some help to get this done before the dumpsters were hauled off. Bob rarely went canning with us, usually it was just me and Carroll. This was one time we were able to talk Bob into going with us, I said, "We just need you to hold the bags open, you don't even have to touch the cans." Remember Bob was a clean freak, so him going with us on this can mission was rare. After a while had passed, we finally made it to the gold mines, the dumpsters.

Me and Carroll propped the metal lids back and literally climbed down into them. We left Bob on the top edge holding the bag while we sifted through the garbage getting the cans out. We knew there would be a lot of cans, but never expected so many. There was bag after bag filled, when all of a sudden while we both were bent over picking up cans, we heard a crash and got dark at the same time. We looked up to see what had happened and noticed the heavy metal lid had fallen closed. We noticed Bob was gone too, so we pushed open the lid looking for him, I said, "Bob, where'd you go?"

Looking down on the ground, there was Bob, lying on his back with his head bleeding. I said, "What are you doing down there?" He said with a pitiful voice, "What do you think I'm doing down here, the wind blew the lid over and hit me in the head and then knocked me off the dumpster." Still standing up in the dumpster we asked him if he was okay, with him holding his head and blood running down his face, getting up off the ground his reply was, "What do you think?" I said, "Do you need some help or will you be able to put something on your head?" He got on his bike and took off towards the boat; we just looked at each other, bent over and started canning again. We said to each other, we might better go see how bad his cut is, and with that we crawled out of our treasure pit.

After we got back to the boat and cleaned Bob's head up I called the office to report the injury. After telling our supervisor how it had happened, he said, "With the lid being metal, just to be safe, you better take him to the hospital for stitches and to get a tetanus shot." Bob told me on the way to the hospital, he knew he should have stayed on the boat, and from now on he would. I said, "Now you know you were having fun with us, we'll get back after it when we get back from the hospital." If looks could kill, you wouldn't be reading this book right now.

The hardest part about the whole incident was Bob's long explanation he had to come up with when he told his wife. When he finally reached her by phone, it was not pretty, after telling her what had happened and that we were on our way to the hospital, that was when the conversation got hot. She wanted to know what in the world was he doing in a dump-ster. He finally convinced her he was okay and was going to the hospital just as a precaution.

I was just glad to hear she wasn't going to meet us there. I knew when-ever I saw her again, she was going to rip me a good one for talking Bob into mine and Carroll's can operation. It turned out to be a very short dumpster diving career for Bob, of which we heard about over and over and over again from him. When all was said and done, the total amount we had picked up was one hundred seventeen pounds of cans that week-end, all with Bob's help; we couldn't have done it without him.

Yvonne IS A FAST BOAT

When Carroll's long run as Captain on the *Palmetto* came to an end, he was transferred to the twin-screw tug *Edna*. Although she had two engines, with two propellers and a whole lot more maneuverability than he was used to, she sure didn't have much speed. If you were planning on a slow trip to China by water, the tug *Edna* would definitely be the boat of choice.

We were on our way back to Port Manatee one night where I was just running along at Carroll's pace matching his speed off his starboard side. You know how sometimes something just strikes you funny, well that night it happened to me. Bob was sitting in the wheelhouse with me talking about how the day had gone, and then it hit me, I said to him, "Watch this Bob." I put the throttle full ahead passing by the *Edna* as if she was tied to the dock. When I was past her maybe two hundred feet, I crossed her bow to get to her port side. I then pulled the throttle back to idle letting Carroll pass by us, then after he had went ahead of us, I did it again. I crossed under his stern with full throttle; again we shot by him on his starboard side, one more time.

When I passed him that time, he called and asked me, "Just what are you doing?" I said, "Who me, oh nothing much, just running circles around my ole Buddy." He said, "Yeah, that's what I thought, go ahead and have your fun." He said, "You know I can't do anything about it," I said, "Yeah I know." Depending on which way the current was running it usually took two hours of running time from Port Manatee to our dock in Tampa, and the same going the other way. Carroll had been dispatched for a job at the Egmont Key anchorage to assist a small ship that had engine problems for the entire transit to the dock. We were dispatched for same job, but our location was in Tampa, where Carroll's was in Port Manatee.

I told Bob to get her running quick; we had to get underway ASAP. We were underway within minutes and quickly noticed we were going with the current. Carroll was underway at the same time, where we had about twenty miles farther to run than he did. We were running about as fast as we ever had, looking at the buoys as we went by, there was a super long tail on all of them. A tail on a buoy was what we called the water that went around the buoys, making it look like the buoy had a tail.

That was also what we used to indicate the direction of the current, the longer the tail, the faster the current was running. A flood tide is an inbound current, an ebb tide is an outbound current, that day the current was ebbing very strong. I knew Carroll would have the same current we had, and was surprised at him arriving to the job just one hour before us. We had made the transit in two hours and fifteen minutes; it had taken Carroll one hour and fifteen minutes. We had also run all the way from our dock up in Tampa, where Carroll had only run from Port Manatee, just one short hour longer. I asked him, "Why didn't he pick up his anchor before he took off, man that's a slow boat?" He said, "I know she's slow but she sure is one comfortable boat." Remember that trip to China I had talked about earlier, this was why I said what I did."

The *Edna's* speed or lack of it, often kept her from being dispatched to certain jobs. There was a sulphur ship that started making a steady run into Tampa one year named *Teoatl*, she needed an escort tug to run along with her each time she came in for some mechanical problem she had. With the tugs *Yvonne* and *Edna* using Port Manatee as our homeport, we were closer to their location whenever a tug was needed for that job.

The first boats to be dispatched for any job that was in our location were the Manatee boats, regardless of that vessels destination. We usually knew well ahead of time of any upcoming jobs that we might have to do. Whenever the *Teoatl* was inbound, the *Yvonne* was almost always assigned to that job because of her speed. At times like this Carroll would say to me, "I sure wish the *Edna* was faster, so we could get that midnight job coming up."

He'd just laugh, slapping his hands together and say, "We'll be holding the dock up when you guys get back, show'em what you got, especially how fast that ole *Yvonne* is." The one thing about it was this; the *Yvonne* was definitely a fast boat, she was comfortable, and no matter what he had tried to do, I was also still her Captain.

First Trip to Boca Grande

While working mainly in the harbor, we were occasionally dispatched to jobs in other ports. The *Yvonne* was dispatched for a job in Boca Grande, although I was off duty, I was called from home to go on this short run as an extra wheelhouse man. Reggie Atkins was the Captain since it was his shift, there was also Jerry Anderson as engineer, and Rolando Gomez as deckhand. Having the passed around Loran reinstalled on the *Yvonne*, we entered the Latitude and Longitude of the Boca Grande sea buoy, topped off with water, secured the deck, and was underway about 20:00 (8 PM).

Reggie or I neither one had been there; we did have the required charts to make the trip though, and after plotting the course, we found it to be only about a seven and a half hour run. In that amount of time we could make two round trips to Tampa and back. The docks in Boca Grande were being reconstructed, which made the docking of a ship necessary for tug assistance.

Since we had never been there before and had limited information as to the docking procedure, or even where to meet the vessel, we planned as we went along. We arrived at the sea buoy about 04:00 (4 AM), and thought we could find a shallower place to anchor. We'd wait on a call from the Boca Grande Harbor Pilot for docking instructions.

Having been informed that the ship would not start in until around 10:00, we chose to anchor outside and wait. What we didn't know was the force of the ebbing current coming out of the mouth of Charlotte Harbor. We tried several times to get our anchor to fetch up, without success. The current was so strong we just gave up and decided to go inside and try to find a place to secure the boat.

We had never seen such a strong current and even seen something stranger, as we approached the construction barge moored close to the dock being repaired. An anchor buoy with a light on it was actually being pulled under the water by the force of the current. After finding an old phosphate dock to tie the boat to, we were finally able to relax and talk about experiencing current to which we had never seen.

Later in the morning we were called, and completed the job we were sent to do around noontime. We were advised we were to stay made up to the ships port quarter, however we could shut down the main engine but be prepared to startup with short notice, we would find out why a little later. Talking with the crew aboard the ship, we learned before the construction project had begun, they never used a tug for their docking procedure.

They would always dock using the flood tide to their advantage. When entering the turning basin they would drop the port side anchor, letting the current swing the stern around. After being positioned parallel to the dock a few hundred feet off, the anchor chain was let out to allow the ship to approach the dock. With the ships wheel turning just enough to hold it up into the current, she would slowly work her way to the berth using the ships rudder. When the lines were run and the ship was secure, the docking procedure was completed. The ship would then pay out enough anchor chain to lie on the bottom directly under the bow of the ship; this would prevent another vessel from hitting the chain. They told us the only reason we were there was because of the construction taking place, the mooring bitts were now anchor buoys with shackles for the ships lines to be secured.

A few hours had past after the sun had gone down; as we were out on deck looking in the water, we noticed something. After getting a flashlight and shining it into the water, we were looking at shrimp by the thousands. The current was taking them right past the side of the boat, ah ha, the dip net was the equipment needed.

Oh No, the dip net was missing and no one knew where it was. All those shrimp and no way to catch them, we even thought about taking a bed sheet and somehow making a net. All we could do was look at what could have been some good eating, had we been able to get some. As many shrimp as we were looking at, we could have gone into competition with the Bubba Gump Shrimp Co. The current changed during the night to an ebb tide, the likes of which we had experienced earlier that morning, we now understood why we were left still made up to the ship. We were told to start our engine and push on the ship about half ahead. The ebb current was causing the ship to put a strain on the anchor buoys, so we countered the strain by pushing on the ship. We pushed half ahead with almost a forty-degree rudder, and that was just to hold a ninety-degree angle to the ship. We were finally told to stop pushing after the current had changed directions again.

When it come time for the ship to depart, we were moved to midship while the ship lines were taken off the mooring buoys, with a flood tide they just simply reversed their docking procedure. After the ship lines were brought aboard the ship, they heaved on her anchor chain pulling her towards the anchor that had been dropped the few hundred feet off the dock during her docking. This was one smooth operation that we had never seen done. After being released, we took off for the southwest channel to the entrance of Tampa Bay, another job well done.

Second Trip to Boca

Grande

A few months later, we were dispatched to do it again, this time it was a Bouchard tug/barge unit. I was on duty this time, and was told I would take a Captain off another tug, Dave Scarborough was his name. Dave was the king of practical jokes; I knew I had to be expecting anything at anytime on this trip. Remembering the current we had experienced from months earlier, I knew what to do beforehand. When we arrived at the sea buoy this time, we went right on in and secured the boat to the same dock.

Everything went as before, except this time, there was a tarpon tournament going on with hundreds of boats participating. When we left the dock to meet the tug/barge unit, we came up on them and couldn't believe where they were fishing. There were wall-to-wall boats completely blocking the channel for what seemed to be more than a quarter of a mile, beginning close to the dock and out the channel for quite a distance.

I just idled through the middle of them to go meet the tug. I picked up the mic to the loud hailer and said, "I can't believe how stupid you people are, can't you see that ocean going tug and barge coming up the channel, you people better get out of the way?" I kept this up through the transit out the channel, I found out later there were some big money people I was sounding off to, I'll tell you later about that bit of information I didn't have.

The tug had to actually run outside the channel to keep from running over the out of touch tarpon fishers. Somehow getting the barge around this offshore marina, we were able to maneuver the barge to her berth. The pilot acted like this was normal during these tarpon tournaments; I thought surely, there are tarpon other places than right in the middle of the channel. Maybe the tarpon were after all those shrimp we had seen down there a few months earlier.

Tied up and secure once more, we could get down to a good card game. Well aware of Dave's antics I was bracing for his first prank to come up. Taking a break, I then prepared a feast for dinner, with a smoked turkey and all the fixings. Dave and I were sharing the same room, so after supper he said he was going to lie down and watch TV. After we cleaned up the galley, I also went to my room to watch some TV with Dave.

With it being dark at my closed door, I opened it with caution, went in and sat down. Feeling something wet on my hand, I got up and turned the light on to see what it was, my hand was all yellow with mustard. I asked, "Now I wonder how that got there?" Dave was just lying there laughing like the cartoon dog Mutley. I opened the door and saw mustard smeared all over the door handle, I asked him, "Is this what I have been expecting from you?" He said, "Don't know what you're talking about, what's up?" Playing dumb didn't fool me; it just made me more leery.

I slept that night not knowing if I would be totally yellow by daylight or not. Getting up and seeing nothing had happened, I was amazed. We made fresh coffee, went to the wheelhouse just to talk and admire the view, "Boca Grande is a beautiful place," I told Dave. I chewed tobacco back then and should have known better from past experience. It was refill time so I volunteered to go down stairs to get us more coffee. Not below but just a few minutes, but long enough for prank number two to take place. Back in the wheelhouse and finishing my second cup of java, it was time for a good chew of Levi Garrett.

I opened my bag of tobacco that I kept in the wheelhouse and squeezed a fair amount between my fingers. When that tobacco hit my mouth and starting beating up on my taste buds, I thought I had just put battery acid in my mouth. My Buddy Dave had put the shavings out of the pencil sharpener into the middle of my tobacco. I went to spitting and choking on a nasty taste that I had never tasted before, and hoped never to again. I said, "Okay Buddy, yours is coming, that was a good one, a real original."

After sailing the Bouchard rig later that day, we once again headed back to Port Manatee. During the transit back, Dave was on the controls for a while which gave me time to find something for him. In our room I noticed he had some shoe polish paste in a can with his gear, I also seen his black baseball cap just lying there on his bunk. Since his head wasn't in it at the time, this had to be it. I smeared some black paste all over the inside rim of the cap and left it in the same position I had found it. I never heard what happened when he finally put his cap on. I just would have loved to have been there when he pulled it off. We returned safe, secured the boat, and waited for our next assignment.

This is the explanation that I said I would tell you about earlier. A few days later, we happened to be in Tampa with the boat. While talking to Jimmy Brantner, who was one of the upper level managers, he asked me, "Weren't you on this recent trip to Boca Grande?" With pride, I said, "Yes sir I was," thinking he wanted to know how the job had gone. He said to me, "You know when you go off to unfamiliar places like that; you might want to watch what you yell at people." I asked him, "What do you mean, what did you hear?" He said, "One of those people y'all were hollering at in those boats is a well-known sport-fishing guide, who also happens to be a good friend of Steve Swindell."

Steve was the top manager, and also the son-in-law of George Steinbrenner, the owner of the company. I could have just melted right there on the spot, not knowing how to respond, I just stood there. Steve's friend had called him and told him one of his boats was down there in Boca Grande raising cane over the loud hailer. I finally said, "Yeah it was me, I was just trying to get the boats that were in the channel to move, I thought they were in the way of the inbound barge." I then said, "I can't believe I traveled ninety miles just to get in trouble." I filed this conversation in my memory banks, for the next time I traveled somewhere.

BOB CATCHING MY CHEW

When we were in Port Manatee secured to the dock, it was also mainly the time we used for maintenance on the boat. After work hours we would ride our bikes, or walk on the docks to get some needed exercise. One afternoon Bob and I were out walking, and talking about nothing in general as we did often. Bob and I were both tobacco chewers those days, so after a while, I thought I'd mess with him a bit. Walking side by side, I would shoot my tobacco juice on the ground right in front of him.

He would say, "Aw man, spit on the other side," then he would change sides. Whenever it was spitting time again, I would shoot a charge right in front of him, right where he was going to step. This went on several more times with him continuing to change sides, every time tobacco juice hit the ground in front of him. After messing with him for quite a while I figured it was time to throw this chew away, so I dropped my chew into my hand at the same time Bob was changing sides behind me.

What happened next was a fluke; I could not have done it again if I were paid a million dollars. Bob was still talking while crossing over behind me, I flipped the chew behind my back, landing right in Bob's mouth. The way he started jumping around, spinning, spitting, and sputtering, I thought a bee was after him and was fixing to get gone myself.

When he told me what had happened, I almost split my sides laughing so hard, and so did he after he got the chew cleaned out of his mouth. I laughingly promised not to do that again, he said, "That was nasty, but it was a good shot, a one in a million pitch." I told him I didn't know what the big deal was, since he chewed tobacco too. He said, "Yes I do, but mine is fresh out of the bag and not ABC," (already been chewed).

Pensacola trip with Dave Scarborough

Back to tugging, telling a Dave Scarborough story made me think about going to sea my first time with him. This trip was long before the trip he made with me, this is where I learned about his shenanigans. Having no Mates on the tugs was the reason Captain's were put on other boats as an extra wheelhouse man. Whenever an offshore job came up for a boat, a Captain was added to that boats crew to run as Mate. Dave was the Captain of the tug *Harbor Island* for this time. The Company was contracted to take two deck barges to Panama City, Florida, from Tampa Bay at a bridge project.

The Captains watch is usually six to twelve while the Mates watch was twelve to six. We departed with the barges around 17:00 (5PM). Dave assigned Mark Swisher, the engineer, to be on my watch. He said he was going to take a shower, get something to eat and be right back up. I said, "I got it, take your time." What I didn't know was that the steering linkage, a round rod, came from the wheelhouse and went right through the shower to the stern of the boat. The steering levers looked like a pair of bicycle handlebars that you pushed side to side to steer the boat.

Dave had been below for about ten minutes, when those handle bars seemed to be possessed. They started moving fast, back and forth, side to side, with me trying to hold them still. Mark jumped up and said in a shaken voice, "What's happening, what's making them do that." He shot out the wheelhouse door and said, "I have to go see what's causing this, I've never seen that before," and slammed the door behind him. I was freaking out; I am now by myself with possessed steering levers, and with two barges in tow approaching a bridge.

With this being my first time on what appeared to be a boat needing an Exorcist, we hadn't even gone under the bridge yet, and I already wanted to get off. This was causing the boat to look like a drunken duck going out the channel. It seemed to start and stop a couple of minutes apart. Finally stopping, I was also ready to let Dave have his boat back. Dave and Mark came back up at the same time laughing. Mark said, "I couldn't see anything wrong with the steering, maybe you were just doing something different."

Dave asked me, "What was making the boat go back and forth a while ago?" I said, "If you guys were doing something just to mess with me, that ain't right. If you weren't, then I don't think we need to make this trip until some repairs are made to correct the problem." They both started laughing and Dave said, "Man, you're going to be easy, then he told me what he had done."

I figured out right quick, this was going to be a long trip. We only made a speed of about four knots, that's just over four miles per hour. I had heard of these trips and was now experiencing one first hand. I took about half a dozen bags of tobacco for this trip, hoping it would be enough. Each time I got a chew out of a bag, I would fold the top down, the same way that you fold a toothpaste tube, about two days out and with nothing else happening since the steering rod, "Here's Johnny."

I came up for the noon watch after getting a bite to eat. Dave brought me up to speed as to our present location and ETA. He said, "Have a good watch, see you at 18:00," and went down below. I looked around at the barges, checked the radar, plotted our position, everything was as it should be, life is good I thought.

Mark come up after a while to hang out in between his engine room checks. Having already eaten, I was ready for a fresh chew. I got my tobacco, and to my surprise was unable to open it. My Buddy Dave had been a busy boy; he had opened all the folds on my bag. When he refolded them, he put drops of super glue on each and every one of them; I had to tear the bottom out of the bag just to get my tobacco.

Mark said, "It looks like Dave was bored his last watch." He said,

"Let's super glue his lighter sideways to the ash tray, that way he would have to empty it every time he lit a cigarette." I said, "Do you have any super glue?" He said, "I learned a long time ago, with Dave around, you fight fire with fire, I keep a tube with me," then he told me some of the things Dave had done.

He has super glued quarters to the deck of the tug, just to see how people would react. To mention a few, putting dish soap in the ice trays, a good one, salt in the sugar jar. More is, pointing the sinks rinse nozzle towards you and putting black tape on it so it would squirt all over you when the water was turned on. After hearing these and so many more, I just shook my head and wondered what I had gotten myself into.

During the trip the weather got pretty nasty; which had became a big concern. Besides all of the smaller equipment, there was also a crane on one of the barges. Although the equipment is usually secured and tied down pretty good, we shined the spotlight on the crane revealing some movement. We finally made it into Panama City around 23:00 (11 PM) with the barges, and securing them at the appointed berth at Harders Construction Company, we could also finally breathe easier.

After being secure, we inspected the barges to see how everything had faired through the rough seas. We noticed the counter weight on the crane was just before falling off the brace it was secured to, our hearts jumped up into our throats. With the rough seas we had just come through, the Lord was with us for sure. If the counter weight had fallen off the brace, the swinging action would have broken the cables and we would have lost the whole crane at sea.

We had also decided to get a good night sleep before departing the dock. We got up the next morning and watched the TV weathercast while we ate breakfast. The report was wave height three to five feet with diminishing seas, that didn't sound too bad. We made a unanimous decision to head back, so off to Tampa we headed. A few hours later we were south of Cape San Blast, where the seas evidently hadn't heard the same report we had listened to earlier.

We spotted some shrimp boats, pointing at them I told Dave, "Those are some crazy guys over there." He said, "They don't even know it's getting rough; shrimpers have to keep going," and since we had gone this far offshore, so did we. Dave had run a shrimp boat in the past, as did my Dad. "If a boat is tied to the dock," he says, "It's not making any money."

The seas finally built to have ten to twelve feet in height, far from what the three to five we had seen on the TV. On a tugboat sixty-five foot long, and although we were heading home, we knew this was going to be a very uncomfortable ride. I would come up for my watch and Dave would ask me how I had slept. I would tell him, "It's like having a nightmare, the whole earth was continually rocking, and people kept coming and going through a hole in the ground." I said, "It was like riding a bicycle in a potato patch."

Since you couldn't go out on deck to get to the wheelhouse, there was an access hole installed to do just that, have access inside the boat. You could come from the galley through the access hole, which was located in the deck of the Captains room. I guess every time one of them would come through the hole it would half way wake me up. That would explain what I thought I was dreaming, with the earth shaking and all.

The seas had knocked the potable water cap loose and contaminated our water tank with salt water. Since Dave didn't want salt water throughout the system, we couldn't even flush the Jon. The trip back took longer than normal due to the rough seas. As we were entering the bay, Captain Sonny Stoll called us form the tug *Gloria* and welcomed us back. Dave told him about our water problem, and said we've had to open green beans just to get water to drink, now that was funny. However, we did make it back without a single prank being pulled too; funny how rough seas can calm some fellows down and change your joking ways.

TUG *Seafarer* AND

Balsa 37 COLLISION

A few years later on August 11 1993, as the tug *Seafarer* and barge *Ocean 255* had just passed Egmont Key, she was involved in an accident. The *Balsa 37* had just departed Port Manatee channel around 05:00. My crew at the time was Bob Taylor as engineer and Steve Parrish as deckhand. The tug *Yvonne* was alongside the inbound tug *Marlin* and barge *Gulf Stream*, heading right back into Port Manatee. No one could have predicted what would happen next, less than an hour later.

As we were pushing the barge *Gulf Stream* to the dock, we heard Carroll come over the company radio yelling. He had panic in his voice saying, "There has been a collision and a barge was on fire, there were people in the water, send help now, get some more boats heading this way." With us knowing which job Carroll had been dispatched to, we couldn't figure what in the world he was talking about. Sounding very excited, he just kept repeating what he had transmitted at first, over and over again. I told Bob to look towards the bridge; it looked like the sun was rising, but we were looking towards the west, we knew that just wasn't right. While still in Port Manatee, we were about eight miles as the crow flies away from the accident site.

The *Edna* was escorting another tug/barge unit up the bay who was down on one of her engines. He was made up to the barge on the starboard bow. Picture this, a small ship, *Balsa 37* was outbound who had just departed Port Manatee, the tug *Capt. Fred Bouchard* with barge *No. 155* was inbound for Port Manatee, followed by the tug *Seafarer* with barge *Ocean 255* who was also inbound for a berth in Tampa.

All of the units involved had already agreed over the radio on how they would pass each other in the channel, a one-whistle pass which was a port-to-port passing. The Pilot on the *Balsa 37* evidently saw something he did not like, and changed the passing agreement with the tug *Seafarer* at the last minute. Changing to a two-whistle pass was now starboard to starboard passing; she then crossed in front of the inbound barges. The tug *Seafarer* had started over taking the tug *Capt. Fred Bouchard*, with the *Balsa 37* ending up in between the two tug/ barge units.

They all met at a location just past the widest part of any of the channels, from the sea buoy to any dock in Tampa Bay. If the ship would have just kept her course and passed both tug/barge units with the agreed one whistle pass, I wouldn't be writing about it now. When the ship tried to go in between the two barges, the result was a collision involving all three vessels. The *Balsa 37* hit the port bow of the barge *No.155* rupturing her forward cargo tank. Just Seconds later with her starboard side, the *Balsa 37* collided with the starboard side of the barge *Ocean 255*, which in turn caused an explosion. We learned afterwards that when Carroll seen what was happening, he told his engineer Doug Bogard, "Turn our line loose quick, we have to get out of here." Doug said later, "I had only taken a few steps when the brilliance of the fiery explosion came right through the porthole, it was unreal, it was like a flashbulb going off right in my face; we were frightened, not knowing what was going on."

The fire could be seen from miles away, with an enormous amount of black smoke billowing into the air. The smoke could be seen even while it was still dark, the enormity of the fire was seen a lot better after sunrise. The barge *No. 155* was carrying 120,000 barrels No. 6 black oil, bound for the power plant in Parrish for Florida Power and Light. Although it was oil, No. 6 oil was hardly flammable in its present state. The barge *Ocean 255* however had a cargo of jet fuel, unleaded gasoline, premium gasoline, and No. 2 diesel oil, totaling 225,000 barrels of the highly explosive liquid. A bulk barrel is measured at 42 gallons; this was many a tank full of gasoline burning up, no matter how you measured it.

We were underway to their location as soon as we could turn loose, and was listening to what seemed to be something Hollywood had dreamt up for a movie. The pilots' boat had been close by and responded to the May Day transmission. The tug *Seafarer* turning to port had also run aground after the collision. Not knowing what ten million gallons of gasoline would do, a decision had to be made. The explosion had already blown a large part of the barge deck up, flipping it atop of the barge. All

Tug *Seafarer* with the barge *Ocean 255*
Courtesy of The Bradenton Herald

of the crew had jumped into the water off the stern trying to get away from the burning barge, along with the twelve-year-old son of one of the tugs crewmembers.

The water seemed to be on fire from the spilled gas and was spreading towards the tug. With a heroic act, the pilot boat operator rushed to the crewmembers with fire circled all around them. He literally rescued them from what seemed to be a certain death from the burning sea. Marshall Ancar, who was the barges cargo Mate had told me that Captain Charlie Chapman had even tried to reenter the wheelhouse in order to disengage the pins to free the tug from the barge. This was impossible to do, since the windows had been blown out from the explosion and the heat from the fire was just too great.

They weren't even able to get on the boat deck to get the life raft, this was why the decision to jump overboard had been made. The tug *Capt. Fred Bouchard* was ordered to stay west of the Skyway Bridge in the Mullet Key channel. The black oil spilling out of her ruptured tank had caused concern. The Coast Guard wanted to keep the barge out of the bay in hopes of lessening the environmental impact. We were dispatched to assist tug *Capt. Fred Bouchard* to help hold her barge in the channel.

The tide was ebbing which helped take the spilled oil away from the beaches or any land. This turned out to be disastrous when the direction of the tide changed, a turn of events, so to speak. We had put a line on the barge *No. 155* just west of the Skyway, and could only see from a distance, the fiery inferno barge we had assisted many times before into the dock. Some oil was transferred from the bow tank to the stern tanks farther aft on the leaking barge. Another Bouchard tug/barge unit just happened to be in the area and awaited the okay to transfer the oil from the barge *No. 155* to her own barge.

The okay was finally given and the transfer was completed safely. Raising the ruptured bow high enough off the waterline; making it possible for a transit up the channel to prevent more oil from escaping. After being

released from the barge *No. 155*, we were dispatched to the heavily damaged ship, *Balsa 37*. The ship had anchored close to the collision site to wait for orders on what to do. Arriving to her location we were now

Balsa 37 with extreme damage
Courtesy of The Bradenton Herald

closer to the burning barge, looking at all the damage from all three vessels, it was a miracle there was no loss of life. The *Balsa 37* had her starboard quarter peeled open like a sardine can, the hull was completely opened to give you visual access to the inside. We could see the whole insides of this one stateroom, with the bed, dresser, cabinets, even the pictures on the wall, just as it was left by that crewmember. With the damage that we were looking at, it was apparent the good Lord was watching out for the crew aboard the *Balsa 37* on this morning. A few years earlier on the Mexican bulk carrier *Azteca*, we had seen some extremely bad damage aboard her too. Although they were both horrific to look at, they were caused by much different circumstances. An open door even exposed the toilet in the head, where, Bob, Steve and I all said at the same time, "Can you imagine sitting on the Jon when the collision occurred." We laughed at what someone might have thought was happening at that particular moment when the collision came through the ships hull. Knowing this was a very serious matter; we went back to reality and were just thankful to the Good Lord that no one had gotten hurt. The bow of the ship did not show any damage at all, not even a small dent. We found that to be very strange, especially after seeing the large gaping V shape hole that the ship had made when she collided with the bow of the Bouchard barge *No. 155*. We had put up a line through the center chock aft of the ship with orders to assist the *Balsa 37* farther into the anchorage.

Get into shallower water and push on her until you're sure she's aground, we were told. I knew purposely running a ship aground was against everything we had ever been told not to do. However, not knowing the extent of the damage, this decision was made to keep the ship from sinking until a diver's inspection could be done and completed. I then understood and told my crew, 'This will be a first time doing this, and we won't even get in trouble."

Having been anchored; she heaved it aboard and we headed for shallower water. I was told, "When she runs aground, come full ahead to push her as hard aground as possible before she drops the anchor." With this little operation done, and with all traffic stopped until safe passage was reestablished, we were told to stay with the ship. *Wow*, what a day to remember this would be.

Throughout the day it looked like a stirred up ant hill, all around Mullet Key. There was oil booms placed everywhere in an effort to keep the black oil from reaching the pristine beaches that were known for their beauty. Boats of all shapes and sizes were hired to help with the recovery of the black oil still floating on top of the water. A deck barge with shelters placed on it was brought out and placed close to the action where a command center could be established.

Bay Transportation even placed tug *Trooper* alongside the deck barge where meals for the workers could be prepared. Karl Workman, a deckhand and a super cook, was placed aboard the *Trooper* to prepare the meals. He was kept busy preparing meals for around two dozen people, for every meal. All these meals were prepared on an apartment size stove that was meant for no more than a four-man crew. A forty-cup coffee maker was also needed for all the coffee being drank. Groceries were delivered almost everyday since there was limited storage space too. Karl did a remarkable job with what he was asked to do in his four-man galley, Bravo Karl.

When traffic started moving again, we went back to ship assistance in the harbor. The port being closed for a short period of time will back up the ship movement in a big hurry. We noticed this because the amount of jobs that we were doing, an extra wheelhouse man was also added on the first day, which was greatly needed. From the time of the accident, we were kept busy with an assortment of different jobs.

The barge fire was finally extinguished after more than seventeen hours of very intense fire fighting. After enough time had been given for the barge to cool down, she was able to transfer the rest of her very volatile cargo to another barge. The heat from the fire had actually fatigued the integrity of the metal, making the barge unstable to move in her present state.

Workers had to install large I-Beams, welding them in a position would replace the missing deck, making the barge almost as it was before the fire. The extra metal beams stiffened the barge with enough stability to pass the Coast Guard inspection, where she was now possible to be taken to the shipyard for repairs. The Tampa Bay area had never witnessed such an impact to the environment caused from an accident of this magnitude, and would surely remember it for years to come. Poor old Carroll thought he was out of the woods, but after the accident had happened, and the messy job of recovering the spilled oil was taking place, the tug *Edna* was put into an oil recovery mode for next few days.

It just so happened weeks earlier, there were some distinguished looking visitors that came to Port Manatee in search of. They were there to look at the Manatee boats, and choose a tugboat that could be utilized at the needed time to aid in the recovery of a major oil spill. The tug *Edna* was very maneuverable with her twin screws, and a big back deck that just filled the bill. This was also a job that the need for speed was not necessary, a quality suited for the tug *Edna*. After she had been labeled the boat of choice, the Coast Guard came down and had previously mounted an adjustable metal arm on her deck that extended out away from the hull of the tug; this is where the recovery boom was attached.

They then removed it for storage until it was needed at a later time. Well, that time had come, and this time it was for real. I had seen smaller oil spills in the past, but this one was a dandy. I in no way envied Carroll and his crew, with what they were going through in this process. I for one was just glad that the company Management at that time, really did know how to run a tugboat company, and also had the foresight to crew the boats with the extra personnel we needed.

TUG *Seafarer* HIT A DOCK

The new company, Bay Transportation Corp., was also called D/B/A (Doing Business As) St. Philip Towing, which was a well-established name in the Marine Industry for tug service. Not long after the buy out, all of the Ports in Tampa Bay were back to doing business as usual. After the last story, I remembered another time that involved the tug *Seafarer* and Barge *Ocean 255* in a collision. The tugs *A.P. St. Philip* with Captain Roy Cannon aboard, and *Yvonne St. Philip* with yours truly at the helm were assisting the tug *Seafarer* with her barge into Old Port Tampa. The *A.P.* was on the port bow, and we were on the port quarter.

As the barge was turning to starboard and started to enter the slip, the tug *A.P.* was told to come full ahead. The flood tide was starting to set the barge to the north side of the slip entrance, right where there were some old rusty clusters of pilings, that is where we did not want to get into. We also called these pilings can openers, that is what they would do if the weight of a barge or a ship ever came into contact with them.

When the barge became broadsided to the current, I was also told to come full ahead and try to push this loaded barge up into the flood tide. All three tugs were working as hard as possible to get the barge into the slip, and out of the pressure of the current, a battle we were losing. The barge was about half way into the slip, but had been set to the north by the current, and is why a slack water docking policy was implemented.

The *Yvonne* was so close I had to come alongside the barge to miss the can opener. Just as I cleared it, I steered hard right to get back on a ninety-degree angle to the barge. Just a few seconds later we saw the newly constructed dock get hit by the starboard bow of the barge. For me, I was just thankful there were no sparks, with the meeting of crunching concrete and the metal of the barge, this could have been disastrous.

Captain Roy and I reported what had happened to the office, and was told not to speak to anyone. They said, "The lawyers will be there shortly, write down exactly what had happened." Since I had been promoted to Captain, this was my first lawyers meeting. I had the misfortune of attending previous mandatory meetings with other sea lawyers about accidents that had happened during the years as relief Captain. I knew this was just part of being a Captain and was ready for the responsibility that goes along with it. Although this was a brand new repaired dock that another ship had previously damaged, it was once again in need of the construction crews.

THE STONE COLD

ADVENTURE

In the spring of 1992 I had a new deckhand come aboard that was like a breath of fresh air. His name was Jim Stone, who let us know he was married to Sharon Stone, not the actress, he would say. She was a very understanding woman though, with what Jim had wanted to do, she sounded like my wife with a go for it attitude. Jim had been working in the white-collar workforce for years, and said he just wanted to have a change in his working lifestyle. He was a very knowledgeable man, and it showed with his obvious intellect. Jim told Bob and me he had applied for this job a few months earlier. Steve Howell had told him to get some experience and then come back once he had it.

Well that is what he did, he traveled the docks looking for a job working on a boat, any boat, where he could get the experience that he was told that he sorely needed. The job application process was not going well, until he was finally told those magical words, you are hired. Jim told us he was pressed for time and was only given a few hours to get home, pack his gear, and get back to the small ship before she sailed, bound for Haiti.

He said, "Sharon was not at home and didn't know I had gotten a job, so I was going to leave her a note." I said, "You mean you were just going to leave and not tell her face to face, you can't do that." He said, "I was writing all the pertinent details down for her, I was leaving my truck at the dock; time was running out and couldn't wait much longer." Just before leaving his home, she came driving up, that was close. He was hired as a deckhand, working aboard a small ship called the *M.V. Pirana*, making runs to Haiti.

He told us, "The ship was only 160 feet long with a gross tonnage of 392 tons." The crew of four was a real life family affair, the Captain was the Son, the Chief Engineer was the Dad, the Mate/cook/bottle washer was the Mom, The other crewmember was a Haitian, who was the deckhand that Jim would be replacing, and would be getting off when they arrived down in Haiti.

He told us they sailed with a crew of four; there would be a crew of five for the trip down only, with the Haitian getting off in Haiti. He was on this ship for eleven weeks without any relief days. Jim would tell us how they conserved their water by recycling it. Mom would start the cycling in the morning, by washing the breakfast dishes with fresh water. Then using that saved water for the lunch dishes, and also the supper dishes. When the crew bathed, that daylong dishwater was once again used and saved one more time. Dad, the Chief Engineer, would then use it for any washing down in the engine room that needed to be done.

There was a very large, thick plastic water storage tank on the stern deck used for extra water storage. He was told, "Taking on water in Haiti was not possible." Jim said how ironic it was for him to start a Maritime career, on a ship named *Pirana*. He had started on December 12 1991, and was aboard continuous until February 27 1992, seventy-seven total days worked without a relief. After just over a week from coming back off his Caribbean cruises, Jim was back on the job hunt, his first stop was Bay Transportation Corp. Offshore Manager Steve Howell must have been impressed with the story Jim had told him, because this time when he applied for a tugboat job, he was hired. His experience was only what he had learned from the dry cargo freighter. He worked a couple of days aboard the tugs *Harbor Island* and *Bradenton*, and then he was sent to the tug *Yvonne*. My boy Bob would have to show him the ins and outs of tug boating, the way we did things our style.

I remember when he first came aboard the tug *Yvonne*, his line throwing skills needed quite a bit of practice. Although Bob could throw the heaving line up on the higher ships when we went alongside, Jim said he wanted to do this job. That was usually one of the deckhand's jobs, tying the heaving line to the tag line and tossing it up to the ship. He really tried hard and wanted to pull his own weight as a tugboat crewmember.

After seeing him attempt several tosses, it was definitely time for class to begin. We had finished a job one day, and after securing the boat to the dock, I told Jim to come go with me and bring a heaving line. We walked over to a light pole that I had used in the past for this very same thing. I pointed at the pole and said, "When you can throw that line straight up in the air using the pole as the simulated side of a ship, you can throw it up on ships." "Practice makes perfect," I said, and with that, I left him to practice his little heart out.

Jim was also a perfectionist with the tenacity of a bulldog; he stayed at the pole, practice throwing until he could place the monkey's fist right over the top of the pole. Maybe I should have found that pole before I took the infamous monkey's fist home with me, it might have saved me the cost of a truck window.

Whenever we would depart the dock for a job, the deckhand would get on the dock to release the lines; Jim would run from one end to the other, now that's wanting to make a good impression. After some days had gone by, we came in for duty one Friday morning, I had brought a book with me about tugboats, called Primer of Towing. I gave it to Jim to read that day and told him that it might help him to understand some of the terminologies, and overall procedures we are required to do.

Jim Stone visits the *Hawk*
Author photo

He came to me Sunday morning with the book, I said, "Keep it until you've read it, I'm in no hurry to get it back." He said, "I have already read it, where do we keep the dynamite?" I said, "What are you talking about, dynamite, where is this coming from?" He said, "On page 164 paragraph 3, (arbitrary numbers), it says dynamite is sometimes used to blow the cable tow wire apart when you get in irons, to keep the tug from tripping." I took the book and flipped it over to the page he had said went to that paragraph, and sure enough there it was. I told him, "I have read this book and don't remember that being in there." He just smiled and said, "It's a gift, I have a very good memory." I later found out that Jim had a BA, in Mathematics and Chemistry. I knew he wanted to work on the water, but with his talents and intellect, he was definitely destined for greater jobs.

When Jim came on the boat, Bob and I had told him of our history, where we three were now swapping stories as we had done with Carroll when I was hired. The subject of cooking finally came up where I had mentioned what a mean spaghetti sauce I could make. He says that sounds like a challenge, not with me, but my Wife Sharon, she makes the best sauce you have ever tasted. He told us that she takes almost two days to make her sauce, and it is worth every minute spent too.

I told him it only takes me about an hour to make mine; he said that's not real Italian sauce. "It's real when I put it on top of some spaghetti noodles and eat it," I said. A time had to be chosen for the event; with the next weekend on duty for the big spaghetti sauce cook off. I knew Sharon is an Italian woman, and probably a good cook, I just didn't think spaghetti sauce had to be cooked for no two days. I thought; shoot, two days, it'd be stuck to the bottom of the pot. We were going all out with this contest, and needed some judges for tasters, so Bob's wife and mine were enlisted for the jobs.

The big weekend was upon us, Saturday suppertime was the planned meal, jobs withstanding. First thing Friday morning Jim tells me, "Sharon started her sauce this morning, when are you going to start yours?" I told him, "Probably tomorrow afternoon, it doesn't take me two days to make my world class sauce." He laughed and said, "You're going to be very disappointed when she gets here."

She was making meatballs on the side, I put meat in the sauce, she used fresh spices, where I poured them out of a plastic container. My Mama taught me how to cook; I had made it the same way for years and never had any complaints. He said, "Prepare your taste buds for the treat of their life." We had store bought garlic bread, and fresh made salad to make the meal complete.

No jobs were coming up, so all parties were contacted and told like they say on The Price is Right, come on down. With everyone there

I gave thanks, the only rule was for all to be honest with their prefer-ence. Can anyone guess who won? That's right, we were both winners with both sauces being delicious, and no decision could be made by the impartial judges. The challenge was lighthearted and fun, which brought us all closer together.

We have been to each other's homes to share meals since, with a friendship that still remains to the present day. Jim only stayed a little while longer needing a more permanent position, instead of the relief list that he had been put on which was a hit or miss when you would be called for work. He stayed for only twenty-five days with us and then moved on to Dann Ocean Towing Inc. He worked with them for a total of eighty-two days, until his short Maritime career finally came to an end. Jim's talents were many; this would become evident in later years. Jim is now a Registered Nurse and has worked in Emergency Rooms for most of his ten year nursing career, his wife Sharon is also a Nurse, not the actress, and is doing well.

Tug *Beverly Anderson* Fire

It was April 16 1992; we were just chilling out and watching a little TV, not quite ready to go to sleep yet. I monitored the radios from speakers mounted in the Captains quarters; I had the volume adjusted just loud enough to hear, in case we were called for a job. While we were secure in Port Manatee one night, I heard the tug *Eagle* being dispatched to a tug on fire up the bay in Gadsden point cut. I shot up the stairs and called the dispatcher, I told him we could probably beat the *Eagle* there since we were much faster than they were and about the same distance away. I told speedy Bob to get her running quick, there's a tug on fire and we're going to see if we can help ASAP.

We were underway in just minutes, with Bob and our new deckhand, Stewart Bradshaw as my crew. We learned the tug *Beverly Anderson* was ablaze with an engine room fire, and was still in the notch of the barge *Mary Turner*. In less than an hour and just beating the tug *Eagle* there by minutes, we pulled up to the port stern quarter of the tug *Beverly Anderson*, making fast to the tug. We had already attached the fire hose to our monitor before arriving in preparation of firefighting. Stewart passed it over to the *Beverly's* crew and Bob pumped the water to them with our fire pump. I told Stewart to stay out on deck and to just stand by close in case they needed anything from us.

The tug *Eagle* had arrived and was told to use her fire monitor to shoot water into the openings of the engine room. She was positioned off the stern of *Beverly Anderson* for a straight shot. The wind was blowing pretty strong that night, so some of the tug *Eagle's* water was blowing right over on the *Yvonne*. The Tampa Fire Department's smaller fireboat had to depart when the seas had gotten so rough, and was unable to stay alongside the *Beverly Anderson*.

The water from blowing over on the *Yvonne* was to where Bob and I could hardly see through the wheelhouse windows. The *Beverly's* paint locker mounted just above the engine room was repeatedly flaming up, even after being extinguished numerous times. With the fire finally brought under control, and with the artificial rainstorm stopped, we could finally go out on deck.

The Captain of the tug Beverly Anderson was Junior Montgomery, whom I had known for years. We looked at Stewart when we got out on deck and started laughing at what we saw. He looked like a drowned rat; there was not a dry thread on him anywhere. I said to him, "I know I said to stay out here on deck, but I didn't mean for you to get soaked, you could catch pneumonia out here in this wind, go take a shower and dry off."

Captain Junior came over to us and shook all our hands and said, "Billy, I believe we would have lost her if you hadn't have got here when you did." He had taken our hose and went towards the engine room where he fought the fire right along with the crew. Now being able to enter the engine room with the fire being put out, it was time for a head count. It had revealed there was a man unaccounted for, and not seen anywhere aboard the boat.

Something every seaman hates to hear is a missing sailor. Searchlights started coming on from every boat, looking for the missing engineer Steve Bodden, he had moved here to Tampa from Honduras. It turns out that when the initial fire had started, he was below in the engine room and was able to extinguish the fire. However, when the fire flashed back, he was unable to extinguish it the second time and decided to leave.

With the fire being overhead, he went up the stairs through the fire trying to get out of the engine room. With his clothes on fire, coming through the hatch he noticed some liquid laying on the deck. Steve mistook the liquid for water; instead, it was either diesel fuel or hydraulic oil. He then rolled in it trying to put the fire on his clothes out which caused the fire to flash all over his oil soaked clothes. He headed for the stern at which time he jumped overboard to put the fire out. Since the fire had started while underway, the fiery tug was rapidly going away from where he had just jumped overboard.

Looking for anything to climb up on, the burned engineer noticed an anchored barge and swam towards it. There was a Sheridan tug/barge unit anchored in Gadsden anchorage awaiting a berth. God must have placed that barge, in that location, for the sole purpose of saving this mans life. Before Steve had been found, and not knowing he had swam towards their barge, the Sheridan tug started backing out of the barge notch in response to the search. He had said later, "When I seen that tug backing away from the barge, I thought this is the end."

He said, "Thinking about my children, my three daughters is what kept me going." He said, "The will to survive just kicked in; the Lord brought me through this tragedy for a reason." Swimming towards the anchored barge, he had said he must have swum for forty-five minutes before finally reaching the barge. With continuous yelling, he was trying to get anyone's attention; at last, a man on the barge heard him and guided him towards the barge's pigeonholes. Pigeonholes are small round recesses made in the side of a barge with horizontal bars inside, used just like a ladder. Having been guided to them, he then started painfully climbing up the barge using the pigeonholes. When he finally made it to the deck of the barge, notification spread fast.

While not knowing Steve had been found, the search continued, and was not stopped until this radio transmission was heard, "We have him over here on our barge, he's burned pretty bad, but he is alive." Everyone was glad to hear Steve had been found; it's always good to hear of finding a lost fellow seaman who is still alive.

With a job well done, we headed back to Port Manatee. We really felt good at knowing what we had just been a part of. The appreciation was shown by the crewmembers with a repeated thank you. I had always heard there had been a sort of hidden rivalry between St. Philip Towing and Gulfcoast Transit Co. With both companies being in the tugboat business, you could really expect nothing less. We also heard that what our company had done by sending the tugs *Yvonne* and *Eagle* to what was a very dangerous situation, was a good thing to patch up hard feelings. With the presentation of this plaque, it was the most treasured acknowl-

Appreciation plaque
Author photo

edgements we were ever presented. I have it in my home today with all of my other tugboat memorabilia that I have collected throughout the years. I am writing this book some thirteen years after this tragic accident had occurred. Although the tug *Beverly Anderson* has long been repaired, with a lot of water having gone underneath her keel, I am still thankful to the Good Lord that no deaths were attributed to this fiery Maritime accident.

It was years before Steve could even get out in sunlight, and the last we had heard, he has yet to have returned to work. God bless you Steve, we wish you all the best and a full recovery. My crew was presented with the appreciation plaque which was kept aboard the tug *Yvonne*, displayed on the galley wall.

The plaque was left on the tug *Yvonne* until years later when she was sold to Moran Towing. I was presented with it from the last crews that was assigned aboard her, and display it proudly on my wall at home. It is a constant reminder for the appreciation given to my crew, for the assistance we gave to fellow sailors.

GROUNDING ON

CHRISTMAS EVE

These fire accidents brought back memories of my *Palmetto* deckhand days, thinking about what would've, or could've, or might've happened, had the circumstances been slightly different on this particular day. Both tugs, *Palmetto* and *Bradenton* had been dispatched to a grounded ship out towards the Tampa sea buoy one Christmas Eve around 17:00 (5PM), a bad time indeed. Whenever we had worked groundings where the main engine was at full throttle for a long period of time, we seemed to have a problem. We looked like we were in a stealth mode after a few hours of hard pushing.

The boats electrical breakers were in the fidley, which is the open space right over the main engines and close to the exhaust stacks. With an open space over the engine room, the heat rose directly past the place-ment of the breaker panel. An electrician had told us that whenever the temperature near the breaker panel reaches around 200 degrees, they would trip. We knew this time would not be any different, if we were there pushing for any length of time.

When we arrived, we immediately started pushing full ahead on the port bow. While still daylight and fairly calm, we thought this won't take long to get her off ground. With the ship not moving at all, and after we had been pushing full ahead for hours, our minds were rapidly changing. Missing our family, and with this being Christmas Eve, this grounded gasoline tanker was rapidly becoming the event we did not want to spend all night doing. Remember the electricity breakers; one by one they started tripping, the deck lights, galley lights, and even some of the engine room lights.

Although they were breakers, we lost lighting only, and never lost any of the operating machinery. We were a ghost boat, a stealth mode we referred to as being in. When the sun had set it started making the seas rougher with higher winds. The windows were open in the wheelhouse trying to get some air, since the heat from the main engine had made it very hot below with no air conditioning. Carroll said he smelled something like an electrical fire, or some rubber burning. Bob took off to the engine room to investigate the source, coming back in a few minutes saying he found nothing burning. By this time, we could smell it like it was in the room with us. Bob and I went back downstairs to trace the source of this smell. We found it all right, the tires we used for fenders right on the bow, also known as the bow pudding, was smoldering.

The *Palmetto* was pushing so hard the bow pudding was stuck against the ship. With the seas progressively getting rougher and the wave height increasing, we knew we were in for a bad night; especially since there was no movement of the grounded ship. The bow of the boat was riding up and down inside the stuck pudding, causing friction between the boat and tires. This resulted in a smoldering tire, with the knowledge of fire and gasoline not mixing; we immediately grabbed the water hose and started pouring the water on it trying to extinguish it.

Carroll relayed this hot information to the Pilot, which he immediately said, "Stop pushing and back away from the ship." The ship that was aground was a loaded gasoline tanker. An open flame would have probably been the catalyst needed to ignite the fumes. A smoldering tire, probably not, but with a tanker full of gasoline you never take a chance. Just to make sure, we kept our smoldering tire away from the ship and put a towline up.

This meant we were now pulling, instead of pushing on the ship. We were also several hundred feet away from the ship. As time progressed throughout the night, the weather worsened, with higher winds and a wave height of eight to ten feet. The *Palmetto* and *Bradenton* both kept breaking their towlines we would send up to the ship, finally making them too short to use as hawsers. The ship began passing their tie up lines down to us, which were also nine inch lines. We would pull away from the ship a few hundred feet, the ships crew would make the line fast, and we would begin pulling on Mrs. Grounded once again. This worked a few times, but with the swells getting higher it only lasted a short while. The ships lines that were sent to us weren't made to be used as tug hawsers, the surge would part them almost as fast as we would make them up and start pulling on them. Around 04:00, the Pilot finally said a decision had been made to cease operations.

He told us, "They were going to wait for more favorable weather conditions and a higher tide." Christmas morning and we were heading back to the dock; we were ready to get home to our families. The office called and asked if there were any volunteers, who might want to go back out to help. With it being crew change morning and Christmas to boot, can any guess how long the volunteer's line was? We all went home that morning to spend some good quality, well-deserved time with our loved ones.

Grounding on *Yvonne,*
Hawk, Condor, and *Tampa*

Working on the water makes the time spent on dry land that much more appreciative. Especially true during the winter months where the weather can turn nasty very fast. The tug *Yvonne* and tug *Tampa* was docking a Del Monte ship in Port Manatee one winter day in early 1996. The wind seemed to be blowing a gale with the way the ship had to crab up Manatee channel. We were on the port bow with two lines, since we were backing the ship into the slip, tug *Tampa* had the port quarter.

The wind was blowing terribly strong out of the north. After entering the main slip and turning the ship to port, the ship was now broadside to the wind. We could tell this wasn't going to be pretty from the get go. The tug *Tampa* has 6,000-horse power, which handled her end with no problem, although the tug *Yvonne* has 3,300-horsepower, I was feeding all 3,300 of them all they would eat.

Backing full astern trying to keep the wind from blowing the ship onto the dock was a battle we were losing. I had never seen a ship yet that we couldn't back up into the wind, no matter how large the ship was. The ship ended up dropping her anchor to keep the ship from hitting the dock. After fighting with the abnormally strong winds, we were finally able to snake her into place and get the Del Monte ship to her berth safely.

Before we had started the job we were informed of a grounded ship loaded with phosphate that we were to visit after we were finished with the banana boat. Millage Harvey was the Captain aboard the tug *Tampa,* he and I both had asked for an extra man to help on deck; this was done often whenever we worked the grounded ships.

The agent for the ship that had run aground had already ordered four tugboats to go to her location, which was about eight miles past Egmont Key. The pilots were even boarding and disembarking off Egmont Key inside the land cut because of the rough seas making it dangerous to get off ships, or to board them outside. We heard this is why the ship had run aground in the first place. The pilot had told the ship Captain not to leave Egmont channel until he had gone passed a certain buoy, well he didn't, see what can happen when you don't listen.

The tugs that were dispatched were the *Hawk*, and the *Condor*, who were already underway. The tug *Tampa*, and little oh me, the *Yvonne*, didn't leave until our other job was finished. I knew with the wind blowing as hard as it was inside the bay, we were about to get a butt whipping from Mama Nature. With 22,700 combined horsepower on the way, this was going to something to see. On the way out there, I was already calling the office informing them of the sea conditions. Wave height was ten to twelve feet with gusting winds from thirty to forty knots, not ideal conditions to work a grounded ship. When we arrived on site the Pilot positioned all tugboats on the ships port quarter to push full ahead. The *Hawk* was closest to midship, followed by the *Tampa*, then the *Condor*, and then the *Yvonne*.

All the boats with the exception of the *Yvonne*, was able to stay in contact with the ships hull. You would think that coming full ahead on a tugboat with 3,300 hp, it would be impossible to be pulled away from the hull by wave action; however, that was exactly what was happening to us. I had the throttle control pushed down as hard as I could get it. Whenever the *Yvonne* came away from the hull I would pull the throttle back to clutch, (idling) then just before we came back against the hull I would push her full ahead again. Some of the ships crew was standing just above where we were pushing, looking right into the wheelhouse at us.

Each time we hit the ship they would just shake their heads, knowing we were causing damage. I called and reported to the office numerous times telling them of the steel plates we were caving in almost every time we hit the ship. The office said, "Yes we know it, but the agent said to keep pushing until further notice." Having the *Condor* on our port-side and the seas coming from the same side, it was only a matter of time until he ended upon my deck. A wave had picked her up and placed her rubber fendering on top of the *Yvonne's* bulwarks, bending them over.

When the two big boats were almost lifted up and put on the deck by the rough seas; that was a scary site and must have been the big decision changer. After that was seen, a decision was made to put up tow lines to pull instead of pushing since it had gotten too rough to stay alongside. The tug *Condor* put up a line and immediately pulled it apart. While we were waiting on the *Condor's* crew to get another line rigged, we were just keeping our bow into the sea.

Karl Workman was the extra man that we had aboard the boat that day to help with the bigger, heavier gear that was used for groundings. The seas had grown in height to where we thought the boat was going to turn over when we turned around and caught a beam sea. Karl had come to the wheelhouse to see what our next move was, he was holding on to the console when one of the rouge waves hit us. The top of the console actually broke loose in his hand, that's where all my controls were located.

About that time, Captain Harvey called me and said, "Hey Bill, I saw your wheel that time when you turned." The weather was turbulent before we departed for the grounded ship and had actually worsened since we had arrived. After a few more failed attempts at putting lines up from the different tugs, someone made the decision to call off the operations. We were told to go back in until the weather calmed down. We also went back to harbor operations as soon as we returned. A job that we had been dispatched to do at the power plant in St. Petersburg, kept us tied up there for the whole night.

I woke up the next morning and called the office to see what time we were supposed to be going back to the grounding. I was told the pilot requested a boat with more horsepower than what the *Yvonne* had. The tug *Challenger* with 3,600 hp was sent in our place, Hallelujah. Although the weather had calmed down somewhat, we could not have been happier to hear that we were not going back out to be shook up by Mother

Nature's washing machine. We had much rather do the dockings and sailings of ships in the waters of the much calmer harbor, than a grounding any day.

DREDGE
George D. Williams SANK

There were many times we were dispatched to a job that the outcome turned out to be entirely different from what it was supposed to be. One blistery winter day, the dredge *George D. Williams* had ordered a couple of tugs to assist them in moving some barges from an impending cold front. The tugs *Yvonne* and *Edna* were sent on this job with Harold Dale as the Captain on the *Edna*, who was also my buddy Carroll's relief, and brother. Paul Coronet was the engineer and Phil Vallandingham was the deckhand. I was working over for Reggie Atkins so I had his crew, Jerry Anderson as the engineer, John Cullen as the deckhand.

The dredge was located north of Egmont channel around buoy number thirteen. They were involved in a beach renourishment project, where they would fill the barges with sand from their location, and then the barges loaded with sand would be taken to the Indian Rocks Beach location where another type of dredge would off load the sand. The sand was replaced on the beach from where storms had washed it away. When we departed Port Manatee it was just before lunchtime. Jerry said he was going to cook some hamburgers and wanted to know if I wanted one. Looking at the wind kicking up the waves at three to five feet going out Port Manatee channel, I told him, "I believe I'm just going to hold off for a while to see what the weather's going to do." He said, "Well I'm going to eat me a couple of burgers, let me know if you change your mind." I had been there before, so changing my mind was not an option with rough seas.

We were getting white water coming over the bow so much, that I had to stop the boat. I asked Jerry and John to secure the lines to keep them from washing down the deck before we could proceed. As we approached Egmont Key and passed the land cut, the seas were really kicking up a fuss. It took another thirty minutes to reach south of the dredge location, but staying in the deeper water of Egmont channel.

We were told by the dredge Captain to depart the channel at buoy thirteen and go north, straight towards the dredge. I looked at the chart where their exact location was and did some quick math in my head. Our draft was thirteen feet; the dredge was in sixteen to eighteen feet of water. The wave height had grown to be ten to twelve feet; taking into consideration the probability of making it to his location, was slim to none.

I asked John to hold the controls for a minute while I used the head. When I opened the door, I realized why I hadn't seen Jerry for quite a while. He was down on one knee getting rid of those greasy hamburgers he had eaten. I said, "Jerry, not in the sink; go out on the back deck." He looked up at me with the saddest eyes and asked, "Ain't we through yet, can't we go home?" I said, "No, we haven't been released to go back in yet, and have to stay here until we get the word."

I had made Jell-O before we had been dispatched for this job, and we had all completely forgotten about it. When we had started getting into the rough waves, yep, you guessed it; we had red unset Jell-O coming out of the bottom of the refrigerator door. Although there were latches installed on each door, refrigerator and freezer, we didn't dare open them while it was rough, cleaning up would have to wait for a while.

We told the dredge Captain that neither of us could get to where the barges and dredge were because of our draft. If they could get the barges to the channel we could put a line on them and take them inside, all other traffic had long been stopped because of the weather. We could not even set still; the wind would turn us broadside to the seas, which made it very uncomfortable, so we would just run up and down the channel from buoy to buoy. We both idled with our bows right into the seas, waiting to see if the smaller dredge tender tugs could get their barges to us.

Whenever we would turn around to go back the other direction, I

would try to pick one of the smaller waves before turning. We did this
for a couple of hours, when Harold called me on the company radio and
said, "I think I'll try to ease over there and get to the dredge." I said, "I've
looked at the chart and don't think there's enough water."

Just as the *Edna* was a few hundred feet outside the channel, the smoke
came pouring out of her stacks. She was coming full astern; a wave had
gone out from under the boat and had sat her on the bottom, my math
was found to be correct. Harold's crew was on his back deck lying on the
stern line. They told us later that they noticed a nut rolling around back
aft. It had vibrated off one of the bolts that held the hydraulic steering
ram to the rudder arm. Had they lost the bolt, they would have lost their
ability to steer. With the nut replaced and ready to work, we then witnessed a very costly weather related casualty.

The dredge was held in place with two very thick vertical pipes called
spuds. They are located on each corner of the dredge's stern in a spud well.
They're picked up and lowered by a cable attached to a collar. Both spuds
were on the bottom when one of them broke, right at the same level as
the bottom of the dredge. The dredge then started pivoting on the other
spud from the wind, all the while turning on top of the broke spud. The
broke spud started poking holes in the bottom of the dredge, and within
a matter of minutes, the dredge boat had sank to the bottom.

With the dredge's sinking, that stopped all operations. That meant
there would be no barges to be pumped out at the off loading site. We
were told to go to Indian Rocks Beach and take the spider dredge to
Johns Pass, south of its present location. With charts in hand, I plotted
a course to our new job assignment. Harold said, "I'll just follow you, go
ahead Big Man, I'll be right behind you."

The rain had started making visibility very restricted which took a
couple of hours to reach the other dredge, which was right on the beach.
The dredge's Captain said for one of us to put a towline on the corner
of the dredge. Harold called me and said, "How about going ahead and
put up a line Big Man, he didn't want to back up there with his stern."
I said, "No problem we'll get it, that hard bottom will make you sort a
gun shy, huh!"

Neither of us could get into Johns Pass with our draft and couldn't figure how this operation was going to work. After we had a line up, I just idled pulling on our line while the dredge was disconnected from the shore. We finally got the go ahead and started easing offshore, going away from the beach minute by minute. After we were offshore a few miles, I was told to turn north; I thought to myself, what in the world are they doing. My thought was answered, a voice said, "Okay *Edna*, as soon as the *Yvonne* turns the dredge north, I want you to put up a line on the other end, we'll tow her from the ladder end. I could only imagine what was going through Harold's mind when he heard that. We got her turned north and were told we would be released after the *Edna* was hooked up. As we were passing Harold, we waved at him and I said over the company radio, "Anytime you need us to make up first on a job, just say the word, we're heading home."

It was a very slow movement, and since the winds were still kicking, I knew he would still be there for quite a while. He did have one thing going for him; they would take the dredge from him when he got close to the pass with the smaller tender tugs. All we knew was that it would be well after midnight before we could tie up and shut down for some well-earned rest. There were many days like this that had turned out to be all niters.

Lost Propellers on

The Tug *Yvonne*

We had just returned from working a job in Port Tampa one night. Just as we were approaching the dock, I put the boat astern to stop her headway. I then heard an extremely loud bang that came from the stern of the boat. With Carroll right off my stern on the *Palmetto*, he called me and said, "Hey, something big just came out from under your boat." He said, "Bob jumped up liked he had been hit with electricity."

I pushed the controls forward to put the *Yvonne* back in gear and discovered I had no forward or reverse. I called Carroll and said, "How about pushing me into the dock; she won't go back in gear." All that the engine would do was rev up, and without any wheel wash coming out from under the boat, this wasn't a good sign.

After we were tied up and secure, Bob had me put the controls forward and astern with the engine still running, while he looked at the gearbox to try and figure out what had happened. The shaft was turning when in gear, but without the prop turning. The only other thing we could come up with was that we had lost our propeller, also referred to as the wheel. I called the office and told them we needed a diver to come look under the boat to help determine what had happened. By the time a diver was contacted and got to Port Manatee, it was day light.

We explained to him what had happened as we came into the dock earlier. He got rigged up, dove down to look, and immediately came back up. He said, "Your wheel is gone, I know the bottom is muddy but I'll go down and see if I can find it anyway." As luck would have it the wheel was right under the boat, standing up with two blades sticking up out of the mud. A four bladed stainless steel propeller, weighing sixty two hundred pounds, standing straight up, now that was luck.

We were told the propeller cost around thirty thousand dollars, and

that was in 1988. I thought this was a good thing, not only finding it, but retrieving it as well. We enlisted the help of a cherry picker crane that was owned by the Belcher

Tug *Yvonne* with propeller on deck
Author photo

Oil Company. The crane operator dropped the block down in the water with a cable chocker attached to it, the diver then went back down and hooked the choker around the two visible blades. When the diver was up and out of the way, the propeller was then lifted up and set on the stern of the *Yvonne*.

There was about six inches of the seven and a half inch shaft sticking out of the propeller. It looked like someone had taken a saw and cut the shaft into, a smooth even cut. The office sent the tug *Harbor Island* down to take us to the shipyard in Tampa. That was the first time I had ever heard of a tug losing a propeller, especially without hitting a bank or backing into something. We had just docked a very big ship into Port Tampa, and then ran at full throttle for an hour and forty-five minutes back to Port Manatee.

That was a scary thought of losing a wheel while doing a job. That was something I wouldn't want to experience, it would be like driving a car without brakes, not a pretty picture. The shaft had to have been split-ting for sometime; splitting a stainless steel shaft like this one was split takes quite a while to do. After we had been taken to the shipyard, the tug itself was not raised on the dry dock until days later. Maybe then we could get an expert opinion as to why the wheel had fallen off the tug.

As many unexplained things are mulled over, like UFO's and Bigfoot, this too could not be determined specifically as to what had caused the shaft to split the way it had. One theory was that maybe a vibration had followed a line left from a lathe when the shaft was made, sounds as good as any I suppose. Regardless of why, when she was dry-docked the whole tail shaft had to be replaced, where the wheel was okay to reuse.

HERE WE GO
WHEELING AGAIN

As most everyone knows, good things come in twos, evidently bad things do too. A couple of years later we were on our way to the power plant in St. Petersburg from downtown Tampa. I had noticed a little swagger in the boat for a day or so, it felt sort a like something was in our wheel, maybe a line or a tire, or something maybe floating that we had picked up.

I mentioned to Bob and Carlo that there is something just not right with the way the boat was swaggering back and forth. I said, "I think we had better get a diver to look under the boat after doing this job." With our job in site, we had probably a half an hour before we went alongside. I told Bob, "I'm going to try something; I'm going to come astern to see if something's in the wheel, maybe I can kick it out before the job." We still had some headway, which was okay; so I pulled her out of gear and coasted for a couple of seconds. When I came astern and she went in gear, I heard that same extremely loud bang I had heard a couple of years earlier. Bob and I looked at each other and said at the same time, "Oh no, not again." We went through the same procedure hoping it was something else.

No such luck, I was just glad we had enough headway to get out of the channel where we had anchored. At that period of time, the company had eight tugs that were crewed, and as it turned out, all eight tugs were within half a mile of each other. There were four tugs on a dead ship that was waiting for the inbound rig going to Florida Power to clear "F" cut.

There were two tugs on a ship going into Port Tampa, just astern of us approaching the "F" and "G" cut intersection.

The tugs *Yvonne* and *Edna* were at the bifurcation buoy at the top of "F" cut on the way to dock the tug/barge unit for the Florida Power Corporation power plant. This meant that our assigned job was forced to use only one tug since there weren't any more crewed tugs available. The office had to call in an off duty crew to bring us back to a dock, we also had to wait on them to get to the call out boat from home, plus time to get to our location.

Having a couple of hours to wait for them, Bob, Carlo, and I put our heads together for a plan. We had a fairly good idea of where the wheel had come off, if that was what it turned out to be. After being towed back in and the diver confirmed what we feared might have happened, yes, the wheel was gone again. He told us the shaft was barely sticking out of the cutlass bearing, as it was before. We were also told to put a mark where we thought the wheel had come off on the chart.

Norman Atkins said the company would pay anyone twenty thousands dollars that found the wheel, retrieved it, and delivered it to the company dock. Several people looked for it with some pretty sophisticated equipment, but all failed to find it, this was the same wheel that had come off before in Port Manatee. As far as I know, it's still right where it came off over a decade ago, that might be a good project to tackle some day.

Training on The

Hawk Class Boats

The company, Bay Transportation Corporation, had the tugs *Falcon* and *Eagle* built not long after they had acquired the company from St. Philip Towing. These two tugboats were the conventional class tractor tugs that were being built in the late 1980's. After a while, the tug *Falcon* was sent to Brazil to work with other tugs docking and sailing iron-ore ships, one being the *Berge Stall*, which was the largest iron-ore ship in the world at that time. The *Eagle* was contracted to the Navy maneuvering submarines in and out at the Navy yard in St. Mary's, Georgia.

In 1995, they undertook the designing and building of the *Hawk* class stern drive tractor tug. The *Hawk* is 110 feet long X 40 feet wide X 17 feet draft with 6,700-horse power. She would be the first tug, of three *Hawk* class tractor tugs that Bay Transportation Corporation would have built in less than two years. Tug *Hawk* was first, the tug *Condor* was second, and finally the tug *Eagle II* was third. They were followed by a smaller version with 4,300-horse power, tug *Reliant*, which is the really the best size boat for harbor service.

The first boat of a certain class or style has the distinction of all other boats built after it, ergo the *"Hawk"* class boats. While I was still on the tug *Yvonne*, all of the Captains were told, "Tractor tugs are the wave of the future fellows, and everyone should spend as much time on them as possible." We were told to learn the operation of these tugs, because they were what the industry was going to be building in the future. I was not above learning something new, especially when it could advance me

within the company. Having spent most of my tug career in Port Manatee, maybe now was the time to branch out.

Although still stationed in Port Manatee, we went up to Tampa one
day to see these tugs we had heard so much about. After being on the tug
Yvonne that had an old Noah's ark radar, this console looked like it had
come off the Starship Enterprise, and was completely overwhelming to
what I was used to. I then thought to myself; Lord what am I supposed
to do with all those electronics, with the *Hawk* also being the first of the
big boats that I started my training aboard of. All the tugs names built

Tug *Hawk* controls console-Author photo

after 1987 started with "Kinsman," which happened to be George Steinbrenner's parent company, except the tug *Reliant*. The Captain's on the
Hawk back then was Denny Cooper and Jerry Borden, with the Captain's
on the *Condor* being my old Buddy Dave Scarborough and Jim Brantner Jr. The two Captains I trained most with were Denny and Dave,
just because of the shift I was working. Living thirty-two miles from the
Tampa docks meant I logged many miles, and made many a trip from

home to train on those boats. I would call the dispatcher on crew change morning to find out if there were any jobs that the big boats would be on that day. If there were, I said, "Call me at home when you get an order." After just a few training jobs, I felt fairly comfortable with the handling and the overall operation of them.

You were not okayed to operate the big boats unless you had Jim Brantner Jr's blessing. This went on for four months, until I was finally able to work a couple of jobs with Jim Jr. It was a Saturday morning where I even remember the job well. We were assigned the sulphur tanker *Teoatl* docking at Pasco Terminal in Port Sutton. This was an easy job on any boat; I had worked the *Teoatl* for many years, she was also the same ship we had to escort in years past because of her undersized anchor chains.

The maneuverability of the tractor tugs was something that utterly amazed me. There was a huge difference after coming off the single screw tug *Yvonne*, which took a forty-acre field to turn her around in. The *Hawk* class boats could literally turn three hundred and sixty degrees, that's a full circle almost within the length of the boat.

With the docking of the *Teoatl* under my belt, and with everything going as well as it could, I received Jim's blessing. He said, "You operate the boat as good as I do, I'll go home and you can have it." "I appreciate the good word, I just needed you to ride a job with me to be checked off, and I'll go back home for the rest of the weekend," I told him. We then sailed a loaded phosphate ship from the Eastern dock in East Bay, with no problem.

I felt pretty good with my performance on those two jobs and was now ready for the next move. Preston Barco was the only other Captain that was checked off on the *Hawk* class boats, besides the assigned Captains already on them. Knowing the tug *Eagle II* and tug *Reliant* were about to be finished with their construction, Preston and I had to be the next two big boaters. There would be four more stern drive tractor tug Captains needed, the way we had it figured. But after the *Eagle II* had arrived in Tampa, she was tied up for some tax reason. We were told she was not to be used for any reason, even if there were no other tugs available for a job, until a certain amount of time had passed, she could not work in the waters of Florida.

PULLED MY FIRST BITT
OFF THE DECK

I was in Port Manatee one day where the *Condor* had been requested to assist in docking a rather large ship. Jim Brantner Jr. was the Captain on the tug *Condor* that day and had asked if I wanted to come out and work the job. I was ready for this show to get started and told him, "Sure, I'd be happy to." It was a pleasure to operate one of the most powerful tugs, not only in Tampa Bay, but probably in the Gulf of Mexico. I hitched a ride with Captain Harvey, and rode out on the tug *Tampa* so I could get on the *Condor* before we had to go alongside.

When the transfer was done, I hotfooted up to the *Condor's* wheelhouse where Jim met me and said, "Get in there on the controls and do us a good job." Getting in the wrap around console and sitting in the track chair just felt natural at this point. The power of this monster boat would show me just what it was capable of doing within a few minutes. Captain Timmel, who was the Pilot aboard the inbound ship called and told me to put up one line on the starboard bow. I replied, "Roger on that, one line on the starboard bow." I went alongside that big ship like putting a baby to bed, with a soft touch, being nice and easy.

With our line made fast and running along with the ship, we were approaching the turn into Port Manatee channel. The Pilot said, "Stop the *Condor*," this creates a drag and helps slow the ship down. As we were going into the turn, he said to back the *Condor* slow, I replied, "Back her slow," which is only about quarter power. With the drives turned back and the line tight, I eased the throttle up to a slow bell. Just as the RPM's had reached the slow bell, we started sliding backwards alongside the ship.

Since the ship was empty, and with us sliding backwards alongside the ship, we thought the line had parted, not being able to see on her deck. I turned the drives forward to stop our backward motion and tried to see what had happened to the line. Jim turned the camera that was mounted atop of the mast towards the ship so we could see what it was. The line had actually pulled the bitt out of the riser mounted on the deck.

I was amazed at the power it took to cause this to happen, and we were only backing a slow bell. This was my first bitt, but certainly not my last. The line dropped down off the ship when the bitt came loose, so I retrieved it aboard with the winch and ran it back up through another chock, and hopefully to a stronger bitt. We were then able to complete the job, after that backing command I was a little leery whenever I came astern pulling on the ships bitt. We were just lucky this incident happened where it did instead of coming into a dock where damage could have occurred.

Another time I pulled a stern chock off a ship, was when we were shifting from one berth to another up in the Tampa harbor. The *Condor* was working her line through the center chock aft, while the tug *A.P. St. Philip* with Captain Bobby Strickland, had two lines on the port bow. This particular berth is directly across the channel from a small airport, with a sea wall on the airport side. As we were backing out of the slip I continually gave the Pilot, Captain Lindsey, distances off the sea wall.

The ship had to sort of wiggle out of her berth, restricted by her length, and not being able to back straight out before turning parallel to the channel. Holding the bow tight to the dock, Captain Lindsey was being extra careful not to touch something that would cause damage. As the stern of the ship came closer towards the sea wall, I counted down the distances away from it, all the while backing the stern up the channel, the desired direction.

I had the mighty *Condor* backing easy at idle speed, as I counted down to 200 feet, 175 feet, 150 feet, finally getting a little closer than I liked. I said, "Captain Lindsey you're coming down to little over a hundred feet back here, do you want me to come up some on the power?" He said, "Okay *Condor*, bring her up to a slow bell and pull me off the sea wall."

As I throttled up and not even reaching the slow bell, the stern chock came loose. I immediately clutched out both drives and relayed to Captain Lindsey what had just happened on the stern. As luck would have it, the bow had just cleared the mouth of the slip she was backing out of, and thinking quickly, Captain Lindsey put the ship hard right and shot her ahead to get the ships stern away from the sea wall.

I was trying to retrieve my line so I could move to another chock and finish the shifting of the ship. My line was tangled up in a metal pipe maze, which became quite a task to be moved around on the deck. The stern had a canopy that covered most of the deck; the framework was made of pipe, which was connected to the handrails, which seemingly was connected to everything else. With everything being tied together, and some of the hand rails welded to the chock, yes it was an instant scrap yard. When the chock broke loose it swept across the deck bringing down the canopy with everything else that was attached to it.

The ships crew had to use pry bars to get to the bitts just to free my line. When all the action had subsided, the *A.P.* had been pinched between another dock and the ship, and had to turn the tugs line loose. We were finally able to get our line and relocate the *Condor* to the starboard quarter of the ship. I could only remember what had happened when I was with Jim down in Port Manatee with my first bitt, and now my first chock. As it turns out not the last for either, losing bitts and chocks will also make you gun shy too. I had heard it said that after the *Hawk* class boats came into the Tampa Harbor and started working, there were several ships reinforcing their center chocks to keep them from being pulled off from the sheer power of these boats.

The Charleston, South Carolina Trip

I still worked on the *Yvonne* as my primary tugboat, and would sometimes work relief on the *Condor* when Dave or Jim went places on company business. There was a tug company up in Charleston, South Carolina that was having problems handling ships when the current was running strong. These were very large, deep draft container ships over 900 feet long. Some type of tugboat had to be found that could assist these large ships, no matter what the current was doing.

Not being able to work in Florida yet, the *Eagle II* was sent to Charleston to show what these boats were really built to do. She was there for thirty days, and proved to be the real deal. They put their tugs on the bow, and the *Eagle II* handled the stern. Preston Barco and I worked on the tug *Condor* while Dave and Jim worked the *Eagle II* in Charleston.

Their thirty-day contract was coming to an end, and needed to have the boat brought back to Tampa. Coming into work on a Friday morning, I was informed I would be driving up with Dave Scarborough and Lawrence LeDuc Sr. early Saturday morning to Charleston. Dave was going to relieve Jim, who had been on the boat for his weekly tour. I was really looking forward to the next morning, and getting this trip started. Until then, I hadn't been out of the state of Florida on a tugboat; this changed that day.

I'd be seeing places different than I had ever seen before, and I'd also be on a tugboat that was doing a maneuver that the old tug boaters couldn't believe that they could be done this way. For me, I had heard of the indirect tows that these boats were designed to do, but had never seen one done, I couldn't wait. The drive up was wonderful; we had taken the scenic route seeing some spectacular looking old houses, with beautiful manicured lawns. We had arrived just after noon with a job coming up later that day. After the usual pleasantries, I was told where to put my gear.

Otis Monteiro was the engineer, and Mr. Ed Harris my old deckhand, was now on the *Eagle II* as their deckhand. Within walking distance, Otis, Ed and I took off to visit some of the local stores. I cannot see why people would want to leave such a beautiful place as Charleston; the history alone would make you want to live there.

First Indirect on The
Evergreen Ship

Back from town with a few souvenirs, we readied the boat for the upcoming job. The *Eagle II* was doing the job that all of the tugs White Stack had at the time, could not do. As with any business, time is money, but within the marine industry it magnifies itself many times over. Whenever a ship has to anchor to wait for a slack current in order to dock or sail from a berth, the cost could be hundreds of thousands of dollars per hour.

When the *Eagle II* was built, a very large box keel was constructed and installed on her hull, as was all three *Hawk* class boats. With a line up to the stern of a ship, the *Eagle II* could actually steer the ship with the tug. That maneuver was called an indirect tow, the tug would pay out about 200 feet of line out of her bows bullnose, and would steer the opposite direction the ship needed to go.

On our way out to meet the *Ever Round*, which is 965' long, Jim looked over at me and asked, "You've never seen one of these indirect tows have you?" I said, "No I haven't, why do you ask?" His comment was, "Alright a virgin, just watch, you'll dig this." Well, since I haven't actually experienced one, I was now wondering what to expect. We came up to the ships stern, put up a line through the center chock, and slacked the line until the length was about 200' feet in length. *Christopher Turecamo*, one of the White Stack tugs was also assisting the ship to the dock.

Passing under the Cooper River Bridge, the Pilot told Jim his first command would be to steer the ships stern to the right. This would make the ship turn to the left; the second command would be to the left. With the ships rudder held to mid ship, Jim started the right indirect tow. The

Eagle II had a strain gauge installed on her bow winch which measured the amount of pull that the line had on it, this is important information to have.

While we were in full indirect I looked at the strain gauge, it read two hundred and thirty four thousand pounds of pull, an unbelievable amount of strain on the line. I looked out on the port side and saw the tire fenders floating up with water almost coming over the bulwarks. The boat was leaning over farther than I had ever seen one lean. Jim looked over at me and said, "What do you think, this is pretty cool huh?"

He steered the ship both directions, and then shortened up the line after putting the brakes on the ship. With those maneuvers done, he brought the line in and shifted to the starboard quarter to finish the docking process. I took notice that the lines from the ship weren't even run ashore yet when activity was starting everywhere, it looked like a stirred up anthill all around us. Some containers were being off loaded while the ship was still tying up. With the docking over, we went back to the White Stack dock and secured the boat for the night.

The next morning we looked their equipment over; their boats were painted to look like wood. They actually look like wood from a distance, but up close, whoa. Jim and Lawrence drove back to Tampa the previous night after the big Evergreen job. Jim had been there doing the jobs, while Lawrence just came to get another perspective.

We had sailed a smaller ship that morning; the big Evergreen ship came later that day. After being dispatched to sail her, we would finally be underway to Tampa when finished with that job. Just as the previous day, the crew was still slinging containers on and off the ship when we put our line up to sail her. I thought to myself; why don't they just spend more time at the dock, at least until they're through with cargo.

I never did understand how they could be put on such a strict schedule to spend no more time than they did at the berth. We were now underway with this big girl, handling her as if she should be handled, with a lot of finesse. We went up stream to turn her around and stayed made up on the quarter until we passed under the Cooper River Bridge outbound. Released from the ship we were finally bound for Tampa, Florida. The adventure was about to begin for me, I was sure the jokers wheels were turning.

TRIP FROM CHARLESTON TO TAMPA

Passing the old Civil War post Fort Sumter was an awesome looking site to see. Here was a structure built out in the water during the Civil War over one and a half centuries ago. If that old Fort could talk what stories it could tell. Being out there guarding the entrance to Charleston Harbor for well over a century was completely amazing. Besides withstanding the Civil War, how many hurricanes has this old weathered beaten Fort endured, I wondered. I now had to refocus my mind to the present, and remember who I was on the boat with.

Master Joker Dave Scarborough and his protégée Otis Monteiro, those two were constantly trying to out do one another. Both of them were very imaginative, I had heard of some things that I had better watch out for with them. You know, things like putting a small piece of plywood between your sheet and mattress, now that'll get your attention when jumping into bed. How about unscrewing the showerhead, putting dry Kool-Aid in it and screw it back on the pipe.

Changing your skin color with just turn of a water valve to a bright green or a bright red can be very funny on someone else. With about three days of running time ahead of us, I thought; this was almost an eternity for these two to come up with some new pranks. Dave told me of a classic joke that he and Delaney Jewel had played on a deckhand one time. While on an offshore trip aboard the tug *Harbor Island* headed for Mobile with a couple of scrap barges, they had placed the hand held radio in the Captains quarters right behind the wheelhouse. They then told Blackie the deckhand, to steer the boat on its present course, they were going downstairs to eat.

They went downstairs to the galley and ate, then waited a while for Blackie to get comfortable. One of them came back into the Captains quarters through the infamous hole in the ground. The other one went back to the wheelhouse and told Blackie he was doing good steering the boat, just keep up the good work; he was going into the Captains quarters for a few minutes. With the stage set, he said they would take turns calling the *Harbor Island* with a Norwegian accent. They would say, "This is the research vessel Oleo calling the vessel at (they would give their position), please Captain, you need to alter your course to the starboard, I am pulling roughly a mile of seismic cables, you are about to run over them, please come to your starboard."

He said Blackie was answering him on the radio and was looking all around, "I am unable to see where you are Oleo." He said Blackie had panic in his voice, especially when they both kept calling on the radio pleading with him to alter his course, please Captain, alter your course. Blackie flung the door open; there they were busted, standing there like a deer caught in the headlights of a car. Blackie said, "Get up here and talk to this guy that's calling us, he says we're about to run over some cable." Dave said, "We couldn't believe it, he never put two and two together, there both of us were standing there holding a walkie talkie, looking wide eyed."

I told him to shut the door and deal with it, which is exactly what he did. He said, "Delaney and I had a good laugh at poor ole Blackie's expense." He said he didn't want to tell me all his secrets, that's all for now. When the story telling ended I just sat back, enjoying the new experience of being offshore. We had fairly calm seas with nothing but ocean all around to look at, which was beautiful.

Dave had put our waypoints into the GPS, (Geographic Positioning System). A waypoint is the predetermined position you want to head for, however, with multiple waypoints, they are also the course change points in a planned route. All there was to do was watch the radar screen, and make sure we stayed on course. With the Robertson Autopilot keeping us on our track line, steering this boat was a real treat. With almost

VAB at Cape Canaveral-Author photo

a day behind us we were still heading south. Knowing that land was to the west, I had noticed something very big right on the horizon, but we were over twenty-five miles offshore. Dave said it was the Vertical Assembly Building at Cape Kennedy, that must be one big building, I thought.

Dave said, "The VAB is five hundred twenty five feet tall, and is also one of the biggest buildings in the world." With our height of eye, we would be able to see it from thirty miles away, of which we were within that range. This was one building I just had to see, which I did later on. The farther south we went the closer to land we ran. Not knowing all the equipment needed for these offshore transits, Big Dave held school, just for me. Most of the electronic equipment is rarely used in the harbor, which was where I had done my training. Dave had made numerous trips up and down the east coast, nothing new here.

A repetitive action makes the learning process easier in the ability to retain any knowledge, with all of his previous trips; it made Dave very knowledgeable in this trip too. Jim and Dave had been on the *Hawk* class boats from the beginning. The *Hawk*, then the *Condor*, and now the *Eagle II*, every time a new boat was built they were chosen as the Captains.

With all three boats having the same style electronics, it made Dave very familiar with their operations, so he instructed me in how each of the instruments worked and how to operate them. I learned more about the electronics from Dave on that trip, than I had in my four months of training in the harbor. We were now running close enough to the coast to see land with the naked eye. At one point off Jupiter Inlet, Florida, I looked through the binoculars and could actually see people standing on their balconies. Dave told me, "Anytime you head south, you want to stay as close to the coast as possible." This would keep you out of the Gulf Stream, which has a very strong northerly current.

I knew the lull before the storm that I had been experiencing couldn't last, I was right. Dave and Ed had the Captains watch, while me and Otis had the Mates watch. There was a Phone-Com system set up for communication; it went from room to room throughout the boat. When I went to the wheelhouse on the second night for the midnight watch, all three of those birds were roosting up there with the lights off; I was also not expecting anything to happen this time of night.

Dave caught me up on everything, as was done on every crew change. All of a sudden Otis took off down the stairs, saying he had to go check on something. We just kept talking about the trip's progress that we had made so far, and then the wheelhouse phone rang. Dave was in front of the console standing with Ed, where I was standing right by the phone, how convenient right? Dave said, "Answer it, and see what Otis wants." When I picked up the phone and pushed it to my ear, it was not what I expected to happen. I jerked it away feeling something very wet, and then I asked these jokers "what is this mess?"

I knew the wait was over, the adventure had definitely begun. I reached over and flipped the light switch on to see what I had gotten into. I heard Otis come running back up the stairs, he could hear Dave and Ed laughing about what I had just experienced. He wanted to know how I had reacted, Dave couldn't answer him, he was laughing too hard. They had put masking tape in the earpiece of the phone, to keep it from going into the holes, and had filled it with Ricotta cheese.

When I answered the phone, I also jammed my ear full of this cold wet cheese; I didn't think I would ever get that mess cleaned out of my ear. I told them I had no idea what was happening when I answered the phone, only that it was wet and cold. Knowing the past pranks with these fellows, if they knew something was done and it really bothered you, the pranks would only accelerate in their frequency, so I just started laughing right along with them, hoping for the best.

The next day coming up on the Florida straights, we were approaching the world famous Florida Keys. The water looked so clean; it was almost fluorescent with a green hue that I had never seen before. I started thinking, after working in the harbor for nineteen years; these are places you can only see outside of Tampa Bay. A decision that I was unaware of had already been made that would propel me into that very position.

Rounding past the Florida Keys, we were about to pass through

Targets on radar screen-Author photo

Rebecca Shoals, just east of the Dry Tortugas. This was also another historical place, the home of Fort Jefferson; this area was also known for its beautiful waters, as were the chain of Keys. I can remember my Dad talking about shrimping in these waters when I was just a puppy. We had one of the radars set on a twelve-mile range, while the other set on a three-mile range.

I had just come up for the midnight watch, which would also be the last one for this trip. Dave said, "After we turn north, it's about a hundred and sixty miles to the Tampa Sea buoy, have a good watch," and went down stairs. I said, "You got it, sleep tight, if I need you I'll call you." Within minutes of making a course change, I rechecked our position to make any needed adjustments to the radar.

When I had looked on the screen, there were just a few targets to encounter. Finally making the course change, we were now heading for our last waypoint, the Tampa sea buoy. Within the first hour the radar screen started lighting up with more targets than I could count. With Otis being up in the wheelhouse, I told him I had never seen so many blips on the radar screen before. He said, "What you're looking at is probably shrimp boats, this area is well known for shrimpers." The Dry Tortugas area was where my Father had shrimped forty years earlier. That is what they were alright, after a couple of hours or so there wasn't even one target to be seen on the radar. It was a wonder these waters had any shrimp left in them, with as many shrimp boats that I saw on the radar screen that night.

SUSPICIOUS INK SPOTS

About fourteen hours later it was mid afternoon, and Otis and I were back on watch. After moving some things around on the console I noticed some ink on my hand. I thought now what, looking at my shirt pocket expecting to see a spot from a leaking ink pen. What, no spot, I thought uh oh, I had to now think back at what I had touched since coming on watch a couple of hours earlier. After careful inspection and going through the process of elimination, I finally located the inky culprit. On the small end of the binoculars was some suspicious looking ink. Looking closer revealed the ink had been put all the way around on both eyepieces; right then I smelled a set up. Otis came up and told me he was going to change the end on the shore power cord to be ready for when we got to the dock, and that he would be on the top deck right behind the wheelhouse.

I wondered if he knew of the latest little prank that I had already discovered, so, it was time for a test of my own to see. I picked up the binoculars holding them where Otis could see that I had them in my hand. Looking at him out of the corner of my eye, I eased towards the back of the wheelhouse. Just as Ole Gomer Pyle used to say, surprise surprise, I had definitely peaked Otis's interest in what I was finally holding in my hand.

Never looking right at him, I would casually look off in the distance as if I had spotted another boat. I would then slowly start bringing the glasses up to my face as if I was going to look through them, only to stop just inches from touching my face. I would then slowly lower them, and look towards another direction. Otis was paying too much attention to me not to know about it.

Each time I would bring the glasses up to look through them, he just acted plum giddy, anticipating the dark outcome that never was to be. After a few more times of almost bringing Otis to the point that he could laugh at me, had I went through with the prank, I laid them down and waited on him to finish with the power cord. When he came in, I said, "What did you expect to see?" He said, "What are you talking about, I don't know anything about that ink," what do you think class, did he know? Dave had taken the ink tube from a pen and pulled the little brass end off it; he then blew the ink all around both binocular eyepieces. Had it been at night, it might have got me, as it did with Ed Harris, that was how Otis knew; Ed had come down stairs where he showed off his brand new pair of raccoon eyes.

We were now off the west coast of Florida just south of Sarasota; that meant within hours we would be secured at the dock in Tampa. I knew we were close when Norman Atkins, my immediate Supervisor, called Dave's cell phone. He told me he had some good news, and some bad news, I said, "Lay it on me, I've got broad shoulders, what's on your mind." He said, "We'll be laying up the *Eagle II* when you guys get to Tampa, we still won't be able to put her into the harbor rotation until the time period ends."

He went on to say, "We're transferring you to the tug *Condor*, where you will be working opposite Dave Scarborough, the schedule that boat works is a week on and a week off, is that something you'd be interested in?" I said, "I guess so, when would I start?" He then said, "Well unfortunately, your week starts tomorrow, since today is Tuesday and they work from Wednesday to Wednesday." Well, it appeared I was now in the big league, I was about to be the Captain of a seven million dollar tugboat. Although I was trained to run the boat, I never seen the fastball heading my way from left field, or else I might have bowed out gracefully until a later date.

TRAINING THE WOMAN
FROM CROWLEY

Where do I begin with this next story? This one was recorded with indelible ink into my memory banks. We had gone home late the previous afternoon after we had secured the *Eagle II*, she would hold the dock up for a little while longer. Coming back into work the next morning, the date was July 16 1996. I had first checked in with the dispatcher before stowing my gear on the *Condor*. Norman Atkins said to me, "Welcome back Captain

The tractor tug *Kinsman Condor*
Author photo

offshore, how was your trip?" I said, "It was educational, and if they were all like that, everyone would want to go offshore." We talked a while about my new-found experience and how beautiful the water was, especially down around the keys. Norman then told Me, "Oh yeah, you'll be training another Captain from Crowley, she's already on the boat." I said, "Excuse me, training someone else, did you say she?" He said, "Yes, her name is Christine Calvert, she'll be one of the Captains on the tug *Reliant* after she goes to California."

I knew there had been talk of sending the tug *Reliant* to the west coast, even before she had been delivered to Tampa. I told Norman, "I can run the boat, but I don't think I'm ready to train anyone yet." He said, "You'll be okay, just do what you do best." I knew this was going to be a challenge because there would be situations come up that I hadn't even done myself. I went out to my new home away from home to meet Captain Calvert.

She was put in the deck hands room where she could have her privacy. Doug Bogard was now my engineer, and Scott Reid, a new, very green young man, was my deck hand. These two would bunk in the engineer's room, since the other room was being occupied by Captain Calvert or Crissy as she told us to call her. Her stature was only about fifty seconds; she wasn't big as a minute. Right off the bat she informed us that her husband was a Long Beach Harbor Pilot, and that she had been given permission to use the boat phone at night to talk to her husband, okay.

She went on with telling us the history of her tugboat experiences, her likes and dislikes, and the foods she would and would not eat. She was already painting a pretty fair picture of what I was about to have to deal with. Having worked with Doug, I already knew of his past who was a seasoned man on tugboats. Scott however informed us that his Dad was friends with our big boss, and that was how he got his job, he was the color of talented nurseryman's thumb. Oh Joy I thought, I was not only now in charge of a new seven million dollar tugboat, I was also now in charge of a day care with these two. The very first job we were dispatched to, Crissy had informed me she didn't want to answer the Pilots commands over the radio. She said, "I don't want to have my voice heard over the radio, because I don't want anyone to know I'm on here training." I thought that was all part of the training and becoming proficient in the operation of the boat, maybe I just wasn't dialed into her west coast procedures yet.

Let's see now, there was Doug the engineer, Scott the green deck hand, and me, all with men's voices aboard the boat. This meant when we were doing jobs I had to be the man answering the radio, and with just three days under my belt, this came into play on the forth day. Crissy had also been getting some training by other Captains while I was on the *Eagle II* coming back from beautiful Charleston, South Carolina. So far, I had to make only a few corrections during some of the jobs.

I had told her she was doing pretty good, and seemed to be picking up on this new technology fairly easy. I should have kept my mouth shut, sometimes its best not to talk too soon. With the stern drive tractor tugs, steering them is like steering a boat with an outboard engine. If you steer left, you turn right, if you steer right, you turn left.

We were starting to go alongside a large ship called the *CSL Atlas*. We were told by Captain Gene Knight, the Pilot, to put up a line on the port bow, I answered, "Roger, port bow for the *Condor*." As the ship came closer, Crissy was at the controls and turned the tug up to start running parallel to the ship for the approach to the bow. As the ship passed, we were about mid ship when Crissy turned both drives the wrong way. We were also only about forty feet off the ship with about half throttle. By the time I was able to take the controls and correct the misdirection, we hit the ship with our stern. Captain Knight called me immediately and said, "Billy, the Captain said he was putting you on notice," I could only reply with, "Alright Sir." Being put on notice meant there could be lawyers talking to me in the near future.

I asked Crissy, "What are you thinking, why did you turn the boat that way?" Her reply was, "Well, you're just going to have to keep a closer eye on me." I could not believe what she had just said, and with such arrogance. With me answering all the commands on the radio, I just knew Captain Knight was thinking that I was running the boat. The stern of the *Condor* had caused a dent about four to six feet long, and three to five feet high at the waterline. I was the Captain on the *Condor* for less than four full days; this woman just took years off my life in a matter of seconds. We finished the job without further incident and headed back to the dock. I had already called Norman earlier to report what had happened. I called him back and told him, "Norman, you have to get this woman off the boat, if she remains aboard I'll just go back to the *Yvonne*." "My nerves cannot take this; will you do this for me?" I asked.

He said, "Let me call Jimmy Brantner and see what he says, I'll call you right back." Within minutes, Norman called back and told me, Jimmy had said, "I want her left on the *Condor* and I want Bill to train her." I said, "You know what happened today Norman, it's probably going to happen again." He said Jimmy had told him, "Damage to the boats is inevitable when training people not familiar with the equipment, and we will just deal with it later." This was going to be a week to remember, with all that had already happened in four short days, this big league wasn't so appealing about now.

We were able to make it through the rest of the week, although using extreme caution. After my duty week, I would be working over for a couple of days covering for Dave Scarborough, who had gone to pick up the tug *Reliant* in Louisiana.

Collision With The Tug *Hawk*

The *Condor* along with the tug *Hawk* with Jerry Borden as Captain, were off again, being dispatched to dock a very large cargo ship named the *M/V Hunter*, inbound for a load of phosphate at the IMC berth in Port Sutton. Harbor Pilot Captain Harry Williams told the tug *Hawk* to put up a line on the port bow, and told us to catch the port quarter. I told Crissy that as fast as the ship was going I had better come alongside this one. I was almost full ahead just trying to keep up with her while putting up our line.

I commented to Crissy, "This is awful fast to be making the turn into Port Sutton with such a big ship." Just about that time, Captain Williams told the *Hawk* to come half-ahead, within seconds, he said full-ahead. We were just running with her as we were negotiating the turn, it appeared we were going to barely miss the entrance beacon. After the *Hawk* had narrowly missed it, within seconds she was run aground. Jerry released the *Hawk's* line and said to me over the radio, "You better release your line and get out of here Bill," I was already bringing the drives around, and had released the brake on the winch.

It was determined that we were traveling over eleven knots when the tug *Hawk* abruptly stopped after running aground. That meant had I not reacted as fast as I did, the collision I had with the *Hawk* could have been a lot worse than it was. Yeah, you know it, with my woman trainee aboard; the tug *Condor* could now log two collisions in less than a week. The lines on both tugs were now hanging out of the respective chocks where we had put our lines through. They pulled out of the stops on both winches, mine at the very instant my bow hit the *Hawk* on her stern. The pilot was yelling on the radio for one of us to push on the ships bow. He said, "Come quick before I tear this dock down." The ship was coming astern hard trying to keep from hitting the scrap dock she was rapidly approaching. The ship stopped within one hundred feet from clipping the scrap dock.

With the events happening the way they had, I told Crissy, "I'm glad you weren't in the console when this took place." We made it back alongside where the ships crew had heaved our lines aboard the ship. They then slacked them down to us where we could make up and finish the job. During and after the incident, we reported what was happening and what had happened to the office. This was more than one incident that involved Captain Williams, and was also the straw that broke the camels back with our upper management officials. We heard that the company refused tug service to Captain Williams from that point on.

As time went on, Crissy seemed to be doing better, seemed to be I said. After docking a ship in Port Sutton one night we were heading back to the dock. Captain Harold Dale was following us from the job when my girl got a wild hair. She just took off out there towards Murphy, turning right in front of him. Harold came on the radio and said, "Boy, you can sure tell when Crissy's on the controls running that boat."

There were two more of the Crowley Captains that showed up for Tractor tug training. These two were men and was assigned to the tug *Hawk* for their orientation. I really think Crissy and I didn't hit it off, I told her she didn't impress me at all and I wasn't about to cater to her every little whim like some of the others did. Babies are cute; butt-pains stand about five foot two.

She really had accomplished a lot in her short career, being a woman and all, in what had really been known as a man's world for so many years. I found out she would be training in Tampa only, and then would be flying back to California to meet the boat there. That was the reason for the other two Captains to be training on the Tractor tugs too. They would be taking the boat through the Panama Canal, where I would like to go someday. With the tug *Reliant* being delivered to Tampa by Dave,

Otis, and others, things were finally getting back to a normalcy. The Crowley crew training also was winding to a completion.

The tug *Reliant* was a smaller version of the *Hawk* class boats, with 4,300 hp instead of the 6,700 hp the big boats had. She was the ideal harbor tug with plenty of power in a compact package. There were quite a few things to prepare the tug *Reliant* for her transit to California. She was a good-looking boat with some nice lines, and had been designed with larger than normal wheelhouse windows for better visibility. There were plates made to cover them should the seas get rough enough as to warrant their installation. I never said that I understood the mindset of big business, but I was puzzled at this move; it seemed to me for what Crowley would pay for a lease they could build their own tug.

I suppose, leasing a tugboat before the company that had built her for use in their own fleet, was normal in the industry. We just knew we would have liked to put her to work in Tampa, instead of sending her away bare boat chartered. After she was readied with fuel, groceries, and all the supplies needed for the long transit ahead, it was time for her to get underway.

Even with the tug *Reliant* gone, with the tug *Eagle II* finally in service, we were still in good shape as far as tugs went. There were some of the older tugs replaced with newer tugs as time went on. With each of the *Hawk* class tugs being built at a cost of six and a half million dollars plus, it wasn't long before some work outside the harbor had to be found so the mortgage payments could be made to the bank holding their hefty notes.

First Offshore Trip
on The Big Boats

Heerema Marine Contractors, a Dutch company who has operations all over the world working in the offshore oil exploration field, was our next customer. I wasn't involved in the first couple of oil rig tows, but I did get a taste of the oil patch in December of 1996. Dave ran as Captain with me running as Mate, he had been involved in a lot more offshore tows than I had and was more senior than I was on the big boats.

Dave and Jim had also worked in Brazil aboard the tug *Falcon* for a couple of years. The engineers for this trip were Doug Bogard and Luis Dixon, with Frank Pavon and Ed Harris as deckhands; both of the *Condor's* crews were aboard for this trip. Whenever one of the big boats would go offshore, the company would double crew them for the trip. We referred to the *Hawk* class boats as big, because that is what they were, big boats.

I had missed more than one Christmas since working on the tugs; this one was looking like it'd be no different. The date was December 19 1996, and was expecting to be gone for several days, with any delay we would definitely spend our Christmas offshore. I learned while getting ready for the trip that there were many preparations to be made when going offshore, so many more than harbor service alone. Extra groceries for six men instead of three, taking on enough fuel for an extended voyage if needed, the different charts needed for the geographical regions that might be transited, and so many more things to learn.

Dave had numerous offshore trips under his belt; this wasn't my first offshore trip with him either, so I felt completely at ease with what we were doing. Since there were so many variables to deal with, you had to take into account a lot of what ifs. Weather usually had the final word in most decisions made when offshore work was achieved. When it came to leaving a berth with a project that could run into the hundreds of millions of dollars, heading into the Gulf of Mexico meant the weather usually dictated when it would be allowed with safety always coming first, this would become evident in about two days. With everything having been taken care of, we were ready for our departure. Mr. Brantner was down at the dock telling us to be careful and to have a good trip. He said to me, "I can't believe you guys are going offshore with this bad weather and wind blowing like it is." I asked him, "I don't think we have a choice do we?" He said, "No, not really, be careful and enjoy yourself."

It was around 14:00 (2 PM) when we departed for what would turn out to be a ten-day trip. I departed with the boat while Dave laid down

until his watch which would start at 18:00. I had Luis and Ed on the Mates watch with me, which was my normal crew. It usually takes close to four hours to clear the Tampa sea buoy, which we had done when Dave come up for his watch. There were already seas of eight to ten feet in height when we went past the sea buoy. My Dad in years past had been a shrimper and had to learn to read the weather patterns. My

Heerema Marine Contractors *DCV Baldor* with 6,000 tons lifting capacity in calm water-Author photo

wife had told me after we had returned home that she and my Dad were watching the weather at home the day we departed.

My Dad said to her, "If Bill doesn't get seasick on this trip, he won't ever get sick, they're fixing to get their butts kicked." When Dave came up on the 18:00 watch he asked me why I had let it get so rough. I said,

"Dave, you remember when we brought the *Eagle II* back from Charleston, we never encountered seas like this." This ole girl was giving us a ride to the likes I hadn't seen before. Throughout the years I had heard Dave say, "Riding the *Hawk* class boats is like riding on a Clorox jug," that statement was absolutely unequivocally pertaining to the tugboat that we were now riding on.

We were supposed to be on location by Saturday afternoon with around 580 miles from the sea buoy to the site to go. With only a few hours since we had departed, we could only hope for the weather to get better and the seas to subside. Mother Nature had turned a deaf ear to our requests; instead of getting better, it only worsened. We finally arrived on location on Saturday afternoon as planned and were told the oil rig jacket hadn't even departed from Corpus Christi, Texas yet.

I was now seeing this huge piece of equipment that I had heard so much about, the *DCV Baldor* (Deepwater Construction Vessel) owned by Heerema Marine Contractors. It was equipped with two huge lifting cranes, with a total of 6,300 mT lifting capacity. It looked to be over five hundred feet long and well over two hundred feet wide. The *Baldor* was used in the assistance of the setting up of oilrigs on their locations.

Besides the floating drill rigs so prevalent in the Gulf of Mexico oil fields, there were also the type we were there to assist. The steel tower that a drilling module sets atop is called a jacket, which was the type of drill rig we were there to assist. Since the Crowley tug with the jacket hadn't even left Corpus Christi yet, we were told to stay within ten miles of the *Baldor*. Standing by and waiting for further orders, was looking like the weather was now in charge of the operations, it was very apparent this could turn into a long term project.

With the seas worsening since our arrival, we would put the bow into the seas and idle on one engine, going away from the *Baldor* about ten miles. When we were ten miles away, we would turn the boat around 180 degrees and idle back the other way, right past the *Baldor* for another ten miles. Although it was a twenty-mile pass, this was keeping us within a ten-mile distance from the *Baldor's* location of which we were told to maintain. We would run with the seas a whole lot faster than we did against the seas, which would most of the time take your whole six-hour watch to travel the twenty miles. It didn't take a genius to figure out the bed was the better of the two places to be, although neither was very comfortable.

It was Monday and just two days before Christmas, we had heard the Crowley owned tug *Patriarch* was finally underway with their barge that had the first of a two-stage jacket loaded on it. The seas were in no way losing their height, which was between ten to twelve feet now. I can remember passing Doug in the galley one morning which took us from one bulkhead to the other in a zigzag direction, and there was nothing you could do about it.

Approaching six days offshore, the newness of the big league boat was rapidly wearing off. I had never been in a rodeo before, but I'm sure I now know what it's like to be a bull rider. Dave said the *Hawk* class boats were definitely the worse riding boats he had been offshore on, ever. I couldn't agree with him more, I didn't get sea sick, but it did make me careful of what I ate. Christmas Eve had come upon us, and when we got up for our midnight watch, we had a surprise waiting on us. Without anyone knowing it, Doug had slipped a foot tall Christmas tree aboard with little lights and all. He and Jean, his girlfriend, had bought gifts for the whole crew, Doug had the tree set up with the gifts spread around it. This gesture was a very thoughtful thing to do I thought to myself. Doug said, "It was Jean's idea, she said from past experience she knew when a boat goes offshore, you never know what was going to happen."

She wanted us to at least feel the Christmas spirit, although we would be in the middle of the Gulf of Mexico and would be so far from home. We all opened our gifts and told Doug thank you for them and the effort shown. When you're away from home on the holidays, things like that just meant so much more.

Christmas morning 1996 that would be memorable to us all, we were now in twelve to fourteen foot seas. We heard the tug *Patriarch* had been told to head south and try to stay away from the bad cold front we were experiencing. Doug had been with Dave on other offshore jobs before and seemed not to be bothered by the rough seas. He had even cooked a turkey for our Christmas dinner with all the trimmings, a feat that was very remarkable considering the boat was rocking from side to side as bad it was.

Dave, among other things was also a poet, and had written a poem just for our present conditions. Frankie had come to the U.S. from Cuba a few years earlier and was slowly but surely getting used to the different personalities there were aboard the boat. When Dave wrote this poem, he definitely had Frankie on his mind, along with the Christmas Season and the rough weather. He's a poet and don't know it, his feet show it, they were long fellows. I have kept this poem from that trip for all these years, I knew there was a reason for keeping it, and here I am putting it in my very first book.

The Christmas Poem, written on 12/24/1996 by Captain Dave Scarborough

> *'Twas the night before Christmas*
> *On board the tugboat*
> *The chance of completing*
> *Our job was remote*
> *Another front coming*
> *Out of the Northwest*
> *Our next chance of working*
> *In two days at best*
> *The off crew was nestled*
> *All snug in their bunks*
> *With wisdom, they've all*
> *Chewed their food in small chunks*
> *When all of a sudden*
> *The crew was awaken*
> *From the sound of the voice*
> *There was no mistaken*
> *'Twas Frankie in the galley*
> *Entertaining the squad*
> *And he cried as he sang*
> *No Feliz Navidad*

There wasn't anyone specifically assigned to cook the meals, so who ever wanted to cook, cooked what they knew. Everyone aboard was good cooks, we just all had different styles. My specialty was making something out of leftovers, and with the carcass of a smoked turkey and leftover ham; I had a lot to work with. I came up with a pot full of what I called slumgullion, turkey, ham, and assorted vegetables which I thought turned out to be a pretty good meal.

Dave had been telling me a lot about the *Baldor* since he had been on other operations with them. We knew we would have to come back out to this same location within days of the first jacket lift. We were also in a water depth of over nine hundred feet, that's why this project was a two-stage jacket, I just couldn't figure out how in the world the two jacket pieces would be joined together. Dave said it was all done by ROV (Remote Operated Vehicle); this was going to be something to see. A couple of years later I would be on a single stage jacket tow that was 1,143 feet long, and was the forth largest in the world at that time, that was progress. The weather started clearing Thursday night; we heard if the weather had calmed down enough, we would do the lift Friday mid day. That's exactly what we did; we went to meet the Crowley tug and barge about three miles away from the *Baldor*.

This was the first time we had the opportunity to see the size of the jacket, with it being my first ever, it had to be the biggest man made structure being transported by barge that I had seen to date. I knew this huge steel structure wouldn't have been brought way out here in the Gulf of Mexico if somebody hadn't made plans. What these Dutchmen were going to do was definitely going to be something to see.

With us having put a towline up from our stern, we were being pulled backwards towards the *Baldor's* location. The Crowley barge with the jacket aboard was eased into position with extreme caution. Cables from the *Baldor* were attached to the Crowley barge towards each end of it making it secure to the *Baldor*. The tug *Patriarch* towed on the bow while the tug *Condor* towed from the stern, the tug *Retriever* who was also assigned to stay with the *Baldor*, had put up a towline mid ship of the Crowley barge to help hold it about a hundred feet away from the Baldor during the jacket lift.

All of this rigging took several hours to complete. After the configuration of the tugs had been set and was ready for work, all three tugs pulled in their respective directions with just enough power to hold position. The boats stayed this way for most of the day until the workers off the *Baldor* did their thing. There must have been thirty men with cutting torches cutting the braces loose that held the jacket secure to the barge deck. When the cutting was done and the go ahead was given, the two multi thousand ton cranes lifted the entire jacket off the barge.

With the jacket clear, all three tugs maneuvered the barge away from the *Baldor* like a well-choreographed dance. With the job at hand being accomplished without incident, within the hour we were released and heading back to Tampa. Although we were under way for home, we had orders to be back on the same location in six days.

Dave sent Mr. Brantner this information over the Boat Tracs communicator that we had aboard the boat. He also requested that we be allowed to go into Fourchon, Louisiana and just stand by there instead of going all the way back to Tampa. Mr. Brantner said, "No, bring the boat back to Tampa." Dave said, "The weather probably made the decision to bring us back; any delay could cost Bay Transportation since we would be off contract when we returned to Tampa."

Dave sent another Boat Tracs message acknowledging we were on our way back to Tampa. We seemed to go east faster than we did west, probably because we weren't bucking those unbelievably rough seas. We passed the Tampa Sea buoy after sunrise Sunday morning, which would put the *Mighty Condor* at the dock right at noon. Dave called Mr. Brantner on his cell phone as we were passing under the Skyway Bridge to personally let him know how the job had gone. With us having the capability of working a job from the bow, Mr. Brantner told Dave to work the second lift in that configuration instead of off the stern.

Secured to the dock back in Tampa and certainly ready to walk on steady ground. It was also time for a phone call home to alert my Sweetie that Daddy's in town, and was coming home. I had more than unopened Christmas presents on my mind that I not only wanted to see, but also needed to see, if you know what I mean. I arrived home where I found my wife with open arms; she had turned one of her many lighthouse lamps on when I had left home. After a kissy kiss greeting with everyone, the children took me into the living room where they showed me the lamp that had their Daddy's guiding light, still shining bright.

Lois told me she had turned the little lighthouse on to help guide us back home. She had told the children not to turn the lamp off until Daddy was home. She said, "Now that you are finally home safe, the light could now be turned off." This little gesture brought tears to my eyes, and is one of the reasons why we have been married for over thirty-six years now, little things like this was done with love throughout our marriage.

Second Offshore Trip
on The Big Boats

We were enjoying some good quality time with our families, celebrating a belated Christmas, and hoping we would be home for New Years Day. Knowing Heerema had requested the *Condor* to be back on their location within days; that was forever present on my mind. I was called on Monday and informed that the tug *Condor* would be departing on Wednesday morning at 02:00.

I was told to be aboard no later than 01:00, with a forty-five minute drive from my home to the boat; I figured I could at least wait until the midnight bell before I had to leave. I already had my gear in the car and was just waiting on the ball to drop on the TV program we were watching. Happy New Years kisses for all at the stroke of midnight, with this done, I was off once again. I made it to the boat on time with the same crew as days earlier, and ready to go back for round two. Since it was my watch again, I took us out the channel hoping for better weather than we had experienced twelve days earlier.

Although at the time of departure it wasn't bad at all, the weather reports however painted a pretty grim picture of what was coming our way. Whenever a cold front came across the Gulf, the only thing we could hope for was that it hit us head on. The *Hawk* class boats rode horrible as it was, but when we were hit with the beam seas, it would rock you from side to side making it almost unbearable, and nearly impossible to sleep.

I could now see why Dave asked to go into Port Fourchon last Friday instead of running all the way back to Tampa. From where the *Baldor* was set up to Port Fourchon was maybe fifteen hours running time, versus almost two days running Tampa. However on the flip side, had the weather turned bad enough to where we hadn't received orders to return, that's when somebody would have been catching it.

Regardless of the circumstances of how we got there, or where we came from, we were still heading right back to the same location to do the same job. Mr. Brantner told Dave we should have worked the first job off the bow. Dave and I had discussed how he was going to tell the Dutch tow master Willem van Woercom, of working the job this time off our bow. Willem's company Heerema would draw up on a set of plans as to how they wanted the tugboats configured for each job.

Although their plans had the *Condor* made up with a stern towline again, Dave said he was going to try to convince Willem to work us off our bow. We were still a day and a half from the *Baldor* site and were enjoying some fairly nice weather this time out. This trip was supposed to only be about five days in duration, but just as the last trip had turned out, the weather was about to change operations as planned for this one too.

After we returned back to the location of the *Baldor*, the seas were rough enough to once again be a virtual déjà vu. We were once again told to try and stay within ten miles of the *Baldor*; this little operation was already starting to get minuteness, although, I was in the Big League now.

I was getting a taste of what Dave, Doug, Jim, Otis and others had been doing since the big boats were built and put into service. With the go ahead given for the second stage of the jacket to commence, now that the sea height criteria had been met, it was time to do some fast-talking. After Dave had convinced Willem that we could do the job off of our bow, we then made up to the second barge much easier than last time. I ran the boat while Dave verbally guided me into position where all I had to do was slack our bowline down to the barge.

The tug *Retriever* had transported the workers over from the *Baldor* for the rigging process. They shackled the wire bridles into our line, we backed away from the barge, adjusted the length of our line with the bow winch, and Walla, we were ready to work. Everything went well, as a matter of fact, it seemed to work better this time around. The second lift when off without a hitch just as planned; once we were released, we were once again heading for Tampa, Home Sweet Home.

The best part of going home after these trips was the reunion with your family. Having worked in the harbor for the past nineteen years really makes you realize how much you miss those precious little hugs. Whenever the seas were calm, that was when the sunsets were the most beautiful and wished they could be shared with your loved ones. I would realize throughout the years that there were a lot more good days than there were bad. That was what really made going offshore tolerable to take. This trip

A view of a sun set from the Gulf of Mexico-Author photo

wound up to be seven days long, two days longer than planned. I was surprised the only pranks that had been pulled on me were salt being sprinkled on my bed sheet and a small piece of plywood placed between the sheet and mattress, at different times of course. Knowing Dave's history of pranks, I would have expected more than those two, but was relieved nothing more did happen. Maybe the rough seas are what kept the shenanigans from happening, keeping him from adding things to his repertoire. Well, we were finally secure to the dock in Tampa and were told we could go home for a day or so. The future for me had already taken a turn, but what was going to happen with the big boats was a virtual coin toss.

Big Boats Headed

for Mexico

With two offshore trips behind me now, I didn't know there had been negotiations to send the big boats to Mexico for some long term contract work with Pemex (Petroleos Mexicanos), which is also the Mexican government. Although the contracts had not been signed, the rumor mill was full ahead as to who was going to be involved with this new foreign-based endeavor. We were told there would probably be at least two of the big boats going to be working in Mexico for a year, and maybe even longer. I had gotten my passport in October of 1996 after being told I would probably need it before too long.

The tugs *Condor* and *Eagle II* were now slated to go to a place on the Pacific side of Mexico called Salina Cruz. The crews were chosen, and oddly enough, my name was missing on the crews list. I asked, "What gives, why am I not going?" I was told, "We didn't know you wanted to work out of the country." I just couldn't figure why I had been told to get my passport, I had received it on October 15 1996. And now to be left out of the so-called loop of choice, it really made me feel like I wasn't accepted.

Even after being one of the Captains' aboard the *Condor* for the past year, it looked like the favoritism monster had reared its ugly head once again. There was another fellow chosen, which throughout his career had been shown extreme partiality, but that's another story I'll not go into. After voicing my position of my interest in this newest project, I was told there would definitely be a crew change made, and that I would now be going with Jim Brantner Jr. as his Mate aboard the tug *Condor*.

I was finally going to see the Panama Canal Zone, which is still one the worlds' best, and biggest achievements known to mankind. This was one trip that I was really looking forward to making; this was also what I had expected after making the move to the big boats. While still servicing the Tampa harbor with ship assistance for the next few weeks, preparations for the impending trip were moving forward.

The Company Sold to Hvide Marine

The tug *Condor* was having some work done in the International Ship Repairs' dry dock. It was October 16 1997, with quite a few of us aboard the *Condor* that day doing long trip prep work. We received a call from the office advising us of some people that were on their way to the boat with an announcement, and to gather everyone in the galley when they arrived for it.

We wondered what the big announcement could be, never expecting, or even contemplating what had happened to us ten years earlier. When our visitors arrived, it was the first string all-pro of the company that showed up. Mr. Swindell and Mr. Brantner gathered all of the employees present, and then gave us the news that would profoundly affect all of our lives.

Mr. Swindell started out by informing us that the company as we knew it, Bay Transportation Corporation, had been bought out by a Fort Lauderdale based company known as Hvide Marine Inc. He said, "It was posted on the Internet this morning and we wanted to tell you men first hand." He continued saying, "They have been interested in buying Bay Transportation for some time now, and they have came to us four different times and increased the offer each time." He said, "You know the old saying guys, they made us an offer we couldn't refuse," I can remember a horse losing his head like that after someone else saying that same thing.

Number four must have been the magical offer, because it was accepted, and the offer that done us in. We were then told of the better changes we could expect from them. "Hvide Marine is a big corporation, and they'll be able to do more for you employees than us at Bay Transportation could do," he said. We were told business as usual would continue, with most of the management positions staying the same. That was a relief to hear because present management knew what the current employees were capable of doing. Having new management come in that did not know the crews was not what we wanted to deal with, this would also change.

We were told of the stock option program offered by Hvide Marine, and that their stock was around $33.00 per share at the time of the sale. We were also told they were a company that was growing and had worldwide operations. Mr. Swindell would no longer be in the picture, something some of us would sorely miss. Some of the information that we were being told was true at the time, but would change at the speed of light within the next couple of years, more on that later.

Business as usual, this meant the trip to Salina Cruz was still going to happen, I would still get to experience going through the Panama Canal zone. Not long after the word of the sale, Mr. Brantner and Jim Jr. had flown down to Mexico to look the Salina Cruz operation over. The contract with Pemex still needed to be signed by our company officials too. Arrangements with the contacts that would be used to obtain supplies, groceries, fuel, and other items needed, would also have to be made before the arrival of the boats.

It also happened to be hurricane season, and as luck would have it, one of the monster storms visited the Pacific side of Mexico. It headed directly for the small Gulf that the city of Salina Cruz, along with all their pipelines and SPM (Single Point Mooring) buoys were located. When the Jims' arrived in Mexico City they had actually changed planes, and waited for the plane to takeoff for over thirty minutes. A decision was made to cancel the westbound flight because of the direction that the storm was heading.

That storm damaged the SPM's and pipelines to the extent the services of the tugs *Condor* and *Eagle II* were no longer needed at that location. Hearing the bad news, it was discouragingly apparent that I would not be taking pictures of the Panamanian landscapes that I was so looking forward in doing. With this weather event having changed the operations of plan "A," we were now hearing the contingency of plan "B" taking shape.

There were two other locations we heard about, Cayo Arcos with SPM buoys, and we were told of a super tanker that was anchored in the lower part of the Gulf of Mexico called *Ta'kuntah*, the Mexicans were using it as a floating tank farm. The tankers specifications alone were spectacular. Seeing that ship would definitely be larger than anything I had seen before, and would be different, should the opportunity present itself. She was 1,267 feet in length with a beam of 191 feet wide, and a maximum draft of 72 feet. *Ta'kuntah* had a capacity of 2.3 million barrels of oil, she was also capable of pumping her cargo at a rate of 120,000 barrels per hour. She is located ninety-miles north of Dos Bocas, Mexico just west of Campeche. Cayo Arcos is thirty miles farther north than the *Ta'kuntah* location, where some more SPM buoys are located.

This was rumored of the new locations that two of the big boats would now call home for a while. The *Condor* headed to Mexico first with Captain Dave, but not before going to Mobile, Alabama and pick up a barge to be taken down there. The *Eagle II* went down to Mexico a few months later for the same type work that the tug *Condor* had been doing since their arrival. She was assisting million barrel tankers to and from the SPM buoys that we had heard so much about. I had once again not been chosen to be involved in the Mexican shuffle that the tugs *Condor* and *Eagle II* were doing, but this was about to change. I wasn't exposed to the south of the border country until late 1997, that's also when I experienced my first big airplane ride too.

With the spending spree that the new company had been on, Hvide Marine had acquired two foreign built boats that were constructed in Singapore. Whenever those boats departed overseas, their goal was what Neil Diamond sings about, "Coming to America," they were both to be delivered by foreign crews to the Hvide Marine towing division in Port Everglades, Florida.

My First Big
Airplane Ride

The names given them had the parent company's name in them, which was Seabulk, tugs *Seabulk Caroline* and *Seabulk Katie* were chosen. Both were like the *Hawk* class boats, they were also stern drive tractor tugs which would be based in Mexico for the Pemex operations. These two tugs had the smaller version Wartsila engines with 4,300 hp each. They

Ta'kuntah **loading a million barrel tanker**-Author photo

also had extraordinary fire fighting capabilities, having two huge monitors atop of the wheelhouses with directional controls on the inside of the wheelhouse. Captains Jim Brantner Jr. and Dave Arata, along with Otis Monteiro and Craig Farrow as engineers went to Port Everglades for the movement of these boats from Port Everglades, Fl. to Dos Boca's, Mexico. While this technology had been around a few years, it was still new to the Mexican Captains that would be operating these boats; it was also now time for me to tread on foreign soil.

With the two Singapore boats having been delivered in Mexico, there were now some modifications being made to both boats which would take some time. Dave and Otis stayed in Mexico to oversee the changes, while Jim and Craig came back to the States. That was when I received word that my very first passport was going to finally get a stamp put into it. Jim and I were going to be training the Mexican Captains on the proper operations of a Tractor tug. I told Jim, "I'm almost forty-seven years old, not only will this be my first time out of the country, this is also going to be my first commercial airplane ride."

He said, "You've got to be kidding, you've never flown before?" I said, "I'd flown on a smaller plane, but not on a commercial plane." I said, "Jim, you don't understand, I'm just an ole country bumpkin that hasn't done much traveling before." He told his Dad, "We'll have to get him a first class ticket," well, that didn't happen. Not knowing the proper airline procedures with luggage size and with what you can carry on and what you can't, I just packed my old ratty ditty bag, the same one I had always used in the harbor.

Jim told me to pack enough for several weeks, I did that very thing, and as I learned very fast, it's okay to have more than one bag, really it is. With all my goodbyes said to everyone at home, it was time to be taken to the office where Jim's wife would then take us to the airport. While making the vehicle transfer, when I picked up my bag and grunted, it showed. Jim asked, "What in the world have you got in there, where's your luggage?" I told him, "This is it; everything I'll need is right here in this one bag."

He said, "You'll probably have to check that bag it'll be too big, it also sounds too heavy for a carry on with all that grunting you're doing." With the phrase never assume coming to mind, I would not make this mistake again. This whole trip was going to be a learning process for me, never having flown before; I knew right away that I was out of my element.

We got checked in and were on the plane, this was like going to Disney World for me. It was also going to be a night flight, which would allow me to see the cities night-lights, and yes, they were spectacular. The flight we were scheduled to take meant we would have a layover in Houston, Texas, and a hotel stay too.

Jim was an old pro at air travel, and had already logged more air miles in the past than I would probably travel the rest of my life. At lift off, I knew I could get addicted to the pressing feeling from the planes take-off. High over the Gulf of Mexico and seeing some lights where I didn't think you would see any, I asked Jim, "What are all those lights down there?" He said, "They're offshore drill rigs, some of them have bridges tying them together, that's what looks like lines of lights you see."

I was amazed at what was visible on the ground from such a high altitude. The ride was way too short for me; however, the landing was just as impressive as the take off. We picked up our bags from the luggage belt; this was where I made my second and very important discovery of my big maiden trip. Without having prior experience, and not doing the math by adding two plus two, it was coming clear as a bell. You have to physically carry your luggage, no matter what you take with you, or how heavy it is, inside the airport between flights.

It was also coming clear to me that all those wheeled suitcases people were pulling around, was definitely making a lot of sense. Hauling this overstuffed ditty bag around the airport would be a real workout I would not soon forget. If I made many of these trips, you could make a sure bet on me buying luggage with wheels underneath them.

At the hotel we ate supper and talked about my first plane ride. Jim said he had flown so many times it wasn't a big deal to him anymore. I told him that I appreciated him showing me the ropes, and there would be some changes made on my part in the future. We had a good night's rest and once again, the next morning we were in the air to Mexico City, Mexico. Our itinerary took us from Tampa Florida to Houston Texas, then to Mexico City, Mexico, and then on to Del Carmen, Mexico. That was three takeoffs and three landings, and that was just going one way. It might have bothered some people to fly but not me; I was enjoying this new sensation too much to worry about a vertical landing.

As we flew over Mexico City, Jim told me over seventeen million people lived down there, and including the out skirts of the city there were more than twenty four million. There were also snow capped mountains down there, which I had never seen either. Back on the ground, we walked through the airport to get our bags where I saw what looked like hundreds of Volkswagen bug's running up and down the streets of Old Mexico. I told Jim, "You can sure tell those cars are taken care of as old as they have to be. He just laughed and said, "Those cars are probably new, the VW bugs are still made here in Mexico." That bit of information I did not know, I just thought this country was filled with proud car owners who were amazingly talented car detailers.

Navigating from one airline terminal to another was also an unforgettable experience. I had been to the Tampa airport to pick up people before, but this Latino maze was not anything like I had expected. We were able to stop at a gift shop where I bought a post card to send home from the airport. It actually took over two weeks to get to my home in Florida. I also bought a throw away camera to start a visual journal of the trip.

Making it to the Mexicana Airline terminal, we boarded the plane. This time at takeoff however, I now had a camera to document my flight. I took some fabulous pictures of an aerial view of the most densely populated city on the planet. Mexico City's landscape went on forever, and with it now being daylight made looking down towards the ground that much more impressive to see everything.

We were served a meal aboard the plane that was not too bad. After eating this meal, the realization of eating Mexican cuisine for the next few weeks was now on my mind. I knew I was going to enjoy this tour, because my favorite food was Mexican. Landing at the Del Carmen airport, and the last leg of our trip, I was seeing what was known as a Pemex town. Jim said, "This town exists because of Pemex, probably ninety-nine percent of the people living here works for them."

James Posey was the fellow who met us at the airport; he was also working for Hvide Marine but lived in Mexico more than he did in the states. We loaded our bags in his truck and headed for Dos Bocas, the location of the tugs *Katie* and *Caroline*. I like to have pushed a hole through the floorboard stomping on my imaginary brake. I suppose if I had local knowledge of the roads like James, it might have been less nerve racking, considering the numerous close calls we had had.

The roads down there were not like roads I was used to traveling. With a lot of people riding bicycles, and not the first bike path in site, they would ride right on the edge of an already narrow road where we would barely miss them being so close, I just knew their name was going to be Juan Statistic. Jim had told me, "Don't bring any expensive cameras, radios, or anything else of value, unless you want to have it taken from you." I had asked him, "Who's going to take them if I do?" He said, "Those Mexican fellows dressed in Military uniforms with the M-16's hung over their shoulders that we'll encounter at the checkpoints." With our nail-biting ride from the airport almost over, we were approaching a little town called Paraiso (Paradise) just outside the port. When we pulled up to the checkpoint, I could only hope the throw away camera that I

The bow of super tanker
Ta'kuntah-Author photo

had those aerial pictures on would not be discovered. Looking through our bags and being satisfied with what they saw, we were waved through. Jim said, "When you take pictures, be careful not to get caught." I thought, a bunch of boats, oil tanks, docks and water, this had to be paranoia at the highest level. We finally made it to my new home for the next few weeks, the tug *Seabulk Caroline*. Jim would be over on the *Seabulk Katie* with the rest of

Standing by on the stern of the *Ta'kuntah*-Author photo

the crewmembers being Mexicans aboard both boats, except us two gringos. These boats also had enough bunks to sleep a small Army comfortably, fifteen of them all together. There would only be about half the bunks needed for this operation, with a crew of nine per boat, including

Jim and I. The Captain's name was Freddy; the Mate's name was Ricardo, as was the Chief Engineer's. The Mate was a lot smaller of the two, so we called him Little Ricardo, while the engineer was a tall lanky fellow; Jim nicknamed him Lurch, like on the old TV show Adams family. The three deckhands were called one, two, and three, just for me I think. They were a good bunch of guys, just trying to make a living like the rest of us. The cook Francisco had been in the United States before, and was also a cook there too while living in the city of brotherly love, Philadelphia.

Leaving the Port of Dos Bocas, we were now underway to the site of the super tanker *Ta'kuntah*, some ninety miles north, which would also be where the twin tugboats would call home until a change was made. I understood from Jim that Pemex would routinely rotate different boats to the different locations as needed. These two boats were contracted for the location of the *Ta'kuntah* operations; I guess it was time for a change, and someone else's turn in the barrel, so to speak. Upon arrival to the largest ship I had personally seen, I thought this baby is one big ship. This ship was so large they would put a million-barrel tanker on the starboard side of her to load the crude oil into. Then with cargo hoses six to eight hundred feet long that floated behind the ship, which was connected to her port quarter, there was room for one more. Another million-barrel tanker would then be connected to the stern of *Ta'kuntah*, with some huge mooring lines and was loaded simultaneously with the tanker alongside her.

There was a large structure installed on the very bow of the *Ta'kuntah*, attached to it were ten chains, one and three quarters of a mile in length, they was taken in ten different directions with some very large anchors on the ends of them and set. This kept the bow end stationary, allowing it to pivot directly off the bow where the oil pipelines/hoses were connected that brought the valuable cargo of oil onto the ship.

When we arrived, we just floated around the area with the boats tied together waiting on orders from the Pemex officials. I realized from the get go, this was a job you had better be a book reader in order to pass the time. Time was something we had plenty of to go around. I was put in the chief engineer's room which only had one bunk; it also had a personal head (toilet, sink, and shower). I was treated like Royalty, the time I spent with my newfound friends was better than you would expect. Francisco would put some meals out that would rival any expensive restaurant.

The galleys on those boats were equipped the way that a professional Chef would have one set up, and that's what he was, professional. There were times with days between jobs, those were the times we would be tied together and spend time watching one of the two movies we had aboard. One of our favorite movies was a Brad Pitt flick called *Dose Monos* (*Twelve Monkeys*), spoken in English but sub-titled in Spanish; the other movie was *Con Air* with Nicholas Cage. Between both cooks, our cook Francisco won hands down, so he would usually cook our supper meal and serve all that wanted to eat while we watched one of the unfamiliar movies.

Jim would ask me during the movie, "Do you think he's going to get shot today?" Knowing we had seen the same movie day after day, I would say, "I don't know, what do you think?" Now if you can't read between the lines, that's what the pinnacle of being bored is like. It was either one of those two movies, or taped Mexican soccer matches; I wonder who's going to win today, yeah right.

I never had an actual watch to pull; this was done by the Mexican crew which would usually allow me to sleep throughout the night. I was up the nights we were doing jobs though, which was a rarity. With me being diabetic I would take my insulin at bedtime, this turned out to be a nightly event with the whole crew wanting to see me stick myself with the needle.

They would literally line up speaking Spanish pointing at me, and seemed to get plum giddy when it was needle time. After putting the prescribed dosage in the syringe, at the point of entry was wild with the way these fellows acted, I thought they need a trip to Disney World. If a man shooting himself with a needle got them that excited, they had better not ride Space Mountain.

Receiving word about a job was always a welcomed event. After assisting the ship and securing it to the stern of the *Ta'kuntah*, we would then make fast with a tow line to that ship. We would tow at an idle speed on the loading vessel, keeping a continuous gentle strain holding her bow off the stern of the *Ta'kuntah*. While pulling on one particular ship all night, the next morning I noticed my sterling silver necklace was tar-

Tug *Seabulk Caroline* in Dos Bocas, Mexico-Author photo

nished almost black, I was told it was caused by the sulphur gases coming off the loading tanker, this meant we were also breathing the same air. The smell of the sulphur gases at times was almost suffocating. The entire operation seemed to work well, however the little sisters did not want to be outdone. When it came to being rough riders, Teddy Roosevelt would have been proud of these two boats. The tugs *Caroline* and the *Katie* did not have the big box keels installed on them like the *Hawk* class boats. These were just top-heavy boats, when the wind kicked up and the seas were rough, they rode like a bunking bronco. You could not be running flat out and turn the drives much over fifteen degrees either direction, or you'd think the boat was turning over.

With the *Hawk* Class boats, the drives could be turned ninety degrees, making the boat end for end. What probably made the Singapore tugs ride so bad was being top heavy, lessening their stability, and making them lean as they did. The Mexican Captains were feeling confident with their training program and was doing pretty good in what they had learned to do, when a job did come along. With Jim calling all the shots, the operation at *Ta'kuntah* had gone on for three weeks and was coming to an end for me.

Jim told me a couple of days ahead of time that he was going to send me to relieve Dave Scarborough on the tug *Eagle II*, which was working just offshore of Dos Bocas at their SPM buoys. While the *Ta'kuntah* was ninety miles offshore, the Dos Bocas monobuoys were located only twelve miles offshore. This might be a Godsend for me, especially if there were some heavenly calmer waters closer into shore.

I had also gotten an ear infection that was getting increasingly worse with each passing day. Jim said he'd get James Posey to take me to a drug store and get some medicine for it. The Captains on the two Singapore boats would be rotating shifts as the other boats were. Twenty-eight days on and fourteen days off, that's eight months out of the year, a long time to be away from your family. When it came time for me to go, I told the crews it had been a pleasure working with them and would probably see some of them again. I thought to myself; with me and my insulin needles gone, the crew would now have to find some different pre-bedtime entertainment.

I was to fly off the *Ta'kuntah* by helicopter from the pad mounted on her stern. The only way to get aboard the ship was to be lifted up by the ships crane in a man basket from the deck of the tug. This would also be my first time lifted up this way, it looked to be a safe practice. The tug was backed up where the basket was dropped on the stern deck; I threw my one heavy bag inside it and stood on the foot ring, anticipating take off.

You had to be pulled up fast to keep the waves from picking the boat up and slamming into the basket causing an injury. Making it safe aboard this very huge ship, I was escorted to a holding area to wait on the helicopter. I was allowed to go to the ships bridge where the view was absolutely amazing. I had heard it took the super tankers miles to stop, even in an emergency. After seeing how much ship there was out there, I could believe it.

I was told it might be hours before a helicopter would come for me since there was no set schedule for them to fly. A crew member told me it was also a hit or miss with them sometimes, I might even have to spend the night. I had waited about four hours before one finally showed up to transport me and one other fellow to Del Carmen. After boarding the helicopter and giving this mechanical marvel a quick inspection, I understood fully well why Dave was scared of flying on them.

There were nylon ties being used in place of door hinge pins. With flying having just recently becoming my new favorite thing to do, I could only hope the maintenance on the working parts of this helicopter hadn't been compromised and replaced with inferior parts too, like the missing door hinge pins. We finally lifted off and headed for the Del Carmen airport. Now I'm no helicopter pilot, but when you can look ahead and see a gas flame shooting into the air from a drill rig, I believe I'd go around it. Not the Genius running this show, he went directly over the flame instead of going around it. He merely increased the altitude just before going over it, and then dropped back down to our first cruising altitude. That fancy move made my hurting ears pop with a pain that I would not soon forget.

Maybe that's how it's done down there, but that little maneuver put my heart in my throat. After I had swallowed my heart back to its proper place, and although I did enjoy flying, I couldn't wait for this bird to find its nest. Land Ahoy, I was seeing a shoreline ahead which thrilled me to no end. Touching down, softly I might add and was a welcomed relief, considering how it had started.

Standing there at the terminal in all his glory was Mr. NASCAR, James Posey, waiting to take me to my latest assignment. I loaded my bag in the back of his truck and told him about my ear pain problem. He said, "I know just where to take you," and off to the local Pharmacia we went. I thought this is a good, until we got there and tried to make the Pharmacist who spoke Spanish only, to understand the problem that I was having with my ears. This exchange should have been caught on tape; it would have been a winner on Americas Funniest Videos. We were finally able to communicate to the old Gentleman that I just needed some eardrops. If you get sick in Mexico you had better speak Spanish, or have a translator with you, write that down. Since I hadn't caught an earlier air ride into Del Carmen, and was over two hours of driving time to Dos Bocas, James put me up in a Motel for the night. This did not upset me one bit, I was looking forward to lying on a bed that wasn't trying to jump out from under me. A restaurant was there in the Motel that billed the room, which made this overnight stay complete. I needed a good night's sleep, knowing that I once again had a nail biting, Mexican dodging ride ahead of me the next morning.

With a night's sleep behind me and an authentic Mexican breakfast under my belt, I was ready for this wild ride to get started. James took me by the office of Oceanografia, which is where the Mexican crews were hired through. This place had to be the ego capitol of Mexico at the highest level. The longer I was there, the more I saw how anyone with just a little bit of authority treated those that had none, and with only a desire to work, I would find out later that these guys were mere amateurs.

Not being impressed with that stop at all, we were finally heading to the Port of Dos Bocas to find me a ride out to the tug *Eagle II*. This was done by Pilot boat, which only took about forty minutes to reach their location. Captain Dave was like a caged lion when we pulled up to the stern of the *Eagle II*, that man was ready to go home. We had little time as we jumped from one boat to the other; Dave told me there was a notepad up in the wheelhouse with instructions on it for me to follow.

Dave had learned to speak Spanish and could communicate in the language that I was nowhere near fluent in speaking. There was only one man that spoke English aboard the tug, the engineer Mark Chabasall. I could only try, plus read the three or four pages of notes that Dave had written down for me. He also had some Spanish to English words written down for me.

The Dave notes were a tremendous help in understanding the operational procedures that I would soon encounter. He had written a cheat sheet too, with most of the commands that I would hear from the Pilots during a job. Some of the words were Para-stop, adalante-ahead, atras-astern, Aguila dos-Eagle II, and so on. The Pilots were supposed to speak to me in English, but sometimes at critical moments during a mooring procedure they would revert back to Spanish. This happened to me on the very first job that I worked aboard the big bird boat *Eagle II*.

Dave had also written that although there was a Mate placed aboard the tug, the Captain that was sent from the states did all of the jobs. They were not trained to operate the Tractor tugs yet and just pulled their watches with minimal operation. The Mexican Mate that was aboard the *Eagle II* when I had arrived spoke absolutely no English, my being impressed level had gone underground.

I was working my first job, and up to a certain point, the commands had been given to me in English from the Mexican Pilot. Something was going on with the operations that must have excited him; this caused him to start shooting commands so fast they sounded like a machine gun going off. Well, I just sat there, since I hadn't heard any English commands I'd recognize. There was also Spanish speaking chatter heard over the radio constantly, non-stop. Since I didn't understand what the Pilot had said and hadn't answered his commands, the Mate came alive with some hand movements, all the time hollering in his native tongue. He was pointing at both controls, yelling like the world was coming to an end. One of the deckhands who was in the wheelhouse with us did know how to say stop. Hearing what was going on, he started repeating stop, stop, stop, which is all I needed to hear.

At that point in my first Mexican tour, I realized the importance of being bilingual. We muddled through this job with me telling the Pilot he really did need to speak English. He said, "Sorry about that Captain Buffalo Bill, I'm used to speaking to Captain Dave, I'll try to remember that he's not aboard the tug." I told him, "Until I learned the language a little better, that would be best." That is also when I learned that Brother Dave had told the Mexican Pilots that a big bearded man, with the name of Buffalo Bill was coming to relieve him while he went home for some down time. We did a few more jobs before the word spread among the Pilots about the importance of speaking English to the new Captain running the tug *Aguila dos*. I sure was glad they understood that and didn't mess with me.

Buffalo Bill with my beard-Author photo

Within two days, Dave had called me on the Sat phone just to see how it was going, and if he could do anything for me. I told him, "Get me a bilingual Mate, this is not working for me." He told me to hang in there; he would see what he could do. He said, "You need a Mate like Jose Bibiano, he's one of the regular crewmembers that work with me." He said, "It's weird, Jose doesn't speak any English but seems to understand everything you tell him." He asked me how I was doing with the e-mail, which is how we sent our daily reports to the Tampa office. I told him, "Those notes really helped me out of a jamb since I didn't even own a computer, let alone how to use one." He said, "You've come a long way in a few days Brother Bill, just think, last week you couldn't spell e-mail, now you're sending it."

We had a good laugh with him telling me just what I needed to hear, I received some encouraging words from him to let me know everything would work out. He must have said just the right thing, to just the right person, because the very next day I had me an English speaking Mexican Mate aboard the boat. When he came aboard, I asked him if he could speak English, he said, "Yes sir, I can speak a little bit." I said, "With those few words you just spoke, I can tell we're going to get along just fine." Whenever the weather kicked up a fuss that shut down the operations out at the monobuoys, the tugs were allowed to go into Dos Bocas. We had to type up a report that was presented to the Pemex officials upon securing the tug in the port.

This form was already in the computer and just had to have the dates and names changed for the current crewmembers before printing it. Louis Dies-Meir, my new mate, told me that he would type the report if I wanted him to. You do not know how sweet those words were, I told him, "By all means, type your little heart out." I typed with two fingers as it was, so with the added surprise of talent that Louis was demonstrating, he was exactly 180 degrees different from the man he had replaced in all aspects.

Things overall seemed to go so well now that there was good communication among the crew. I learned a lot about these guys with the short time I had already spent with them. One thing I knew, there was some outstanding cooks working on this tugboat. It seemed that there were different schedules worked for almost everyone with the different faces passing through the boat. Once I figured out who did what, it was the same as the guys I had left at the tanker *Ta'kuntah*. There were some of the crewmembers that passed across the decks of the tugs who turned out to be some of the hardest working people I have ever seen, anywhere.

Although they weren't paid as well as the Americans were, they gave you a good day's work for a day's pay.

There were times in the morning when one of the deckhands would come to the wheelhouse to see if I wanted breakfast. He would gesture with his hands like he was eating, and say, "You eat." I would tell him, "No comida Para mi," (no food for me). He would take off down stairs, after about twenty minutes he'd show up with a breakfast fit for a King. Tortillas with scrambled eggs and tuna fish mixed together, eggs and shrimp, quesadillas, but at different times of course; no wonder I gained weight down there.

Time seemed to just slip by with things going as well as you'd expect, then it was time for crew change. This was when I met Jose Bibiano, the Mate that Dave had said I needed to work with. My old engineer Luis Dixon had come to relieve Mark Chabasall. It had been a while since I had seen Luis; I did remember he spoke Spanish and was from Honduras. Mark Chabasall, Doug Bogard, and Louis Dixon were the three engineers that worked aboard the tugs *Condor* and *Eagle II* on a schedule of forty days on, then twenty days off.

They would rotate from one tug to the other, Dave worked a schedule unlike the others since he didn't like to fly, he figured the longer he spent aboard the boat, the less he had to fly. The remainder of the *Eagle II* tour was coming to an end for me as well, after forty-two days, I was ready to go home.

When we had crew change this time, Dave and I were able to talk for a few minutes before I departed. He asked me how I liked this part of the world, to which I replied, "It is different from the States, that's for sure." I told him he had a good bunch of guys to work with, and thanked him for all the notes he had left me. He said, "I'm glad they were of help to you," then we talked a bit about the times he used to spend on the docks of Port Manatee with my Dad, who he called Pops.

That's where the name Brother Bill came from, he would spend hours on the dock talking with my Dad. He was a tankerman that loaded the oil barges that Dave pushed around Tampa Bay years earlier on the tug *Harbor Island*. Dave told me my Dad would tell him stories and jokes that made him feel close to him as he did with his own Dad. Whenever we would add Brother to the front of our names when we talked to each other, it just seemed to bring us closer, like a real Brother.

I once again needed to be transported to Del Carmen, where I would fly from the next day. I was taken to the same motel I had previously stayed in, but driven by Amador, another employee of Oceanografia. I had talked to Amador several times during the three weeks I was on the *Eagle II* and got to know him somewhat. He set me up with a room, told me to enjoy my supper meal at the café, and he'd see me in the morning.

I remembered the menu being printed in Spanish and thought I'd give it a whirl on my own. I sat down, picked up a menu, and saw several words I could recognize immediately. Having gone over the grocery lists with Luis and Jose during their tours, which were also written in Spanish, I recognized some of the foods we had ordered. The one that caught my eye most was camarones (shrimp); Camarones Diablo was here as an entrée jumping out at me. I thought this must be hot and spicy shrimp, I also wondered how many there were on an order.

After a comedic exchange with the waiter as to how many shrimps there were, he finally held up eight fingers, I could eat eight shrimp by accident, I thought. The cost was eighty pesos, about eight U.S. dollars, and since it was being billed to the room, I told him dos platos (two plates). When he went to the window and placed the order, the woman cook peered around the corner with a weird look. I could only imagine what he had told her with the funny look she had on her face.

When he began bringing a double order of everything else that comes with two plates of the entrées, I then figured out why the look of, are you kidding me, that I had received from the cook. I got a double order of chips and salsa, two salads, two huge piles of rice with diablo sauce atop of them, and sixteen of the biggest shrimp I had ever laid my eyes on. The waiter said something in Spanish when he was through bringing me my double order shrimp meal, I just smiled and said, "Gracias," (thank you).

I started in on my heart stopping meal, which I ate everything that was brought to my table, right down to every grain of rice. I can tell you this much, when I was finished, I had to take a long walk just to try to settle the very large meal I had just eaten.

When my walk was over, and as I was heading to my room going past the front desk, another comical dual language exchange took place. I wanted to make a collect phone call to my home, not much to ask for, right? The front desk girl could not understand, no matter how I said it, as to what it was I wanted. A bilingual man came by and heard our exchange, and within minutes I was talking to my wife. Hearing the voices of my family made me want to see their smiling faces. I was now ready for the bed; I needed to rest up for that heavy bag-carrying task ahead of me the next day.

While up in the airplane the following day, I tried to remember the route we had navigated through the airport so I could reverse it. Three takeoffs and three landings later, I was finally home in Tampa, Fl. I took a couple of days off and then went back to work doing harbor service. I also went out and purchased a computer so I could communicate with my home, if I went back south of the border.

After a few days had past, Jim Jr. told me that Dave was looking for someone to relieve him on a ninety-day schedule; he wanted to work sixty days on, and then take thirty days off. I told him, "If he would send me to the tug *Eagle II*, and let me come right back to my boat in the harbor without missing any days, I would do that for Dave." He said, "If you'll do that for me, that will take a huge load off my mind." I said, "You got it, I'll do it for you too."

This would also mean that I would be working eight months out of the year too, the same as Dave, but I'd be home more often. The extra money was always nice and could definitely be put to a good use. Norman Atkins had called me into his office a little while later where he said to me, "With you agreeing to relieve Dave on the *Eagle II*, your stock just went up big time with the Brantner's." He said, "Finding a relief for him to work that schedule was worrying Jim, you have just taken a big weight off his shoulders." My so-called stock in reality had not changed one bit, which proved to be true later on down the road when it came to choose a new team.

Tractor Tug

Winslow C. Kelsey

The new company, Hvide Marine Incorporated, appeared they were definitely either loosening their purse strings, or borrowing a lot of money from somebody. It seemed that they were either buying and/or leasing, just about everything floating in salt water. They had also bought other tug companies, ships, and offshore supply boats, besides the two Singapore boats.

The Tampa Division was told that since two of the big boats were working in Mexico, they would be receiving another Tractor tug. It was

Tractor tug *Winslow C. Kelsey*
Author photo

a lease boat from Groton, Connecticut named tug *Winslow C. Kelsey.* A company called Electric Boat had been using her in the movement of Submarines for the Navy base. Captain Denny Cooper along with Lawrence LeDuc Jr. who ran as Mate, were sent to Connecticut to bring her down to Tampa Bay. Paul Roush and Craig Farrow also went as engineers, they were going to be the Chief Engineers when the boat got to Tampa. Paul was going to be my engineer, when a replacement on the tug *Challenger* was found for him.

With two of the big boats now stationed in Mexico, I had been working aboard numerous boats, jumping from one boat to another like a grasshopper on a fresh mowed lawn. When the tug *Kelsey* finally arrived in Tampa in the month of January 1998, Lawrence LeDuc Jr. and I were to be the Captains. Some of the Tampa Bay Pilots had seen her at our dock and told us they were going to shorten her name to just *Kelsey*. Since they give their commands along with the tugs name in the radio transmission, it would be too much of a mouth full. I could not agree with them more, and was glad to hear of what we had already talked about between ourselves. Could you imagine having to say the whole name of the boat along with everything else you repeated, sometimes as many as a hundred times during a job, depending on which Pilot you worked with.

I was at home on a Saturday morning when I was called into work to be aboard the tug *Kelsey* for her very first job. JR, as he liked to be called, he would say like on the TV show Dallas. We were to meet the tug *April Moran* with her barge at the sea buoy, which needed to have an escort since the tug was having some sort of engine problems.

The *Kelsey* could sleep up to twelve crewmembers; she had one of the nicest, most spacious galleys I had ever seen on a tugboat. Her length was ninety-eight feet, with a thirty-two foot beam and had 4,300 hp. which was a good combination. She was an older boat, but seemed to handle pretty good. The only thing that was different between her and the big boats was a winch for the bow line; the line would have to be made up on the bitts. She had a good 360-degree visibility with her three-deck height, something I had grown used to having. The tug *Kelsey* seemed to be just the right package for harbor service, as was the tug *Reliant* which also had the same horsepower.

We had just been running along staying off the barge a hundred feet or so matching her speed. With this being our first job and not having a line on the barge, it gave us an opportunity to get the feel of this submarine tug. As we were approaching the Port Sutton turn, we made fast with one line on the port bow of the barge. Most everything went well during the job, with the exception of the leaning bow bitts.

Whenever we came astern the bitts would flex forward, and that was just working on an easy bell. JR and I agreed that some braces would definitely have to be welded to the bitts to strengthen them. We couldn't believe someone hadn't noticed it before now; maybe they had, and just thought it was normal. Whenever I came astern while doing a job, I did not want to see the bitts fly off the deck, like happened to my old Buddy, Captain Carroll Dale one time.

Lost Bitts on The

Tug *Palmetto*

While Carroll was still on the tug *Palmetto*, they were sent to a grounded ship one night. His engineer was Gary Louderback, who had a little stutter when he talked. It was a little hazy when they departed the dock, with heavy fog expected anytime. He said when they finally arrived to the ships location the fog seemed to just drop like a curtain. He said they pushed on the ship for quite some time with no results. With the tug pushing on one side, then to the other and yielding no results, the Pilot made the decision to do a little dredging. This was a common practice we had done dozens of times. They put up a tow line to pull on the ship, pulling aft, or at least towards the stern.

The tugs wheel wash would then be directed down alongside the ship removing the material, causing a digging action like a dredge would do. We had been on groundings that had lasted days before, if the suction from the mud could ever be broken, the grounded vessel would usually come right off. While the tug was pulling and dredging, that was the ultimate goal on a grounding job, to float.

Carroll said it was so foggy he could hardly see the ship, even as close to it as they were. They had been pulling on their line for sometime, when the boat just took off. He called Gary to the wheelhouse and asked him to go to the stern deck and see what had happened. He said, "I thought maybe the line had parted, or maybe the ship had broke loose and was floating, I just needed to know." When Gary got back to the wheelhouse, Carroll said he was stuttering so bad he couldn't make heads or tails at what exactly he was trying to say.

Carroll told Gary, "Calm down, stay here and standby the radio, I'll go see what the problem is myself." He said when he went back aft and looked, there was nothing to see, absolutely nothing. The metal plate that the bitts were welded to had come loose from the deck. With the line being made up to the bitts, when the plate came loose it cleared the deck, plate, bitts, and their line, all gone overboard.

He said they were able to retrieve their line, since the eye of the line was made fast to the bitts on the ship. The ships crew winched the line aboard and then let it back down to the deck on the *Palmetto*. He said all he could do then was push, after the ship was off and they made it back in, what a story he had then. He would brag about the power that the *Palmetto* had to have had in order to pull the bitts off the deck that way. I would say, "I guarantee you Carroll Dale, that boats got some power." Thinking about this story made me cringe when we worked a job with the *Kelsey*, at least until the welder was able to install the bitt braces, which then stiffened them properly.

THE RUSSIAN SUBMARINE

We had been working the tug *Kelsey* for quite a while in the harbor, when out of the blue, the type of job comes along that this Ole Gal was made to do. For the past few years the *Kelsey* had been used to move submarines, it seemed her sub moving days was still around. There had been an old World War II Russian submarine brought into the Port of St. Petersburg.

The owner of the sub wanted to use it as a tourist exhibit, but had not anticipated one big problem he was about to encounter. On the St. Petersburg side of Tampa Bay was another tourist drawer extending outward into the bay, known as the "Million Dollar Pier." It was an angler's joy to fish from, also a beautiful view of the bay that photographers frequented. That location is where this fellow wanted to shift the submarine to from the Bay Boro Harbor. The tugs *Kelsey* and *Ybor* were chosen to make this planned move. Although the weather was not going to be cooperating, it was a job we were going to doing safely.

We had to make this move at the highest tide, which was a particular date and time; the high tide time was also going to be late at night. Mr. Jimmy Brantner, his son Jim Jr., and their wives met us in Bay Boro for this impending

My family aboard the *USS Alabama* in 1989-Author photo

circus. Larry Shelton was the Captain aboard the tug *Ybor*, who had been told he would tow the submarine over to her anticipated new home. My crew was Paul Roush as the engineer and Jose Navaro was the deckhand for this move. When we arrived at Bay Boro, we secured the boat and were told we could take a tour of the submarine.

I had taken a tour of an American submarine moored with the battle ship *USS Alabama* in Mobile, Alabama. Although this submarine was Russian made, I still expected to see about the same design I had seen before, in the U.S. made submarine. The access hatches from one compartment to the other were round instead of an oval shape. With the bottom of the access about two feet from the deck it made passage a little difficult, especially for a larger fellow as I am, and have been all my life. A quick exit for me was completely out of the question, don't anyone yell fire, I thought. I'm satisfied to believe that the men who crewed these close quartered vessels, whether friend or foe, were, and are, a special breed of people. She was at least sixty some odd years old, and you could almost sense what it must have been like in the war years.

Capturing that feeling was probably what the big draw of going aboard an old submarine was all about, the experience of pretending to be there was really exhilarating, but at the same time, it was also sad. With the sub-tour being over, it was now time to get this challenging movement started.

With the charts having been gone over to find the deepest route we could take, it showed there was a shallow area that might cause a problem. The submarine owner had been notified that because of the sub's draft, there was a few feet difference on the shallower sandy lump that just might prevent us from getting across it. He said he still wanted to try anyway; it was only that one lump that would cause a problem. With the tide height being at its highest, if the sub was going to cross that terra firma, now was definitely the time to try.

The Brantner wives rode on the tug *Kelsey* with us to observe the workings of the job, Jimmy and Jim rode the submarine to Pilot the job. It was a humid summer night with the weather turning bad, and as it has so many times before, it started showing us some major water falling from the sky. We started out with Larry towing, while the *Kelsey* was made up alongside the starboard bow with two lines, but facing aft. This way we could maneuver the sub like a barge if we made it past the infamous lump, and with any luck.

It was apparent this whole operation was going to be done with restricted visibility, since the rain was coming down increasingly harder as time went on. Thunder and lightening that comes along with these summer squalls was also increasing with intensity.

We had made it out of Bay Boro harbor safely, turning north; we now just needed to make it over the sandy lump. Making it to the area that we could turn west and go towards the "Million Dollar Pier," the tug *Ybor* headed in that direction. Larry was pulling and I was pushing, as we approached the area we had hoped to slide the sub across without too much aggravation. Murphy's Law would be showing up, very soon.

As we had suspected, we found the sandy knoll, and like the grassy knoll of times past, this one would also be talked about for a long time to come. Jimmy and Jim were getting soaked since they didn't have any rain gear, and a shelter that was almost non-existent atop the sub where they were communicating to us from.

Their wives kept asking with great concern about both Jims' status. We could only try to assure them saying, "They are safe, they know what their doing." I said, "This isn't their first rodeo." When it had reached the point that it became unsafe to continue, and with the submarine not going anywhere being aground, the operation was stopped. Hoping the weather would pass before the tide started ebbing; the lightening had also gotten pretty fierce.

When a strike would hit, it would light up the whole area with the brilliance of a sports stadium having a nighttime event. Jim's wife Janet, who was already nervous, was sitting atop of the filing cabinet we had in the wheelhouse. We were watching the fiercest light show that Mother Nature had put on in quite awhile. About that time, a lightening strike hit very close to the boat with a deafening clap of thunder that seemed to shake the whole boat. We all jumped, then Janet asked, "That was too close for comfort, if lightening hits the boat will it hurt us?" Paul said, "It won't hurt you at all, unless you're touching metal." Bless her heart; she jumped off that metal filing cabinet as if she had been shocked.

We all started laughing and told her she was okay, although the squall was still upon us, that little laughter seemed to ease the tension. When the weather started clearing, we got started with the task at hand once again. Relocating a few hundred feet from the first tried location, we pushed and pulled for quite a while, until it was evident that this underwater behemoth was not going over that sandy hump.

Both tugs ending up working pretty hard removing the sub back off the sand bar, the last try was finished up by taking her right back, where hours earlier we had undocked this World War II relic. After securing the sub back to her berth in Bay Boro Harbor, we were released and told to go back to Tampa. I wondered to myself, what would happen to this piece of history now. It was a sure thing that this Russian made submarine would end up as a tourist exhibit somewhere, just not in St. Petersburg, and certainly not this night.

FLYING SOLO TO MEXICO

With it being almost two months since I had came back from Mexico, I was informed that it was time to fly again. Receiving my itinerary from Jim, he also told me I was going solo. I would be doing the same airport shuffle but with one difference, I would be going to another airport with the final destination being in Villahermosa, Mexico.

As I packed my two bags, yes, I said two, the bigger one with wheels; see I remembered, and anticipated a future flight. Three more takeoffs and three more landings, this was the best part of these trips for me. I knew with this schedule, I wouldn't be away from home as long as I had the last trip. I got me plenty of hugs with the whole family seeing me off at the airport. I acted like an old pro, checking my bags and heading for the gate terminal. It was also pre 9/11, so the whole bunch went right with me, even riding the shuttle and going as far as the hallway to the plane.

I left early enough this time that I would be at my destination by late afternoon. Everything went off without a hitch, making it to the bigger airport of Villahermosa. Just like clockwork and with a sigh of relief, there was my ole Buddy Amador. He seemed to not be in such a rush as my other chauffeur, which was the way I liked to travel, nice and easy down these roads that had almost as many bicycle riders as there were cars. These bikes had been modified with longer bars sticking out of the back axels, allowing someone to stand right behind the peddler.

This was done on almost every bike we had seen, one person peddling, and one riding while standing up. I even saw some people cutting their yards, bent over with a machete. Amador said they could not afford lawn mowers, and probably couldn't afford the gas that it took to run one. I saw some poor people there in Mexico, when I had made it home from the first trip, I had told my wife of the poverty that I had seen.

I told her, "It was no wonder the Rio Grande had so many visitors swimming north, the United States is truly a blessed nation." We have taken so much for granted and really should take a look around us. We should give thanks to the Lord each and every morning that our feet hit the floor when we get out of our warm comfortable beds with food to eat.

We made it to the port safe and sound, slower, but safer. I didn't have to wait for a ride this time either, there in all her glory was the mighty *Eagle II*, her and the *Condor* was the big dogs working in the Mexican oil patch. There in Dos Bocas and every other place they worked, there were no other tugs with their horsepower or with their increased maneuverabil-

Eagle II **with rough weather fendering**-Author photo

ity, at that time. Dave was a happy man when he saw me, and told me how the Mexican Pilots were also happy to hear that Captain Buffalo Bill was coming back. He told me that I had impressed them with how I had operated the boat, and had picked up on the operations so quickly overall. That was an unexpected good report to hear, I also had some books on Spanish with me to study.

This time we also had a good crew exchange, with plenty of time to talk about any changes or projects they were working on. I also saw the Mate Jose Bibiano back aboard, and was told there would be a Mexican crew change take place in a couple of more days. I just wanted to know who Jose's replacement would be, and if he spoke English. Dave said he

Standing by on the stern of a loading tanker-Author photo

didn't know, but was sure I would be alright, I'll tell you why later. With the next two days flying by, there they were, crew change for the Mexicans.

The bow fendering that these Mexican boats had installed on them looked like they had a hairy mustache, but was needed for the rough waters they were working in. My main man Luis Dies-Mier showed up for crew change along with two more crewmembers. This was going to be a good tour, seeing the crewmembers that were aboard. There was one particular deckhand that really shined; he was a Mexican Ed Harris.

His name was Efren Morales, a young fellow who was also learning to speak English. He would come to the wheelhouse early in the morning, as if he was searching for the words to say, he would gaze upwards toward the ceiling. When he had searched his mind and collected the words he wanted to say in English, he would say to me, "Good Morning Captain, how are you doing?" I replied, "Very good Efren, you're doing good with your English." With his limited English, and, my very limited Spanish, at times it was plum comical watching us trying to understand what we were saying, all the while, trying to teach each other our respective languages. On my last trip to Mexico Efren had gone to school and had taken an English class, he now spoke as good as any English speaking person; I was impressed with what he had accomplished all on his own.

The jobs at the Dos Bocas SPM buoys were for the most part, a standby job. After assisting a ship to the buoy, we would make fast to the stern of the ship with a long line and standby in case we were needed. The SPM buoys, like the tanker *Ta'kuntah*, had floating hoses attached for the loading of the oil. There would hardly ever be more than two ship assists per day, since there were only two buoys to moor the ships. The loading would usually take around twenty-four hours to complete.

When finished loading, the ships would usually disconnect, and then depart from the buoy on their own power without any tug assistance, with the exception of the much larger tankers. These were repetitive jobs, so with the Mexican Pilots being as knowledgeable as they were with their trade, most went without any problems. One drawback to working in Mexico was the weather, which is when some problems would surface. Working where the seas would pick the boat up and down sometimes six to eight feet, meant you needed a lot of extra fendering for the cushion needed to keep from causing any damage. We also used a fifteen-inch shock line, shackled into a wire pendant that we sent up on every ship for the mooring procedures.

Working in this type of environment kept you on your toes as well, making sure your deck crew was safe was always a high priority. I could not bear to have one of these guys be killed on my watch, let alone having one of them injured. The incident that had happened on the tug *Yvonne* years earlier with the drowning of that poor man was still much on my mind. I am thankful to the Lord that no injuries ever occurred in all the times that I had went to work in the Mexican offshore oil fields. The rough seas will make you think as a ballerina dances, always on your toes.

With more time spent standing by than actual working jobs, Louis had started a home project. He was making this huge hammock during the times he was up on his wheelhouse watches. He was using the unfurled strands from lines that we were discarding. I told him the story about those two large shrimp meals I had eaten the last time I was in Mexico, which he thought was hysterical. I told him that while walking around Del Carmen that evening, I could actually see right through some of the houses as I walked past, and saw hammocks just like he was making, hanging in them. The one he was making was so big; it could probably sleep a whole family. Luis even made the needles he used to weave it with out of some old wood planks he had picked up in Dos Bocas.

I also told Luis that when I had gone home last time, I had bought a home computer to keep in touch with my Wife. This was some modern technology that I had only been introduced to just two months earlier. I had already contacted Brother Dave aboard the *Eagle II* using this electronic marvel, just to make sure it would work, I said I was just an ole country bumpkin.

Jim had sent news releases to the boat about all kinds of news stories. Even with our Commander in Chief's Lewinsky problem that was front-page news back in the States. The Mexican Pilots called him Slick Willie; they would actually quiz me on what I knew about that was going on in the States.

I figured a computer was a good investment for me to stay updated with happenings on my own home front. Before I had left on this trip, Jim had told me it was okay to send e-mails home when I sent the morning reports over the Internet. Using the satellite phone for the Internet connection, and at a cost of $1.19 per minute, was indeed costly. He said, "Pass on to who ever you e-mail to not send pictures because of the time it takes to download them. Luis asked me if he could send e-mails to his girlfriend, I said, "I'm sure it would be okay, just no pictures."

I know just about everyone has seen the short movie clip that circulated on the Internet of a baby chimpanzee, smelling his finger after wiping it on his backside, then appears to faint and falls out of the tree. Do y'all see it coming, me and Louis sure didn't, and then there it was after floating around in Cyberspace for a day. I sent the morning report to the office along with two more homebound letters, when they were finished; I started receiving the e-mails that were sent to the boat.

This was when I knew there was a problem, something big was trying to be downloaded, at a very slow snails pace. I stopped the downloading a couple of times, because at $1.19 a minute, this was going to be a hard one to explain. I just kept thinking of what I had been told, no pictures. Whenever we went back to Tampa, we were told to bring a copy of the phone log with us for review.

The look on Jim's face kept bouncing around in my head, when I knew the time would come for me to tell him about this pictured long-winded e-mail.

I couldn't figure out how to get rid of it, so I just let it download, which took over thirty-eight minutes to download. Sure enough, it was about ten seconds long of a chimp running his finger across his butt, smelling himself, and then falling out of a tree. It wasn't until after it was downloaded on the computer, that we could finally see what Louis's girlfriend had sent him.

I liked to have had a heart attack when I saw what she had sent. I suppose in her mind, she really hadn't sent a picture, as Louis had told her not to do. I downloaded this mini-movie to a floppy disk as evidence to show Jim why there was a thirty-eight minute sat phone time in our phone log. Louis just kept apologizing and said he would tell her again, why she could not send things like that to the boat because of the expense.

I still had to tell Jim, which when I did, he just laughed and said, "Don't worry about it," I had worried about it all that time for nothing; Jim had always been understanding and easy going. I also didn't realize how much difference having a home computer during my out of country tours would make to my family. Although computers weren't new, it was new to us, sending and receiving e-mails was a great way to communicate.

I learned quite a bit about the Mexican culture from the many tours that I had spent with the crews. There were shrimp boats docked in the port of Dos Bocas; quite a few of them had dogs on them. I was told their dogs were the security alarms, whenever the crews were at anchor sleeping, the dogs would bark when a boat approached them. I would never have thought to take a dog shrimping with me, but they did.

Just as the United Nations program of food for oil in Iraq, we traded food for fresh fish quite a few times when I was in Mexico. These poor fishermen would come by the tug in their little fish boats and hold up some nice size fish. The deckhands would get some leftover food and fix up a care package to trade with them. The trade was made, and everyone was happy with their exchanged goods. Maybe it was just me or being in a different country, but these guys could make a fish taste like a gourmet meal with how they prepared them.

Periodically we would have times in port when there might be a day or two of just standing by. Paraiso was a small town located within a ten-minute drive of the port. Some of the crew would go into town just to get away from the boat for a while. Sometimes a couple of the deckhands would tell me they would just stay aboard the boat; I knew how they liked going to town too. I also knew that meant they didn't have any money to go.

My Lifetime On The Water

They worked hard for the meager wages they were paid, and would do whatever and whenever was asked of them. I felt like these guys weren't paid enough as it was, so I would give them five dollars each out of my own pocket, to go enjoy themselves. That was like fifty pesos, they had to work four weeks for their fifty-eight hundred peso paycheck, about $580.00.

It was hard to comprehend the difference between our wage scales. I made more in two days than the deckhands did for their twenty-eight day tour. It wasn't long before the wage difference was noticed by the cost of certain charges made. From the first trip I made, to the last trip, was noticeably different in the taxicabs alone. They had gone from a twenty-dollar cab fare to more than sixty to eighty dollars, for the same distance driven. This particular tour was winding down to a close, the crew change would be different than we had ever done before too, or ever did again.

Being out at the SPM buoys while holding on to the stern of a ship, all we needed to see was the Pilot boat with our reliefs. Packed and ready to get gone, it seemed to be taking longer than usual for the fresh crew to show up. In the distance we saw one of the local little fishing boats heading towards us. We said to each other, that's not the Pilot boat with the crew we're looking for. How wrong we were, that little boat was making a beeline straight towards us. Looking through the binoculars we saw a boatload of people on it. This in reality was our next mode of transportation for crew change.

With the choppy sea conditions, just getting out of the little bouncing boat was a challenge. Brother Dave was not a happy camper, when he set foot aboard the deck of the *Eagle II* you could tell where water had splashed onto them and their gear. He said with a loud angry voice, "I will never again come in a fish boat for a crew change; I'll be making a phone call to make sure this crap does not happen again." I said, "Have a good tour Brother, it looks like it's started out bad for you already."

Running late, we once again didn't have much time to talk about the boat; we loaded our bags aboard the water taxi and took off. Louis was with me on this crew change and I was glad he was, with what lay ahead of us. About half way into shore the Mexican water taxi driver slows down,

224

he then picked up the gas tank that the outboard motor was getting it's fuel from and shook it over his head to see how much gas was left.

Me and Louis looked at each other with utter amazement, wondering if we were going to make it to shore was now a coin toss. He spoke to him in Spanish; the man told him he thought there was enough gas to make it all the way. Seeing the direction we were going, it was plain to see we weren't heading to Dos Bocas. When he was running full throttle, it was splashing too much water on us, so just over half was as fast as we could run. We eventually made it to a little fishing dock with a sort of snack shack near by. We departed the water taxi, but there was no vehicle in sight waiting for us.

The Lord was with us though, getting us safely to shore and providing a phone at the little shack. Louis called the office at Oceanografia inquiring as to the whereabouts of our transportation. They said the driver should be there and to just wait, he'll probably show up before too long. This is not what we wanted to hear at this point in time, we were supposed to fly out that day.

When the van finally showed up, the driver had went to pick up his girlfriend to ride with him, he told Louis. With everything and everyone loaded into our land taxi, we were airport bound. We were also going a different route that I had not traveled yet. I asked Louis, "Why does this road have so many speed bumps, and why were they so high?" He said, "With limited resources and not being able to have all the roads patrolled, these speed bumps were installed." These road mounds were about four to six feet across and six to eight inches high, and were very plentiful. These speed controllers were called "Tope" in Spanish, with warning signs posted a few hundred feet before their locations.

I didn't read Spanish, and apparently the van driver didn't read it either. He needed to get the Spanish version of Hooked on Phonics with the way he ran up on them. He would slow down somewhat, but after the front tires cleared the mound; he would push the gas pedal to the floor. After bouncing our heads off the van roof a few times, he was told by a very loud, head rubbing Mexican crewmember some very harsh words. One can only assume what he had said, I know he quit driving crazy, and went over the road hills a lot easier after the heated tongue-lashing he had just received.

There must have been twenty-five to thirty of these bumpers on that road, now I knew why James "Earnhardt" Posey went the other route. The airport was in site, we pulled up, and only Louis and I got out, the others were going to Oceanografia's office. Buying some souvenirs and stowing them in my checked bags, we only had a short wait for our flight. After boarding the plane, Louis and I was only a seat apart, he persuaded a man to trade seats with him so he could show me something.

Having flown this route before, he knew we would be flying right over the *Eagle II*, the direction towards Mexico City. Within a few minutes after takeoff, sure enough, there was the *Eagle II* right where we had left her. Louis would be going to the city of Vera Cruz from Mexico City, where he would meet up with the chimp lady. I called my wife from the Houston airport and gave her my flight number and time into Tampa; it would be almost midnight before I landed there. My shift was off duty on the tug back in Tampa, so I could try to catch up on events the next day with my Wife, and family. It was now the end of January 1999, and having spent some time in Mexico; this would also be the year that I would remember the most.

The Trinidad Trip

to Remember

It seemed that Pemex didn't renew the offshore contracts for the Singapore boats first contract which was coming to an end, so other contracts elsewhere were looked for. With the addition to the fleet of the tug *St. Johns*, she was one of the first of three SDM's built, I was also moved to the tug *Hawk*. However, the time for another foreign tug project was now upon us with the tug *Seabulk Katie*.

Hvide Marine had gotten a one-hundred day contract working in Trinidad. Jim Brantner Jr. had came to me and told me about this job in Trinidad, and the plans he had for us. He said a Mexican crew would take the boat down there; he would meet them there and work the first thirty days or so.

He then wanted me to relieve him, and work for about the same amount of time, or more. Then, he would come back down to finish the hundred days with what days there were left. I told him, "Me and my Dad are very close and he's not doing good with his health, I don't want to be where I can't get to him fast if he takes a turn for the worse." He assured me, and said with a promise, "Bill, if you go down there and something happens to your Father, I'll jump on a plane and come right back down there if I have to, in order to get you home." I told him, "If you'll promise to do that for me, I will agree to go." With that agreement and shook on, things were set for us to go. Jim had told me they wanted this hundred-day contract to go off without a hitch, so with a good performance it would be extended.

He said, "I want the two best Tractor tug Captains available at the time to go down and make sure everything went well." After Jim had been there for just over three weeks, he was hollering for the calf rope, he was bored out of his mind and was calling for some relief. I was still apprehensive about going with my Dad's health worsening, but with Jim's promise about coming right back down there, I decided to take a chance. A decision I would regret forty-three days later, and for a long time afterwards. I had also made a promise to Jim, which I kept, and went to Trinidad to relieve him.

I was scheduled to leave on April 24 1999, with my Father heavy

on my mind; I went by to visit and say my good-byes. I told him, "Get better while I was gone so we could go fishing when I got back home." As I turned to walk out the door, he told me, "Son, you'll never see me alive again when you leave," I started crying, hugged his neck and left. I didn't know it at the time, but

My Mom, Dad, and Me before leaving for Trinidad in April 1999-Author photo

those were the last words I would hear my Dad say to me, face to face.

My Wife, Mother-in-law, and my oldest daughter saw me off at the Tampa airport. All of my children looked forward to riding to the airport, whether picking me up or dropping me off, I think it was just getting to see the planes up close. I would fly from Tampa, Florida to San Juan, Puerto Rico, then on to Port of Spain, Trinidad. Not leaving until mid-morning the next day, I thought this is cool; I'd get me another one of those airplane meals. Having a layover and changing planes in San Juan, just after when the noon meal would have been served foiled that.

The plane touched down around 16:00 (4pm), and with me not having breakfast, or lunch, I was looking to sink my teeth into some food. A fellow that looked like he was from India was sent there to pick me up and take me to the boat. After clearing the air terminal and loading my bag in his car, we were underway.

I asked him how long it would take to get to the port that we were going. "About two and a half hours," he replied. I told him I was hungry since I had not eaten all day. I asked if there were any fast food places close by, to get something quick. He said, "There's a KFC right here in the airport, you like chicken?" "Love it," I said, so he wheeled around and pulled right back into the airport and parked. I asked him if he wanted something too, "No thanks, I'm okay," he says. I told him, "I'll pay for it if you'll eat it," he said, "Alright, just a regular meal then."

I bounced right up to the counter not even looking up at the menu marquee, since I already knew what I wanted. I told the girl, "Let me have two, three-piece dinners, mashed potatoes and gravy, coleslaw, and two sodas." When she left to get my order, I just looked around the airport not looking at anything in particular. She was back with some good smelling chicken that I was ready to tear into, and said, "That'll be $47.85 please."

I said, "Excuse me, how much did you say?" That's when I looked up and seen the prices that they were charging, I could have died. I said, "Lady, I don't know if I want chicken that bad or not," she asks, "Where are you from?" I said, "I just flew in from the States." Reluctantly, I pulled out a fifty-dollar bill to hand her, she said, "I don't think we can change that." Looking confused, I said, "You're only going to give me a couple of dollars and change back ma'am."

She took the fifty and said, "I'll see what I can do," returning, she asks again. "Where did you say you were from?" I told her, "From Florida, in the United States," she says, "Oh, are you familiar with our exchange rate?" I asked, "What exchange rate?" She tells me, "You get six TT dollars for one US dollar," they call their money dollars too, Trinidad and Tobago dollars. I did some quick math in my head, and said, "Shoot, that's only about eight dollars for this chicken, I can live with that." I paid for the KFC meals with a US ten dollar bill and thought, this is going be one to tell when I get home.

The driver was driving from the right side of the car, and within a matter of minutes made me realize that he had a relative in Mexico. Trinidad has some very deep mountain ridges that drop off very close to the edge on some of their roads. With the absence of any guardrails, when coming up on a sharp right hand turn and being on the left side of the road, it makes the sight of those steep cliffs seem to come right inside the car with you.

There were some little ridges pushing up through certain sections of the road, when asked what caused them, I was told, "It was tar coming up out of the ground." They would use front-end loaders to cut the tar ridges from the roadways, making them smoother to drive over. He said, "That was how rich the oil deposits were that Trinidad was sitting atop of." Making it to the boat, there were three of the four-crew members that I had worked with in Mexico waiting for my arrival. The Captain was Felix, the Mate was Little Ricardo, the Chief Engineer was Big Ricardo, or Lurch, and the assistant engineer Felipe, a new man.

Jim and I talked about the operations where he said was the most boring job he had ever been on. I told him about my Dad's health, he said, "Let me know if you hear anything." With Jim gone, my Mexican family and I had a lot to catch up on. They said only a few jobs had been done, since this installation was a brand new natural gas processing plant.

If there was a lot of standby time, this brought me to ask, "How is the TV reception?" Big Ricardo said, "Most stations came in snowy," so I contacted Ashard Mohamed, our agent in Trinidad. I asked him to send a TV man to the boat, I had also brought some petty cash that I was sure would buy some better TV reception.

The next day, a man showed up early and diagnosed the problem, "We needed a new high-resolution TV antenna," he said. The cost was $175.00 US dollars, that's $1,050.00 TT dollars, see it does make you swallow hard. I told him, "Get'er done, and today would be just fine to get started." He jumped on this little project and had it knocked out in no time. He told me, "Try it out and see what you think." I went to switching the TV channel changer, and with a surprised look on my face, we were getting every channel that there was clear as a bell, all three of them. I said, "Are you kidding me, that's it, three channels are all there is."

The Miss Universe contest for 1999 was being held right there in Trinidad. Of the three TV channels we were now receiving without any interference, one of them was dedicated to twenty-four hours a day of nothing but Miss Universe coverage. With as much standby time as we had, it didn't take long to have the boat painted up, with plenty of restless time on our hands. Taking turns going into town to check out what was offered; there in all her glory was another KFC. I told the two guys I was with about my chicken dinner story. We also made KFC a regular treat, at least once a week for the forty-three days I was in Trinidad.

I just had to mention KFC, I'd say, "Who wants chicken today?" Little Ricardo would start calling Felipe; he would start whistling, snapping his fingers, and saying, "Here puppy, come on, let's go." That sounded sort of like when I called Bob Taylor back in the old days. It was funny to see how the letters KFC would excite a grown man. I would give him the needed money, and to town they would go. Two, twenty-one piece buckets with all the fixin's is what we got, every time. That much food would last us through the next day, especially served with our daily dose of black beans.

Working with a Mexican crew, we had black beans almost every meal, with whatever else was served. It's a good thing I liked beans, they were on the table more than anything. They would do as we did in Tampa, take turns cooking the different meals. Big Ricardo was cooking one day where I asked him if he needed some help, "Sure," he says, "You can make the picante sauce," also eaten each and every meal regardless of what was served.

They would take a dry fry pan atop of the stove and dry roast some tomatoes, onions, peeled garlic, and one congo habanera pepper, I used two. Ricardo questioned the use of two peppers, I said, "Will two be too many for you?" He said, "No, maybe it'll be fun to watch the other guy's reaction when they put it on their food." After it was cooked, all of the ingredients was put into a blender with some salt, and switched on to puree.

It has been said for years that when working on tugboats, the more you eat the more you make, so we all tried to make a good living. As we were eating, you could see beads of sweat popping out on everyone's face, maybe two of those very big homegrown congo habanera peppers was a little too much. They would wipe sweat from their faces and say, "I no

Damaged bull-nose-Author photo

remember this picante be mucho hot." Ricardo and I would just look at each other, shrug our shoulders, and keep on eating. The jobs working the natural gas tankers would sometimes be a week apart between them. Although some jobs required using little power, there were those that put your equipment to the test. While docking a ship one day, we were told to "Come astern, back her full," the Pilot says, this resulted

Repaired bull-nose-Author photo

in ripping the bullnose apart like opening a can. When this happened, it was necessary to reconfigure the line being used to assist the ship to the dock. There had also been a new Spectra line installed on the bow winch, this type of line is made from Kevlar, which is the same material used in making law enforcement bullet proof vests, that's some pretty tough stuff and makes a very strong line. All the damage that was done to the line was a few strands tore as seen in the top picture. Even though there had been considerable damage to the bullnose, we were able to finish the job safely. The next thing we had to deal with was to convince everyone involved in the operations, we could indeed sail the ship when she was ready to sail in two days. Everything went well with the sailing, just as we had thought. We now had several days before the next job to make the needed repairs with welders lined up for the repairs; I was told they would put as many men on this job as needed.

I was surprised to see two truckloads of workers come to the boat, for what I thought would only take six to eight hours to repair the damaged bullnose. I should have known better, I was in Trinidad, a laid back Caribbean nation. These fellows stayed with it though, cutting and welding just the way I asked them to do, only in a slower motion for right at twenty-six hours non-stop. The whole tug crew took turns watching the repair process, in case something was needed. I thanked them for the superb job they had done when they were finished. I was then presented with the bill, which was not at all what I had expected, no sticker shock here for what I really thought should have been more.

Knowing what it would probably have cost back in the States to do the same repair, I thought it was very reasonable. The total cost for eight men working twenty-six hours each, with all the materials used, three welding machines plus rods, and the cutting torches, was only two-thousand US Dollars. That had to be the deal of the Century, even at six TT Dollars to one US Dollar. The job was also done right, this time the modifications were made to higher standards. We were ready to put it to the test on our next job, now four days away.

I was learning the Spanish language more and more from time spent with my Mexicrew. We spent many hours' playing cards, which was running a close second behind eating, and watching rented movies from town. We were playing cards one Saturday night/Sunday morning, it was around 03:00. I looked over at Felix and asked, "Felix, what are five grown men doing playing cards, thousands of miles from our families, at three o'clock in the morning?" He just cocked his head, smiled and said, "Because we can." We all laughed, and the card game went on for several more hours.

I had long gotten over the shock of the cost of things too; I now knew the exchange rate for TT dollars. For instance, when you picked up a can of Vienna sausages that cost $3.50, in US currency their cost were $.59. We could rent 20 VHS tapes for little to nothing, which we did often.

I could see why Jim was so bored down there, of course I didn't have the same agenda as he had facing him, and this wasn't found out until a later date. I made the best of what we had to deal with, and actually enjoyed the experience of being there. Meeting other people with cultures that was foreign to me was all part of it. I also kept in touch with my wife through the e-mails sent back and forth to each other. Throughout my Trinidad tour, of which thirty-nine days had already gone by, my wife had sent e-mails to me with progress reports on my Dad's health. She had written me that he had been placed into a Hospice House, since my Mother could no longer care for him at home. My wife had said in her e-mails that the Hospice did not install phones in the rooms, however cell phones were acceptable for use in the patient's room. It was a Saturday afternoon, June 5 1999; I used the boats satellite phone to call my Dad on my cell phone that I had left at home, I didn't need it in Trinidad. My wife was waiting with my Dad at Hospice at the prearranged time that we had agreed on. When I called, she handed him the phone, we both started crying, hearing each other's voices. As we talked, I could hear the weakness in his voice, and then he spoke the words that summoned me home.

My Dad told me, "Son, I need to see you, I'm not going to be here much longer." I told him, "I'll call Jim and let him know that I need to get home as soon as I can." After our talk, it took a while for me to compose myself. When I called Jim and relayed to him what my Dad had said to me, he told me, "It might be a few days before I can get someone down there." Puzzled at his reply, I asked him, "You're not coming back to relieve me?" He tells me, "There are some things going on that I have to attend to which will not allow me to come back to Trinidad." I said, "You're kidding, you're not coming back like you promised?" Then I said, "Do what you have to do, I just need to get home." He said, "Since it was the weekend, it would be Monday before anything could be done."

I remembered the promise that I had been told, I could only pray that my Dad could hold on until I made it home. I read in Monday morning's e-mail that Mark Featherston would be coming to relieve me. Jim wrote that it wouldn't be until Mark was able to get the proper paper work before he could leave. Jim already had the necessary paper work, I then realized his promise had meant nothing; I just wanted to see my Dad.

Trying to keep a lighthearted mood, I told the Mexican crew that this fellow that was coming to relieve me was bi-sexual, which he isn't. I thought what the heck, this worked before, I'll spread it thick and quick just to see what happens. I told them that he was married and had five children, but liked men too. I told them that I don't claim to understand it, but do know he has never been forward with any of the crewmembers in Tampa. Wednesday, June 9 1999 had arrived; this was the date when Mark finally made it to my location, we had a routine crew change. I was also taken to the airport that evening where I would spend the night at the airport. Having my Dad on my mind made the minutes turn into hours, dragging the time out as if the morning would never come. It was the next morning before my flight would depart; I must have walked twenty miles that night.

Early morning June 10, I was in the air again and was going to see my sick Dad, or so I thought. I flew into Miami where I would take a smaller shuttle flight to Tampa. I must have looked questionable with my full beard and long hair because my luggage was sniffed with electronic monitors, and then my bag was physically searched. I could have died when I saw something that was totally unexpected, something I knew I had not put in there. My boys on the boat had put some cans of soup, Vienna sausages, and crackers in my bag. When asked about them, I just told them the truth, what else could I say? The Customs officials just laughed and said "Have a good day."

After we landed in Tampa, I walked up the ramp and seen my Family standing there crying, I just knew my Dad was gone. I asked my wife, "He's gone isn't he?" She said, "Yes, he is, I'm so sorry." She said, "He passed away yesterday, we knew you were on the way home and didn't contact you because we didn't want to upset you, more than you already were."

There was nothing I could have done different to prevent the death of my Father. However, I could have been with him when he did pass, if promises by others were kept, or if I had not kept my promise to go to Trinidad with the bad feeling I had had. There were many things passing through my mind at a very fast pace during this period of time too. I had been told things like, my stock with the Brantner's had really went up when I agreed to do what Jim wanted, and I'll come right back down there if I have to. I remembered I had to almost beg to be put on the crew list going through the Panama Canal, things really aren't always as they seem when you sit back and reflect on them.

Forth-largest Jacket in The World

After my Dad's funeral, I had gone back to work after a few days off to grieve. I talked to Jim about how disappointed I was, and of what I had been deprived of, which was being with my Dad when he died. He could only tell me that he was sorry to hear of his passing, nothing else as to why he hadn't flew back to Trinidad. With these feelings off my chest, I could only wait for the next promise, to see if it too would be broken.

I had been told all of my life; time is the healer of all wounds. It's just the memory of being hurt that makes them seem to drag on. I still had a job to do, so when one came up that would take us across the Gulf of Mexico, I was ready for the challenge.

Our old friend Willem with Heerema had a job for the tug *Hawk* to do, and since the other big boats were still in Mexico. The crew was myself as Captain, Mike Zahorsky as Mate, Roger Strickland as Chief Engineer, Scoot Tyoe as assistant Engineer, with Alvin Anderson and Chris LeDuc as deckhands. Before we departed I assembled the crew into the lounge, and reviewed the job with what everyone would be doing. After this, I told them to hold hands, I then asked the Lord to go with us with good sailing graces, keep us safe from everything we would encounter during this trip, and to bring us all back safe and sound to our respective homes and families. Afterwards, Mike told me; this is the first time I've ever done that.

I told him, "I want everything to go smooth, praying and asking God to watch over us will definitely help." The *Hawk* was loaded down with

85,000 gallons of fuel, and over $2,200 dollars worth of groceries and supplies was also bought for the trip. There was not always accessibility to a grocery store at some of the docks we went to, and had always been

Jacket loaded onto barge
Courtesy of Mike Zahorsky

standard procedure to take enough stores with you. We had been told, "Groceries are a very important part of an offshore trip," a policy that would later change with different management. After checking all the gear that would be used for this operation, I was satisfied with it. A plotted course of just over eight-hundred miles, we were ready to depart. The job we had facing us was to assist the launch barge *Intermac 650*, with a very large oilrig jacket atop of it. We were to come from the Aker Marine yard in Corpus Christi, Texas, out through Aransas Pass,

Jacket on its side from ¼ mile away, 1,143' long-Author photo

and then to her final destination. It was less than one-hundred miles from the southwest pass in Louisiana, which is the most southern entrance to the Big Bad Mississippi River, coming from the Gulf of Mexico. On the barge *Intermac 650* would be the forth-largest jacket in the world, and the second largest to be set up in the Gulf, at that particular time in 1999. This jacket was 1,143 feet long lying on its side, 362 feet high and 342 feet wide at the base. Total weight was 25,000 tons; this very large steel structure was built on shore and would be hydraulically jacked onto the barge for transport.

It would take the Mighty *Hawk* three days to transit the Gulf of Mexico before we were able to see this manmade marvel of engineering we had heard about. The trip across was like running on a duck pond with the weather being just glorious. Upon arrival to the Aransas Pass jetties, we could actually see the jacket looking through the binoculars from a distance of over ten miles away, and that was with it lying on its side. I was excited to see such a big structure and to know we were going to help transport this behemoth across the Gulf.

This jacket was much bigger than the jacket project I had been on with Brother Dave, and that one was a two-stage jacket, which had a total height of just over 900 feet when put together. I could not believe something this large and cumbersome could be moved by man. Once loaded on the barge, from the deck to the top of the jacket was 36 stories high, and 342 feet wide, sticking off on each side. The launch barge *Intermac 650* itself, was 650 feet long and 170 feet wide. The jacket free hung over the stern of the barge some 447 feet, and off the bow 46 feet on the wide end.

The big plates that the jacket stood on were called mud pads, and were almost 100 feet by 100 feet squared. This jacket would be set in 1,130 feet of water, leaving only 13 feet of this massive structure sticking up out of the water. When we arrived at the Aker Marine location, the jacket had not even started being loaded onto the barge. We were told the loading process would take about three days; this would give us plenty of time to check out this big piece of steel. We were told that every joint where two pieces of pipe were welded together, had a hole cut into it that made it possible to put air throughout the jacket. The jacket would be purged with twelve pounds of air pressure, making it able to float whenever it was launched.

This particular jacket had taken two years to fabricate; the drilling module was built in another yard and wouldn't be taken to the location until the jacket was set and secured to the Gulf floor. This would leave just a partial part of the yellow painted area that would be seen. That was also, where the drilling module would be placed, and the rest of it would be underwater. The Empire State Building is 102 stories tall, where this jacket is 114 stories tall, that's some contrast.

The lead tug for the tow was to be the tug *Seacor Vision* with 12,000 hp, the outboard tugs was the tug *Crusader* with 7,200 hp, and the tug *Hawk* with 6,700 hp. We three would be the tugs that would tow the barge to the final location, where the jacket would be set up. There were several smaller tugs that were enlisted to also assist the loaded barge through the Corpus Christi ship channel and out past the jetties in the Aransas Pass ship channel. We had plenty of time to catch up on some maintenance, and with a double crew, the boat was shining like a new quarter. Having been aboard for quite a few days, Mike and Scoot had caught a ride into town. There imagination must have run wild with them with what they had brought back to the boat.

I'm a fairly light sleeper and thought I kept hearing something during the night out on the deck, when I got up in the morning I saw what I must have been hearing. They had went to Wally World (Wal-Mart) and bought a little kids swimming pool. What I had heard was them walking around on the deck while filling our new swimming pool with water on the boat deck. We all had a good laugh at what we were looking at that morning. Knowing this was also a Kodak moment, I asked a man off the tug *Crusader* to take a picture with me and my whole crew in the *Hawk's* new pool. You have to admit that this is one of those classical, memorable moments, caught on camera. This picture also reflects happier times when an offshore trip came our way, indecisive policies was not an option, or was tolerated those days. I had made a "No Diving" sign and taped it in front of the wheelhouse to

Six big men in a pool-Author photo

make it look realistic; it does look real don't it. Scoot had put a block of ice in the water to cool it down, and then cut a piece of watermelon, he crawled right into the pool saying, "Man this is the life, and they pay us for this too." We were standing by, secure to the dock for seven full days. Fishing, eating, sleeping, watching TV, chipping, and painting, we were just trying not to get bored. The one thing we had done was enjoy the

camaraderie we had with each other. This was a dandy crew that had been put together for this trip.

Working the grounded barge-
Courtesy of Mike Zahorsky

We were finally told that we would be getting underway the next day. The pre-sail meetings that were held with the Captains and Mates, lets everyone know how the operation was to be done according to plan. With the many variables that had to be met, such as minimal current, the wind speed could not be more than a predetermined maximum speed, there also had to be good

visibility for a certain distance. The criteria for so many things had to be just right; something was bound to go wrong.

The day of sailing was a little windy, but acceptable for the tow out, at least that's what everyone thought. We came off the dock just as planned, when the

Oilrig jacket on the 170 foot wide barge
Intermac 650 -Courtesy of Mike Zahorsky

barge was turned to go outbound the main ship channel, we stopped. That little wind was just strong enough to set the whole rig over to the north side of the channel, aground we were, and would be until more tugs were brought out to help get her afloat. The little Brown Water tugs were lined up on the same side as the *Hawk* was made up. After one of the larger harbor tugs had arrived, we were able to get the barge with her very expensive cargo, back into the main channel and underway without further incident. We would have never thought the wind would effect the barge the way that it had, evidently the powers that be thought the same thing too.

Regardless of how it started, once we had cleared the jetties the tug *Hawk* was moved to run alongside the port side of the *Seacor Vision* for the three-tug tandem tow. After we were made up and towing, that was a combined total of 25,900 horses now pulling on this barge. We had a

Tugs *Crusader* & *Seacor Vision* switching positions
Courtesy of Mike Zahorsky

few days to go and just settled back into our six hours on, six hours off watches. I remember someone called over the VHF radio one day and asked the tug *Seacor Vision*, "What in the world is that you're towing?" It was then, and still is now, the longest single piece of anything; I have ever been involved in moving, on land or by water, and even in my imagination. Although within the next few years, I

would be involved in some projects that would be the same type of job; they too, would be just as demanding. In addition, the experience that I was now gaining would be invaluable for the future projects that the tug *Hawk* would be called on to assisting in. This particular trip into Corpus Christi was just the first, of many more to come in the next few years. We were told that the pilings used to anchor the corners of the jacket, were 450 feet long. They would actually sink into the ground under their own

Pre-launch view
Courtesy of Mike Zahorsky

Sliding off barge
Courtesy of Mike Zahorsky

Post-launch view
Courtesy of Mike Zahorsky

weight approximately 150 feet. Then the fifteen-million dollar underwater pneumatic pile driver would then be used to drive them down to their finished depth. One of the designers told us the guides that were installed on the legs of the jacket, were just for the pilings to slide into place, and the cost for them alone was fifteen million dollars. Whenever money is spent like it is in the Gulf of Mexico's oil patch, you can bet drilling for oil is not for the faint hearted. So far, we were blessed with good weather, unlike my last offshore trip to the Gulf. With the arrival to the jackets final destination, we anticipated seeing the launch of these 25,000 tons of steel, costing millions of dollars sliding off the stern of this barge. The tug *Crusader* was going to be towing the barge Intermac 650 into Port Fourchon, after the jacket was launched, and then ballasted to an even keel for towing. With the exchange happening in the daylight hours and with the barge almost stationary, everything went as planned, which was always a plus. The tug *Crusader* was now the lead tug until launch time. I had been on other offshore oilrig jobs, and worked in other countries doing all type of work, this particular project just seemed to be on such a grand scale I didn't think I would ever see anything else as large as this jacket.

Although this would definitely be the largest oilrig jacket I could say I had ever worked on, there would be larger pieces of oilrig equipment that I would be involved in, in years to come. With so much to be thankful for on this trip, we were enjoying the experience of the calmer seas. The only difference of being offshore and working in the harbor, especially when it was calm, was that you were guaranteed at least twelve hours off duty. With taped movies to fill some of the time, instead of sleeping or

Baldor in the up righting stage
Courtesy of Mike Zahorsky

constant eating, because you certainly couldn't take a walk up the street.

When we had went aboard the *Seacor Vision* back in Corpus Christi, just to see this very impressive piece of equipment, we were told of her many uses. They said she could hold tens of thousands of gallons of potable water, drill mud, drill stem and pipe, not to mention her towing capabilities and anchor handling abilities. The tug *Seacor Vision* was needed to help the

Baldor with jacket vertical
Courtesy of Mike Zahorsky

tug *Retriever* relocate some of the *Baldor's* anchors. It was in the plans from the beginning to make the switch when we arrived on location. The tug *Crusader* and us, towed on the barge until the *Baldor* was ready to start the launch sequence. This would turn out to be an all day process in itself, from the beginning of the launch, to when we would be released. The *DCV Baldor* was fitted with a series of anchors that held her in place. The *Retriever* was also the same tug that was assigned to the *Baldor* as before on other projects. The tugs *Retriever* and *Seacor Vision* were equipped to handle long line anchors, the relocation of them would allow the *Baldor* to be placed at the jackets template location. The seas were nearly calm the day of the launch, so the top of the jacket was secured to the *Baldor* with a line, probably half a mile away from each other. All of the braces were cut from the jacket and were welded down to the deck of the barge. This prevented the heavy braces from coming off the barge at the time of launch and damaging the jacket. This 1,143-foot tower of steel would float when it came off the barge; with the twelve pounds of air pressure would keep it buoyant, until it was ballasted down to the vertical position.

When it was ballasted down to the vertical position, then it could be set. What they would do was flood the stern of the barge down with ballast. I remembered during the loading of the jacket that the workers had mopped grease onto the skids when the jacket was slid onto the barge. The sheer weight of the jacket caused the grease to smoke from the friction. With the line from the *Baldor* being attached to the top of the jacket, and the tug *Crusader* towing on the barge the opposite direction, this started the slide we were looking for. Allowing the jacket to stabilize after it was floating for a while, the *Baldor* then started the long process of pulling the now buoyant jacket towards her.

The *Hawk* had been made fast with a line off our tow winch to where us, and the tug *Retriever* could help to keep it steady during this stage of positioning. The ballasting down of the jacket was not started until it had stabilized in the horizontal position, which took a few hours for that to take place, even in calm waters. We were told; the weight of the jacket would only be an estimated 2,000 tons when buoyant. With the cranes on the *Baldor*, being rated at 2,700 and 3,600 mT, one of them could handle the jacket when ballasted to the vertical position. The 3,600 mT crane was chosen for the job, this was definitely another Kodak moment. Early the next morning we were released from the jacket. After bringing the line aboard that was attached to the jacket, we went alongside the *Baldor* so they could use their crane and lift the line and gear off the *Hawks* deck.

With the line off and being released off the whole job, we put her in the wind for Tampa. This had been one of those jobs that you were glad to be a part of doing. Besides the little hiccup we had right at the start, it had gone just as it had been laid out. Those few grounded hours spent back in Corpus Christi really hadn't made a big difference in the big picture. "The Big Picture," that was a phrase that was used excessively by certain office personnel in the near future. This job was like I had said many times before, it was like a trailer, it was behind us. Mike said to me on the way back, "You know Bill; I don't think I've ever been on a job that has had beautiful weather as we have had on this trip." I said, "Do you remember what we did before we left Tampa, Mikey?" He smiled and said, "Yes, I do." I told him, "Remember to pray before you go on any trip, it does help."

The Good Lord done as we had asked, we did have some beautiful weather, and we all came back safe, with everyone still having ten toes and ten fingers, pats on the back for everyone with another job well done. After securing the boat in Tampa and reporting in to the office, a few days at home was next on our agenda.

MARINE TOWING OF

TAMPA WAS BORN

As we eased back into the harbor schedule after being back to work for a while, we were then hit in the face with something out of left field. For some, it was an actual life-changing event that would affect the whole Maritime community in Tampa Bay, and beyond. On October 29 1999, all of the employees were gathered together outside by the dispatch office. We were told by James Kimbrall, that himself, Jimmy Brantner, Jim Brantner Jr., Norman Atkins, Dwayne Keith, and Phyllis Hudson, would be leaving the company for good, effective that day.

Mr. Kimbrall told us they could no longer work with the way the company was being ran from Fort Lauderdale, Hvide Marines' main office. He told us, "We will be starting a new company, we want it to be like it was in the past, we don't want the whole company of Hvide Marine, just the Tampa harbor tugboat division back." With full attention he said, "You men stay right where you are, and keep doing the good job you have done in the past." He said, "We'll be back, it might be six months, it might take longer, but we will be back."

When this little speech was over, I thought wow. For me, it was like the air had been taken out of my sails. We were asked to help load some of the furniture out of the main office onto a truck, which we did. Some of the employees had been taken off to the side, and had been told what the scoop was. At that time my engineer was Otis Monteiro, he came by and shook my hand, and then said, "It's been good working with you, I quit, I can not stay here any longer either." I said, "You're kidding, what are you going to do?" With a shrugged shoulder and a wave bye, he gathered his gear and left the boat.

There was a lot of kayos in the next few hours around there. Mark Barthle and I had gone to Orlando to get our FM 3, which is the work visa needed to work in Mexico. Dave Scarborough must have been told of the walkout, because he called from the *Eagle II* in Mexico and told the office he had also quit. When Mark and I got back from Orlando, it wasn't the same atmosphere we were accustomed to having. Some strangers had come in from Fort Lauderdale and tried to assure everyone that nothing would change, does the term 180 degrees different mean anything.

Mark Barthle was sent to relieve Brother Dave in Mexico; I would be going to relieve Mark later. Having their phone numbers, I had called over and talked to Norman when the dust had settled. I figured since I had been told that my stock had went up when the Brantner's was with Hvide Marine, it might carry over with this new company that they were putting together. I was told they only had two boats to start the new company with, and with the men that had also left, a Captain's position was not needed at that particular time.

"More boats would be added to their fleet as their business grew, that was when more Captains would be needed," he said. I was also told, "Stay where you are at and we'll see what happens later," later never came for me, until only one position was left to fill. With all the phone calls going only one way, from me to them, it seemed obvious by now, I would be working for Hvide Marine a while longer. Although hope remained in my mind in the early days for the longest time, my phone never rang.

I had gone to Mexico on my birth date December 14 1999, and relieved Mark Barthle aboard the *Eagle II*. With everything that had happened two short months earlier back in the states, wondering what was going on took up a lot of my time. With uncharted waters in regards to this new management, the Y2K thing that was looming over our heads was the least of my worries. I was now in Mexico with this new management, as for Y2K, I wondered if Hvide Marine was going to have a shutdown.

The first ten days went wonderful, we were even told to come into the Port of Dos Bocas for Christmas. I had asked Amador to see if the engineer Ricardo was at home, since he lived only minutes from the port, and to let him know I was back in Dos Bocas. He brought me word that he was returning from Trinidad that very day, and his wife would tell him. To my surprise, he came to the boat about 17:00 to take me to his home and spend Christmas Eve with him and his family. I was honored to go with him, and was really looking forward to see how the Mexican people celebrated our Blessed Savior's birthday.

When we arrived, he gave me the grand tour of their home that he was very proud of. Ricardo with his wife Santi, their two young sons and myself, spent one of the most memorable Christmas Eve's ever, together as a family. I even called my real home to wish them a Merry Christmas and to let them know, I too was with family. A turkey cooked in a tomato sauce, and served with spaghetti noodles was on the menu. After we had our wonderful meal, just after midnight was when they ate, yeah I know. I had asked Ricardo earlier, "When are we going to eat?" He said they celebrated from Christmas Eve midnight, to Christmas night at midnight, so when in Rome do as the Romans do. This Roman enjoyed every minute I shared with them too.

Ricardo took me back to the tug about 02:00, I slept like a baby, knowing I had been invited to share quality family time with a man and his family, on the second most Glorious day of the year, Easter being the first. I had also made a memory that I would remember for more Christmas days to come.

Back to the Single Point Mooring buoys we went the very next day. With a few more days under our belts, and Y2K approaching fast, would it cause the shut down the so-called experts had said it would. Engineer Doug and I both were wondering about the Y2K problem, neither of us could have guessed what was about to happen. On New Years Eve we wondered if we would once again be treated to the dockside for the Holiday. We were finally told to leave the buoys, and come into Dos Bocas around 17:00. We thought this is great, that way if anything happened we would at least be close to shore.

We watched the ball drop in Mexico City on TV expecting the worst, we looked at each other and said, well nothing has happened so far I'm going to bed, and off we went. I was awakened about thirty minutes later by a loud knock on my door. It was a Pemex official telling me to go to a

Tidewater boat, and transfer 12,307 gallons of fuel to them. I woke Doug up and told him what I was just told. He said, "Something is screwy with this, we have never given fuel to a Tidewater boat, they're our competition, and where did they come up with that amount, 12,307 gallons?"

Now you know what we had found out, the *Eagle II* no longer had a contract to work for Pemex, as of 00:01 January 1 2000. This was a complete shut down, but not the one the world had expected. We gave the other boat the fuel and secured the *Eagle II* until we could contact the office to see if they had any idea of what had happened. This was New Years Day, we were not docking tankers, since the company didn't have a contract, we thought now what.

Ricardo came down to the Port to see if we were there, and yes we were. The Mate was going to stay aboard the boat as he had on Christmas Eve, so I was once again invited to spend the Holiday with the Ruiz Family and their friends. I was seeing things and doing things that were completely foreign to me, and loving every minute of it.

We went to his friend's house for the day's festivities. I had always had black-eyed peas and hog jowl for New Years dinner. That day we were having fish stew, with oysters and vegetables mixed together, different, but tasty. A blessing was said, and I was told to sit and eat first. I told Ricardo, "No way, I will eat when everyone else eats." He said, "My friend says since you are his guest, you have to be served first."

I felt very funny, with me being the only gringo there, and now being shown such preferential treatment, I expected nothing less. This is how Ricardo made me feel just a week earlier when I spent Christmas Eve with his family; I did talk him and his wife into eating with me. There were about thirty people there, and every one of them had their eyes on me when we started eating. I suppose this was how a guest was made to feel at home; well it worked for me, because I was completely overwhelmed. We spent the rest of the afternoon listening to some Mexican music and talking. For me I just listened, with my limited understanding of the Spanish language, Ricardo stayed busy translating though.

All good things must come to an end, and this day was no different. Through Ricardo, I told them thank you for their wonderful hospitality, and how that I will remember this day for years to come. On our way back to the boat, Ricardo told me that his friend was a fisherman. He said sometimes he loses his direction when he goes offshore, then asked me if I could buy him a compass for his fish boat when I got back to the states. I told him, "I'll buy one and get it to him, I guarantee it."

That was one of the first things I did when I got home too, that was the least I could do for him, with the graciousness he had showed me. Back on the boat, I didn't know it yet, but we were now in a standby mode, and would be for the next twenty-one days. During this standby period, I had received a phone call from Jim Brantner Jr. He said, "I was just calling to see how you were doing," with him being on the other team, I wondered if this was the call I had been waiting on. We talked for a couple a more minutes and then he said, "Get with me when you get back, I'd like to talk to you, and have a safe trip." Not even three months had passed since the big walkout, thoughts of different scenarios were going through my mind so fast that Don Garlits dragster couldn't have kept up with it. I could only wait and see; I sure enough had a reason to get out of Mexico now.

While I was in Mexico, I had witnessed what giving just a little bit of authority to someone could do to them. It was sort of like what had happened back in Tampa, with the swelled heads and all. Some of these fellows that thought they were the bosses, belittled the actual workers to a degree that was very hard not to say something to them, then that Roman thing come to mind, when in Rome, do as, well you know.

I had always heard that a little knowledge is a dangerous thing to have, well so is a little bit of power. Doing nothing but standing by gave me ample time to just watch and listen at how some of these people were treated. It must have been no different with the people that really did have authentic authority. I had asked the Mexicans, who were supposed to be in charge numerous times, "Why can't we just leave, give me some fuel, a crew to take the boat to Tampa, my clearance papers, and let me go?"

I was told repeatedly, "The officials will not come to Dos Bocas to give you the needed clearance papers to depart Mexico." Even though it was just about a two-hour drive from Del Carmen, they would not make the drive. I would have to take the boat there, and then I would be given the release papers. It seemed the new management back in Tampa had their hands tied too.

Every time I would ask them what was going on with getting the *Eagle II* released, "We're working on it," was their reply. All that was really happening was that the company was losing money, with us down there and not being paid, someone should pay for the boat being there. Twenty days after Pemex had taken the boat off their contract, we were finally given enough fuel for the trip back, along with groceries, and a Mexican crew. We were told, "Have the boat in Del Carmen tomorrow morning by 09:00, they'll have the officials meet you outside the harbor in a boat." We were there by 06:00; I didn't want to upset their apple cart by being late, I was ready to see some American soil.

We waited, and waited, and waited, until around noon when we saw a Seabulk boat coming our way. We were contacted on the radio and told they had a package for us, I told him that I hoped he had the Mexican officials with him to release me. He said, "Nope, just a package." When they came alongside, we were told, "Here are your release papers, you can now go back to the states."

Puzzled, I asked, "Why didn't the officials come with you?" The Captain said, "They told me it wasn't necessary, just to give you this package and to tell you that you were released." This had to be the highest, most arrogant abuse of power I had seen yet. They could send the papers out to us on a boat, but could not put them in a car weeks earlier for the same purpose, and be handed our release papers then. The Mexican Mate told me, "They probably had not come to Dos Bocas by car, just to show us who was in charge, them, and not us."

That was just the way things were done down there I suppose. I can remember an incident that happened to us one night, but on a smaller scale. Amador was taking me to a motel in Villahermosa one night after one of my tours when we were pulled over by a police officer. Amador went to talk to the police officer to see what the problem was; he came back to the truck just a cursing. He asked, "Do you have any US dollars?" I said, "Sure," having only four ones, he took two of them. He said, "I'll be right back," turned and went back to the officer. I could see they were arguing about something, not knowing why he had stopped us, the thought of a Mexican jail flashed across my mind. Maybe I've seen too many prison movies, who knows.

Amador came back to the truck, started her up, and off we went. He told me the officer had claimed we were speeding, and if Amador would give him ten dollars US, he would let us go. That's when he came and got the two dollars from me, he told the officer to take them and be satisfied, or write him a ticket, his company would pay it. He wanted more but Amador said, "That's all there was, take it or leave it." I told him, "You have to be kidding, why don't you report him to his superiors?"

He told me, "Reporting him would do no good, that's why he wanted ten dollars, because he will have to split the money with his superior." These low-level police officers hardly make any money, so this is how they make their salary, by making bogus charges. The people they stop had rather pay them a smaller amount, than what they would have to pay the courts if they actually wrote the ticket. This "little bit of power" syndrome, seemed to run in all nationalities, not just in the U.S.

We finally departed Del Carmen January 24 2000, bound for the Tampa sea buoy. Just after twelve noon, we now had about seventy-two hours of running to go, and that's all the way to the dock. The first two days were absolutely beautiful, and then we started getting spanked. It was probably because of all the nasty thoughts I had had. They had been directed at the Mexican officials, with their I'll show them attitude, which had made it possible for me to have the unwanted extended stay, and to last three weeks longer than it should have been.

I had been here before, having twelve to fourteen foot seas while riding on these 110 foot long Clorox jugs was no fun. They were something that my Mexican crew, had also experienced while working at the SPM buoys. We arrived at the Tampa sea buoy around 07:00 on the morning of January 27 2000, and since we had came from a foreign country, I had to have a Tampa Bay Pilot aboard by law to transit the bay.

I had contacted the Pilot office earlier and had been informed that my Pilot would be Captain John Timmel, and that he wouldn't board the tug until we had reached the Egmont Key lighthouse. I thought this is great; I had worked with Captain John for several years, and had even been to his island house out at Egmont Key for a family picnic. As I approached the lighthouse the sat phone rang, it was Jim Jr. calling again. He said welcome back to Tampa, looking around to see where he could be, I said, "Where are you at, and how do you know where I am?" He said, "Me and Dave are up here in Tampa working a job, we always know where you're at."

He then reiterated, "When you get settled in, come by and talk to me." When I pressured him once again about employment, he was also once again, very evasive about it and just said, "Come by so we can talk." I thought well maybe that stock was fixing to pay off after all. The Pilot boat came alongside and put Captain Timmel aboard. When he came to the wheelhouse, I was given an envelope with documentation papers to fill out.

Captain Timmel and I shook hands, he said, "Welcome back Bill, if you want me to, I'll steer the boat while you take care of your paper work," I told him, "You got a deal." That Sunshine Skyway Bridge sure did look pretty from where I stood. The Office had also called, and said not to arrive before noon, that's when the US Government officials would be there. You mean they were actually coming to the dock? I thought maybe I should take pictures and send them back to Mexico when the Mexican crew went home.

My wife had been called, and was sitting next to the dock when we arrived; she sure was a sight for sore eyes. After we were secure, Captain John took off, everyone else had to stay aboard until Customs, Immigration, and the Agriculture officials were done with their inspection. No one was allowed to come aboard the boat either, not until the officials were through. I just hoped I had done the paper work right, since I had never come in from a foreign port before.

I also wanted to give that good-looking redhead who was literally within a hundred feet from the boat, whom I was married to for almost thirty-one years, a great big kiss. What had taken the Mexican officials three weeks to do was now done in less than an hour. I felt like Martin Luther King, I was free, free at last, thank God All Mighty, I was free at last. It was now Friday, and although it was my week on duty, well you know, I had some catching up to do. I told my relief on the *Hawk*, "I'll be in on Monday morning to finish out the week," it would only be for two days and then I would be off for a week.

I went home and enjoyed the time with my family, who I had thoroughly missed. The weekend shot by like a rocket, then back to work. I had been kept up with the rumor mill grinding away while I was gone. Mike Zahorsky, my Mate on the *Hawk*, had called me on the single side band radio several times and had apprised me as to what was taking place back on the home front.

I had also not been contacted by the other team yet, and since I had came to work on Monday, I was very anxious to see what Jim had to tell me. It had been discussed about trying to get a Union to come in and negotiate a contract for the employees. Back when the big walkout occurred, the personnel that were sent to assure everyone things would not change and everything would be as usual, well, they must not have read the manual.

Things were not as usual, and haven't been since. On the day that I went back off duty, it was Wednesday February 1 2000; we had a vote in the crew room on company property. The vote was to either give the company a chance to show the employees what they would do for us, or bring a Union in to act as our bargaining Agent. The company was not in a good position for this vote. Since the new managers had been in charge, it seemed nothing, and I mean absolutely nothing was done in favor of the present employees, a few of them tried, but their try was futile.

I had been in Mexico since December 14 1999, so many of the stories that were told to me were while I was south of the border, or when I first got back. For the past twenty-three years that I knew of, we had always had a company thrown Christmas party that all employees and their families really looked forward to attending.

The very first year that our new management had the chance to actually show the employees that they truly cared, they blew it; there was no Christmas party. It might be a small thing to some, but with the memories of past parties, this was definitely not a point making beginning for the new team. I had been told of the non-party event while I was down south. With the absence of past management that some had grown to appreciate, the new kids on the block was just not making the grade. It seemed that the constant miscommunication, and their indecisiveness in decision making that was being made, must have been just the catalyst needed to spark the necessity of contacting a Union.

On my way home after the vote I had gotten a few miles down the road, with the Jim calls still bouncing around in my head. I thought, should I, or shouldn't I, well I did. I called Marine Towing, and asked to speak to Jim, when he came on the phone I said, "Bill here Jim, do you still want to see me?" He told me, "Come by now, and yes, we will talk."

I had always heard that curiosity killed the cat; I had to go see what it was before my cat died. I turned around and went back to see what he had on his mind. I went into their office, shook hands with them all, and said, "Well, what's the big secret, what you got to tell me." Jim said, "When Dad gets off the phone, we'll take you out to lunch." I said, "I don't think I want to be seen with y'all right now, there's a lot happening over at the other place, being seen with the competition might not be healthy for me."

I said, "Do you have a job for me or what, why did you want to talk to me?" He says, "No, no job; I just wanted to see how you've been doing." We talked for a few more minutes, as we had when he called the boat in Mexico, I said my goodbyes, and left. Driving away from there I thought to myself, I must be a glutton for punishment. When was I going to realize, my supposed stock that Norman had told me I had earned, must have done like the real stock back in 1929, it must have crashed.

Although the guys that were already working with Marine Towing were our competition, I still tried to be as friendly as possible. Who knew, I still might be part of their team yet. Through my unanswered prayers it struck me one day; maybe it was my Glorious God that kept me working for the company I was already with, maybe a job change was not in his plans for me. God will give you your needs, not your wants, I sure wanted to work with Marine Towing of Tampa at the time, but this was not to be.

Our company had signed a contract with the American Maritime Officers Union to be the bargaining agent for the employees to go into effect on September 1 2000. With what the Union had promised they would do, here was probably where I needed to stay, to be more beneficial to my family and me in later years. We can't see what's down the road, but God can, and as soon as I realized that, I was better off. It still bothered me that someone says one thing, and then does another though.

I had found out through talking to certain people that their hiring policy was now dictated by the likes and dislikes of the employees that they had worked with before. Since some of their present employees didn't see eye to eye with me, I then knew why I hadn't been contacted. Maybe the thought of fifty-watt light bulbs would be sufficient, and a hundred watt bulb would not be needed, who knew. With a fleet of four tugboats finally achieved, and eight Captains needed to operate them, I was finally contacted by Jim Brantner Jr. at home on a Saturday afternoon. He told me he had been given the okay to call me and offer me a Captains position, the eighth one.

I told him I was aware of their past hiring practices and couldn't understand, why now. He said he had heard that I knew and it was a mistake, that policy had been stopped. I had a good talk with Jim and respectfully declined the job. I'm sure everyone at one time or another has been offered something that just didn't seem right, that job offer just felt like having a bone thrown to a dog. That was the way I felt when that particular job offer came my way.

My wife had heard my end of the conversation, afterwards she said, "I love you, because you are who you are." I also think I had been shown through Devine Intervention; the right decision to make was to stay where I was at, especially with the benefits that the Union had agreed to give us as their newest union members. I still have the highest respect for the Brantner's; making a move then just didn't feel right.

Theodore Too Visits Tampa

With the notion finally gone of me working where there was an abundance of testosterone, I got on with doing what I was good at, operating a tugboat. With the crews being switched around periodically, I now had another crew that was a crew to be proud of. My Mate was now Keith Tyoe; he had told us earlier, "Just call me Scoot, that's what my grandfather nicknamed me when I was a young boy." Scoot had also been my engineer in the past, as I had done early on; he too discovered where the best place on the boat to be was in the wheelhouse. We had just finished a job one night and were on our way back to our home base dock, when Scoot called down below and said, "Get up here fast, come quick, you gotta see this." When I got up the stairs, I couldn't believe what was coming down the chan-

***Theodore Too* in Tampa**
Author photo

nel towards us. Having seen the Tug *Theodore* Show on the local PBS TV station, we just didn't think he'd ever come for a visit to Tampa. His eyes were going from side to side;

his whole head was lit up to where it actually looked just like the little fellow on TV. Scoot pulled the throttles back to an idle so we could get a good look at this little guy. As we passed in the channel that night, we all knew we were going to have to find where he was going to be tied up. Our

interest in *Theodore* was for the kids, and we all had a little kid in us when it came to something like this. Scoot had a small son that just had to see this, and when he did,

Tugs *Hawk* and *Theodore Too*-Author photo

he was tickled pink. Carroll had even called me at home one day to let me know *Theodore* was on TV, and which channel it was showing. The

boat was run like any other boat; you would look through one of the portholes that was under his face, that's where the wheelhouse was located. Since it wasn't an actual working tugboat, the height of the wheelhouse was not that important.

Kayla with Captain Bill Stewart-Author photo

The Captain of the Theodore was contacted and given permission to tie up at our dock. He could take on water, get stores, and even used a car that belonged to a crewmember to do their running around.

I called my wife and told her to round up the kids, and come see who our guest was. With the crowd that showed up, it was evident more than one phone call was made. With it being pre 9/11, visits like this were a normal occurrence. Carroll's girlfriend Shelly, had also brought her daughter to visit, and got her picture taken with the Captain, she felt like she was a little princess. Up in the face part of the tug was all of the information about little tug *Theodore Too.* They had started up in Nova Scotia, Canada, and was on a public relations tour with the tug going into many of the major ports along the way.

Captain Bill Stewart was an actual retired tugboat Captain, enjoying life. He said, "Whenever we pulled into a port we always get the same reaction, just different faces, but with the same smiles from everyone." They stayed for a few more days and then went on their merry way, continuing with their goodwill tour.

I had swapped e-mail addresses with the Captains son, who was also one of the two deckhands aboard this sixty-five foot life sized, kids show tugboat that had came to life. I received some e-mails later, with some pictures of the rough Canadian waters that his Dad had been in, those pictures reaffirmed why the North Sea would never be graced with my presence. The big bad Gulf of Mexico waters were rough enough for me.

KEY WEST TRIP FOR TANKER

Gus W. Darnell

There were some surprise jobs that came down the pike that was pleasurable to do. I had only seen Key West one other time, and that was for a short period of time. Me, my wife Lois, my best friend Carroll Dale, and his daughter Chaleena, had taken a cruise on the *Regal Empress* back in January of 1996. We had only gotten a small taste of what Key West at night was really like.

When I was told the *Hawk* was going there, I couldn't wait to get the trip underway. We were going to assist the government tanker *Gus W. Darnell* into the Coast Guard station. We would be needed around 09:00 on May 16 2000, after we docked her we were to wait for around twenty-four hours, then sail her. After we were released we would head back to Tampa. I would have plenty of time to check out the sites, and hopefully tour the Mel Fisher treasure museum that was closed on my last visit.

We departed around 02:00 on May 15, Dave Arata was my Mate, Doug Bogard, and Scoot Tyoe were the engineers, and Phil Vallandingham was the deckhand. I was told to save fuel every way we could, so I calculated the distance to run at a slower speed than normal. The time needed for the speed we would make, should be just over twenty-five hours. Leaving a few hours early for any problems that might arise; we made the trip, from dock to dock, in twenty-five hours and forty-five minutes.

With two tugs needed for the job, the tug *Dorothy Moran* was brought from her home port of Miami. The job went just like any other docking; I just got to show off a little bit.

We were placed on the port bow, as the ship approached the dock I had to position the *Hawk* alongside the ship, this was a common maneuver in Tampa when we got in close quarters, so I held her against the dock by thrusting sideways, Mr. Pilot was impressed. When the docking was finished, the Pilot told us it would be about twenty-four hours before she sailed. We secured the tug at the Navy dock where a big decision had to be made. Who was going to town first, since me and Scoot wanted to see the gold museum, you guessed it, we went first. Scoot had been to Key West many times before, and told me he had bought a piece of jewelry every time he went, as long as the museum was open. We were in luck, the doors were open, and we were now inside.

Now these are some people that are awfully proud of the treasure they had found. I saw some prices on some pieces that like to have made me swallow my tongue. Scoot says, "I don't look at those pieces; this is the less expensive counter," pointing at where he was standing. He was definitely browsing in my neighborhood; we still bought our respective loved ones a pair of ear rings, but still drooling as we walked out the door.

After being relieved of about three quarters of the money I had brought with me, we headed for the world famous Duvall Street. Scoot says, "You've heard the term, between night and day, well this place is where that applies." There is just about anything you can imagine to eat down there, with seafood everything. I knew we had food aboard the boat, but I just wanted to get something, anything, from one of these little street cafes, just to say that I had. The grouper sandwich and fried taters that I bought was definitely worth the museum price that I had to shell out to pay for it. It was like Campbell's soup, it was Mmmm Mmmm good. After spending a couple of more hours, just walking and looking, we went back to the boat to let the second shift go to town.

We wanted to time it just right, when they returned to the boat we would go back to town for when the weirdo's was out lurking around. Just sitting aboard the boat and watching the boat traffic was unbelievable, I knew there were quite a few cruise ships that came in and out of Key West. If they were not equipped with thrusters, and actually needed tugboat assistance, somebody could make a lot of money with the volume of ships I witnessed coming and going. Scoot had brought some of those little gasoline powered scooters to get around on while we were there.

Yes I did, I ordered me one as soon as I got back home. If this Key West thing was going to be a steady diet for us, I was going back with a ride of my own. We sailed the ship the next day, and headed back to Tampa. After we were released from the ship, the Pilot said to me, "*Hawk,* you can stay around here if you want to, that is one impressive piece of equipment." I told him, "I would love to stay here, anytime you need us we will certainly come right back down here." I put her on the same rpm's we had went down there on, and couldn't wait for our next trip back.

THE AIRCRAFT CARRIER

USS Enterprise IN PENSACOLA

The company seemed to have feelers out, always looking for work that the big boats would be suited to do. The tugs *Hawk* and *Falcon* were dispatched to dock the *USS Enterprise* in Pensacola, Florida. One of those new management decisions was made that would require the *Hawk* to tow the tug *Falcon*, from Tampa to Pensacola in order to save fuel.

We departed just after midnight on June 7 2000 towing the *Falcon*. My crew was Jason as Mate, Scoot as Chief Engineer, and Uncle Bob as assistant engineer, and Phil Vallandingham as AB deckhand. On the *Falcon* was Captain Bobby Strickland, with Captain Andy McDonald as Mate, Frankie Pavon and Wormy as engineers, Travis Muse was their deckhand. When we got underway, I asked Jason to head her down the channel; we were making a speed of less than eight knots. I knew after towing for the first ten hours, that this fuel saving idea was not going make the grade. Scoot had come to me and said, "We are burning a lot of fuel." I made the decision to call the office to let them know about our fuel consumption. I told them I was going to take in my tow wire and release the *Falcon*. Captain Bobby could run light boat and we still would not use as much fuel as we had. As it turned out, we used less fuel the next twenty-five hours running, as we did the first ten hours towing the *Falcon*. We made it to Pensacola the next day around 20:00. The big show wasn't suppose to take place until the next day, and we knew since this was a big time deal, we were going be a part of it, and probably even on the local TV. There were also two more boats coming from Pascagoula, Mississippi to

USS *Enterprise* Entering Pensacola
Author photo

help assist this vintage aircraft carrier into the dock. The two Navy Pilots and one State Pilot that would be running the show came down to the boat that morning, to go over the operation with us. The *Hawk* was chosen to make a run out the channel with them, this was also done so we could be told how the maneuvers would be implemented and the placement of the four tugs on the ship. All during that Friday morning, we noticed helicopters doing a

Placement of tugs *Falcon* and *Hawk*
Courtesy of Keith Tyoe

lot of flying offshore and back again. We were told they are hauling dignitaries out to the ship; so that they could ride it back in. I thought the Mighty *Hawk* had quite a bit of pull with her 6,700 hp, compared to what those people had, it was nothing.

We met the *Enterprise* out in the Pensacola ship channel, the tug *Hawks* line was placed in the center chock aft of the vessel, that's right in the middle on the back of the ship. The Pilots had told us they wanted the strongest tug back aft, we could be used to slow down the ships forward motion that way. They had asked me, "Does the *Hawk* back pretty good?" I said, "Yes Sir, she'll put the brakes on you." The site of this old war ship coming up the channel was an impressive site to see. Just like I had seen before, the crew on this ship was also decked out in their dress whites, standing around the flight deck like a proud bunch of Sailors. With us having navigated the channel safely, and with the other three tugs finally made up at their assigned places, we approached the turning basin.

This time period was also pre 9/11, with a visiting aircraft carrier not being an every day occasion, the smaller boats were out in force to see this historical ship that was visiting their state. It looked like there was an enormous boat show in the area, and it just so happened to be at the dock that we were going to tie this carrier to. As we approached the last turn towards the dock, one of the Pilots told me, "Back the *Hawk* half," "back half *Hawk*," I replied. Within seconds he said, "Hook up *Hawk*, back her full." I said, "Back full *Hawk*." It wasn't ten seconds later when he says, "Stop *Hawk* stop," I said, "Stop the *Hawk*." He then says to me, "*Hawk*, you stopped this ship, now we're going to have to come ahead on the ship to get some headway." I said, "Yes sir, I told you she'd put the brakes on you." That little bit of backing sure impressed these cats, big time. I also never did back full, not wanting to relieve the "*Big E*" of her small looking bitt that my line was placed over.

We finally got the ship moored safely to the Navy dock, where she would be on exhibition for the next four days. We had been told she had come into Pensacola for one reason and one reason only, because some politician wanted it to. The Navy was going to have an open house aboard the ship and give tours over the weekend to the public, which was a better reason.

We finished this job at noon on Friday June 9, then were told to tie up close to the ship and to get comfortable. The ship wasn't going to depart until June 13, the next Tuesday. Well, that meant we had some time on our hands, and with this great big Navy ship next to us, it was tour time. Me, Scoot, and Phil went to the ship to see if maybe we could be shown around. We found a fellow that looked like he had a high ranking, we told him we were part of the crew off the tug *Hawk*, and asked for a tour.

He told us, "Come back early in the morning before the public tours begin, I'll see that you get a VIP tour." The Officer that had told us this also had a chest full of medals and was being saluted by everyone that passed him; we had evidently talked to the right man. We had noticed one of those expensive cigarette boats there in the plane bay. Before we had left the ship, we asked about what that particular boat was used for.

It turns out that the boat was found floating off the East coast, with no one around. They reported what they had found and then they brought it aboard the ship to keep it from getting hit. A half-million dollar boat had to belong to someone; through the numbers on the boat they revealed its owner. He never did tell us about the circumstances that put the boat where it was found, but that it was owned by the CEO of one of the big cookie companies, like Keebler or Nabisco, you know, one of the big boys. The boat owner showed his appreciation for its return by sending a truck to the ship, with pallets of cookies inside of it for the crew.

After a good nights sleep, Me, Scoot, Phil, and Uncle Bob left Jason sleeping, well, somebody had to stay. We left early and went to the

On top of the "Big E" with big eyes
Author Photo

Enterprise for our promised VIP tour. When we got over there, this same Officer was close to where we had seen him the day before. He told us, "Good morning," and called a man over to where we were standing. He told him, "Take these men on a tour of the *Big "E,"* the engine room, crews quarters, and galley are off limits, every place else is okay."

This was definitely going to be a VIP tour; we even went to the warroom, where the guys wrote on the glass backwards. They had a model of the ship that showed where all the planes were positioned at all times, they called it the Ouija board. We were then taken to the bridge, where there was another fellow; he was actually one of the quartermasters that steered the ship. He went to telling us all about the *Big "E,"* and of all her big accomplishments, and the history of the ship as he knew it.

On some of the older tugs that I ran in the past, they had a steering wheel mounted in the wheelhouse that was used just like steering a car. This huge aircraft carrier also had a wheel used to steer with. This fellow went to pounding on the wheel saying, "No one, and I mean no one, can steer this ship the way I can." Scoot had his video camera on, and captured what this fellow was telling us. He told us what he could, but wouldn't tell us about the speed, where they would be going next, he told us anything classified he could not answer. At any rate, we felt very privileged at what we had already been shown on our VIP tour.

We left the bridge and went on top of the wheelhouse where we found some very large binoculars, you could see for miles with them. And looking at the crowd that was gathering below, I was glad we weren't with them. We then went out on the flight deck where there were some planes on display. I owned three and a half acres of land, and I have mowed it, this ship had almost five acres of flight deck surface area; now that would be a lot of grass to mow. The sight of standing on one end of the deck, and looking to the other end, was almost unbelievable. Thinking about these ships, and what they were used for, it struck me; this ship was really just a floating airport and was only one of many in the fleet.

We were given some brochures about her dimensions, with all of the unclassified information available that was permissible for the general public. After a while, we were ready to go back to the boat, we were then treated to a ride down on one of the plane elevators. That thing dropped so quickly our ride only lasted a few seconds. There should be a warning sign posted, letting you know that the swallowing of gum is a possibility.

**Looking aft from the bow of the
Enterprise-**Courtesy of Keith Tyoe

We couldn't stop talking about what we had just seen as we walked back to the boat. For me, I experienced

Me playing a tour guide for the *Hawk* –Author photo

the same feeling that I had felt when I had toured that Old Russian Submarine. If these old war ships could talk, what stories they could tell. It was coming up on noontime, and since we had left Jason on the boat, we figured he'd have lunch fixed for everyone. As we approached the boat, we saw Jason up on the boat deck painting some spots that needed to be covered. We all started telling him, man you should have seen what we just saw, it was unbelievable, you should have went with us, and oh yeah, you got lunch ready, we're hungry.

That was like throwing gas on a burning fire, he exploded. He held some fingers in a certain shape, and then told us some certain things. I looked at Scoot and said, "I think Jason's mad at us." I just added some more fuel to the fire and said, "Since you didn't cook anything for lunch, you just keep working, we're going inside to cool off." I guess being mad can make you work like you're on a mission, because he didn't stop until that part of the deck was completely painted. Jason cooled down during his painting tantrum, I told him he did a good job, now take the rest of the weekend off. Scoot broke out his motorized big wheel scooter like we had in Key West, and with an extra can of gas to run through it, we had hours of fun riding that thing around. We took turns riding around; I discovered that the Pensacola Naval Base is a town of its own, with manicured lawns and all. I also passed by their cemetery while I was there, and although I've never been there, it looked just like the cemetery at Arlington. Those were some somber few moments as I drove past, and

269

saw row after row of white crosses. I thank each and every fallen soldier for keeping our country safe with their sacrifices.

There were people coming by the boat all day long, and looking it over just like we were part of the open house. They asked us all kinds of questions about the Mighty Tug *Hawk*. Some couldn't get over the size of the tires we had mounted on her for fenders. I told them, "Those tires are just some old pay loader tires, nothing special." I thought, surely there are some big tired machines up here in north Florida to look at. At any rate, our mini tour went on for the rest of weekend. I'm sure we made memories with the little children, when their wide eyed faces looked the *Hawk* over.

Just laid back and enjoying the down time, Tuesday had come upon us before we knew it. The tugs were placed in the same positions when the 10:00 time came to sail this ship, this would also be a memory for us too. Everything went smooth as silk, and we was now on our way back to Tampa. We had bought some trolling lures and line while we were in Pensacola; we just hoped it would be worth the cost of the ninety dollars we had split.

Nothing hit the first day, but Wednesday morning was just what the Doctor had ordered. Two big Wahoo's found those trolling lures just too tempting to let them go. Two fish was it too, after they were cleaned and put in some zip-loc bags, we figured those two better be some good fish. With a ninety-dollar investment, they were some very expensive fish. After we made it back, the boat was once again secured and everyone went home, what would be next?

Puerto Rico Trip on

The Tug *Eagle II*

The tug *Hawk* was put into the shipyard for her five-year ABS inspection. All boats have scheduled inspections every year, the five year ABS (American Bureau of Shipping) is just so much more extensive than the yearly ones are. The *Hawk* had gone into the shipyard just days after we had gotten back from Pensacola, and was doubtful of making the long trip to Puerto Rico that had came up.

There was a new LNG (Liquefied Natural Gas) power plant coming on line in Puerto Rico. We had heard that there were only two ship Pilots that worked the ships coming and going in the port of Guayanilla. They were also granted the authority to require a certain amount of tugboats, with a minimum amount of horsepower for the jobs there. Since this was a new installation and never having a ship alongside their dock, rumor was the required cumulative horsepower this Pilot wanted for this particular job, was 15,000.

If the *Hawk* was ready, she would go with the tugs *Eagle II* and *Condor*, with a combined total of 20,100 hp. The *Falcon* with 3,000 hp was the tug going to replace the *Hawk* if she wasn't able, the horsepower criteria would still be met. The tug *Condor* had been working out of Mobile, Alabama almost continuously since she had come back from Mexico. As the details for the trip were told to us crews that were making the trip, it sounded a little strange from the get go. Just like when we were in Mexico, the only American crew members were the Captain, and Chief Engineer, all others crewmembers were to be Puerto Rican.

The two Puerto Rican tugboat company's that worked in Guayanilla had formed a Consortium between the two of them. This way, both companies' would be getting a piece of the pie from this new Power Plant. The ship we were going to dock was one of the LNG tankers I had worked while I was in Trinidad, just thirteen months ago. The *Matthews* was a good size tanker with 98,000 gross tons, the two tugs that worked her in Trinidad had a combined horsepower, of less than 9,000 hp.

I told John Collins, our Operations Manager at the time, the three boats for this job was a big time over kill. The *Hawk* was oh so close to being finished, but with the time having run out with the date of departure being July 3 2000. So, the tug *Falcon* was now her replacement for this long run job. I was assigned to the *Eagle II* with my old Buddy Paul Roush as the Chief Engineer. The Mate Francisco Padilla was a son of one of the owners of South Puerto Rico Towing, who also had part of his crew to round us out.

With an estimated 120 hours of running time, the tugs *Eagle II*, and *Falcon*, departed right on time. The *Condor* had already departed Mobile; hopefully, we would rendezvous around Rebecca Shoals off Dry Tortugas, some 200 miles south of Tampa Bay. We were running together out of Tampa Bay when Captain Dave Arata called and said, "There is a problem with the *Falcon*." His Chief Engineer Harold Perkins had reported that he had been adding water to the main engines at a steady rate.

He had told Dave, "I don't know if there's enough water on the boat to even make it down there." Reporting this to the office, Dave was told to bring the *Falcon* back to the dock and to put all their gear and provisions on the *Hawk*. Paul and I just looked at each other with puzzled looks. Both turbo chargers off the *Hawk's* main engines had been completely rebuilt during her shipyard down time. We thought surely there would be a break-in period, especially before being sent on a 120-hour steady run, that's five full days of non stop running at high speed.

She was still my boat; I just hated to see something go wrong because not enough time was allowed for a break-in. There must have been controlled chaos aboard the tug *Hawk* for the three hours it took the *Falcon* to get back to Tampa. Paul and I couldn't imagine how she could be ready to go offshore when just hours earlier, there was no way.

I had plotted around 1,273 miles for this trip, I figured the route to be ran was the same as Dave, and at a steady speed the tug *Hawk* would surely catch up to us within five days. These fellows all spoke English which made communication a breeze, or so I thought. About the second day out, Mr. Deckhand asked me if it was okay to thaw some shrimp out. I told him, "By all means, as a matter of fact, you can be the designated cook for all the meals."

He said, "I am going to fix us some shrimp and yellow rice, Puerto Rican style, it will be a meal like you had never had before," he would even share his recipe with me. Now I know when I want to impress someone with a special recipe, the first thing I would do with shrimp, is to peel them. Not this fellow, five pounds of unpeeled shrimp were added to two large bags of yellow rice, and cooked. That was it, nothing special, such as onions, spices, or anything else to make it standout. When I sat down to eat and crunched down on a shell on my first shrimp, I thought well, he must have just missed one. When he had told me he was going to fix a meal to remember, he wasn't far off. He hadn't knocked the hide off the first shrimp, and yes, I would remember it. Not wanting to hurt his feelings, I let him down easy. I told him it was good but, I was stripping him of his newly designated cook title.

During that second day we had ran up with the tug *Condor*, with Captain Cliff Currci, and Chief Engineer Doug Bogard aboard. The tug *Hawk* was steaming our way with plenty of catch up time left. Sometimes we would make a speed of almost fourteen knots, while other times we made just over nine knots. The sea currents made a big difference in the speed, I had also figured the entire trip at an average speed of eleven knots, and wasn't concerned.

We passed close to Cuba on the east end of the Island Nation, just south of Cayo Romano; we could see land by looking through the binoculars. The one thing we didn't want to see was the Cuban gun boats that I had heard so much about. I had never been in that part of the world by boat before, so I could only go by the stories that I was told. So far, we had traveled just over 500 miles, and all three boats were now running within a few of miles apart. Departing the coast of Cuba, our next sighting of land would be Haiti and the Dominican Republic.

Paul had been down to Puerto Rico before having spent several years on offshore tugboats, and yes, that's where I heard some good offshore stories. Our weather was relatively good with the seas being no higher than three to five feet, so far. Paul kept telling me to enjoy it while it lasted, because the 150-mile stretch of Mona Pass was coming up. He told me he had been through the Pass many times before and had gotten tore up every time. We were making pretty good speed and were even ahead of our ETA, and then we received a phone call. After running for almost four and a half days, we had now been told not to get to the dock until after daylight. We had to pull the throttles back to almost idle speed. Doing this for about nine hours, and through Mona Pass to boot, I was glad to see the sun peeking over the horizon.

It was a beautiful Saturday morning July 8 2000, we had also managed to stretch my estimated 120 hours running time, into 120 hours and 30 minutes dock to dock. We came in one by one with the shore cameras rolling, a daylight entrance now made sense. All three boats were in bad need of re-hanging some tires that Mona's Pass had put on the deck with her rough water. The tug *Hawk* was the only boat out of the three that did not have a lifting crane mounted. We spent the next few hours doing the flip-flop shuffle, turning the boats end for end, to where the cranes on the *Eagle II* and *Condor* could reach all the tires that needed to be lifted on all three boats.

After the tires project was finished, Hector, who was Francisco's father and part owner of the new company, came by for us three Captains, we were invited to go for lunch. This was an offer we all accepted, and I was glad we did. I couldn't pronounce what I had ordered to eat, but it had seafood in it and with peeled shrimp too. I thought during this meal my deckhand had better rethink his shrimp cooking procedure, or just maybe, he wasn't a real Puerto Rican. I had given Hectors wife some money to buy some souvenirs, just in case I didn't get a chance to. She came back with a sack full of little trinkets, probably things I could not have found on my own, and my kids loved them when I got home with their presents.

The next morning we were told that we would be meeting the tanker in the early afternoon, but would only be assisting her into the inner anchorage. The actual docking of the vessel wouldn't be until Monday, July 10. Dave, Cliff, and I talked about them dragging this job out, maybe this junior Pilot was a little gun shy. So far, the *Eagle II* had been nothing but an observation platform for the dignitaries.

Finally, the day of the big job that we had traveled almost 1,300 miles to do had arrived. As we prepared to depart the dock, our dignitaries were back aboard. The tugs *Condor* and *Hawk* were the tugs that actually assisted the *Matthews* from the anchorage to the berth. The *Eagle II* was once again the boat of choice to observe the job from, after the ship was positioned at the dock, we were then called over to push on the ship around midship. I would hate to know that we had come this distance just to hold a ship to the dock while the lines were put out, well we had.

The ship was secure and the big hoopla was over. Somebody had spent a lot of money for us to come all the way to Puerto Rico, just to do what a pontoon boat could have done. Regardless, we as employees do as we're told, and go where we're told to go. I'm just grateful for having the opportunity to make the trip.

After all, if I had not gone I would have never gotten to eat shrimp and yellow rice, Puerto Rican style. We found out she would only be at the berth for around twenty-four hours. I sure wanted to tour this island, but time had slipped by before I could. The sailing had been set up for 15:00 on July 11; the sailing also went like clockwork. We then went back to the South Puerto Rico Towing dock where different crews were put aboard the boats for the return trip.

All three tugs departed at 21:30 that night, with the tugs *Hawk* and *Eagle II* headed for Tampa, and the tug *Condor* heading for Fort Lauderdale. We had five days running to get back to the Tampa Bay area. One of the first things I did was to find out who could cook and who couldn't. I was hoping the run back would go as smooth as it had going down there. For the first four days everything went well, and then we turned up into the Gulf.

Although the last day was a little bouncy, just getting closer to home made it alright. I had plenty of time to reflect back on the last couple of years. I had been all over the Gulf of Mexico; I had worked several tours in Mexico, and also worked forty-three days in Trinidad in 1999, plus the big jacket tow out of Corpus Christi, Texas. After the big walk out, I made another trip to Mexico December 14 1999, I had then brought the Eagle II back from Mexico in January of 2000.

The month of May 2000, brought the beginning of my Key West adventures. Less than a month later was the trip to Pensacola to Dock the *USS Enterprise*. A short three weeks after that now took me on a trip of almost 1,300 miles from home. I thought to myself, Bill, you have been a busy man. Maybe this was one more reason I never received a call, from you know who. I was put on a mission to gather material for this book, thank you Lord.

I don't know what it is, but it sure seemed like we always made better time going home, instead of leaving home. We made the run back to Tampa, 6 hours faster; of course, we didn't have to slow down for a picture taking session this time. We had made it back safely, secured the boats at 16:00 on July 16 2000. The Puerto Rican crew had a ride waiting to take them to the airport for their return trip home. Now that's a quick turn around, not even time to sight see a day or two.

The Next Few Years, Not The Same

There were some jobs that came along through the years with the safety factor having slipped some minds, they were to rescue some vessels that had broken down, or one that comes to mind had just been abandoned. The tug *Hawk* had been placed in Port Manatee, to be what we used to call the Manatee boats. What had happened as told to us was the crew of an older 60-foot tugboat the *Jean T*, was on their way to pick up a small barge in Louisiana. When a cold front was forecasted to come into the Gulf of Mexico from the north, they turned south to get away from it. We heard they had run past the Dry Tortugas, turned back around, and once again started heading north.

When their position was off Fort Myers, Florida they were now running out of fuel. They had already used up all of their fuel filters due to being back in the rough waters from the cold front they had originally ran from. Whenever a boat is rocked around from rough seas, it will stir up the fuel in the tanks and anything else that is in them. The end result of their detour was they had to abandon ship. The Coast Guard was called to rescue them, with their EPIRB (Emergency Position Indicator Radio Beacon) switched on, they departed the boat. This was done so the boats position could be tracked by satellite; this is where the Mighty *Hawk* came into play.

Here we are, a 6,700 hp Tractor tug, 110 feet long, who was now dispatched to go rescue this abandoned tugboat with a length of 60 feet, we were 40 feet wide. I questioned management about the decision to send us out to what was surely an accident waiting to happen. I said, "You know there are only three men aboard the *Hawk* right," "Yes, we know," was their reply.

With prior management, this was a non-issue. It was clear to everyone; management had not weighed the negatives in this job. We were expected to go on this night search with three men where the seas were six to eight feet. We departed on a Saturday night, Frankie was my engineer, and Victor Ramirez was the deckhand. Victor was one of those fellows that got sea sick very easy, sometimes at the dock. Frankie and I had talked about what we were supposed to do with this little tug, if we could even find her. We had been given the position that the EPIRB signal was sending to the Coast Guard. I also had the phone number of the Coast Guard station, just in case we didn't find this needle in a haystack we would be looking for.

The absence of daylight didn't make the search any easier either; also whenever the seas get to a certain height, a suspected target on the radar screen was harder to pick out. Although radars have a sea clutter feature which aids in making the screen clearer, the location we had been given had netted nothing. So, I called the CG number using the Sat phone, I was now being told the EPIRB signal was coming from miles of our present location. I told Frankie, "This thing must be running on its own," the wind was blowing hard which was probably the big difference.

With two radars aboard, I would put one on a three-mile range and the other on a half-mile range, and still nothing at the new position. Allowing enough time to figure out we were alone, it was phone call time again. Another call to the CG and yet another position farther away from where we were located again. After going to that position, and still being unable to locate the hide and seek tug, it was time to call the search off.

It was now around 01:00, all we were able to do for the last few hours was to burn some fuel and get spanked by Mother Nature. I still hadn't figured out how we were going to safely get a line on this tug with two men and one of them so sick I hadn't seen him since we had left the dock. While heading back in I reported what we had done to the dispatcher, and went back to Port Manatee securing the boat at 04:30.

Later that day I was informed of plan B, this one had more crewmembers, but still didn't sound good either. The little tugs owner and the tugs Chief Engineer, who had been on her when she was abandoned, was going back with us for the second search. I also had a Mate, Bill White and another engineer, Scoot Tyoe was added to the crew. This plan had the owner and his engineer being put aboard the little tug when, or if we found her, with a gasoline powered pump and a bag full of supplies. With the weather worsening my concerns really didn't matter, because we were making money, as I had been told many times before when these bonehead jobs came up.

We departed the second time at 02:00 on March 4 2002. With a new EPIRB position, we were in search of a very elusive little tugboat. I slept during the ride out, and when I went up for my 06:00 watch we had still not arrived to the tug. Around 07:00, I called the CG to get an updated EPIRB position, guess what we did after the phone call. I made a course change of almost forty-five degrees, and headed for the newest position. At 08:45, we found the little girl, over forty miles southwest of the Tampa sea buoy. *Jean T* had her wheelhouse door latched wide opened, right next to the EPIRB. This tug owner liked to have had a heart attack when he saw that. With what he said, I'll bet somebody lost their job over that move.

This was probably one of the most delicate maneuvers I had ever done on the big boats. The seas were now eight to ten feet, and would require me to time it just right to come alongside the tug without causing any damage. I positioned the *Hawk* parallel to the much smaller tug and put her in a walk mode.

With *Jean* on my starboard side, the *Hawk* shielded the little tug from the seas somewhat. As we came alongside our two passengers jumped onto their tug with the ever-moving deck. My crew helped them with their gear, pump, and gas can. As soon as they were safely aboard, I immediately got away from her. I kept on thinking how unsafe this was, regardless if everything turned out good. The worry that the owner had, seemed more important, since *Jean T* had been abandoned; all that someone had to do was to put a line on the little tug and claim her for salvage rights.

My thoughts were now that we had found her, we could stay close until the weather had calmed down some. This wasn't even an option, we were told to put a line up and tow her to shore. With only two men on the little tug, there was no way they could pull our tow gear aboard to tow on. There was however about 150 feet of tie up line that we had put on the boat, just in case, and was really the only size line these fellows could handle anyway.

With an eye spliced on each end of the line, I backed up to the baby tug where Scoot threw them the line. They dropped it over their bow bitt, and then Scoot dropped the eye on our end over a fairlead on the tow winch. You could tell there wasn't much fuel aboard; she was sitting on top of the water like an air mattress. After seeing how high she was off the water, and with the wind blowing twenty-five plus knots, that would help explain the different positions reported thirty-six hours earlier.

I started out barely pulling on her in a minimum mode, I then clutched one engine out of gear to ease the strain on the line. The seas was lifting her up to where the line would come tight, then lunge forward putting a lot of slack in the line. When those fellows jumped aboard that little tug, they never could have guessed the ride that they were now getting. Running on one engine at idle speed, we weren't breaking any speed records. Because our heading was east northeast, we were also catching the seas on our beam, that's when you really have a nasty ride. With almost forty miles to the sea buoy, it was going to be a slow go.

I was just hoping the small line we were towing with wouldn't break with the way it came taught when all the slack came out of it. At 21:00, twelve rough hours after we had started in, we were now in sight of the Tampa sea buoy. With ship traffic coming and going, I gave my security calls and stayed well out of their way. Within a mile of the sea buoy my biggest concern happened, the line we were towing with broke. It had chafed on the bow of the little tug; my crew pulled it aboard and put a bowline knot in it, not having time to splice another eye.

I turned around and put the line back out, and then proceeded in. The only difference was now that the line was shorter it wouldn't take the surge as well. This proved to be true for the next two hours, with four more line breakings. It had finally gotten so short with the bowlines being put into the line with each breakage, we now had to come up with something else to tow with, since the line was now not long enough. We had also reached a point outside the Egmont ship channel where we had to enter the channel due to swallow water ahead; grounding at this point was not an option.

We had constant communication with the boat people that had been following us for the past fourteen hours with their handheld radio. The owner now informed me that there was a line they used for towing underneath a cover on their boat. I would liked to have had that bit of information when we found this floater, we wouldn't still be out there if I had known. They were both fatigued to the point that when the line was passed to us, they were having a hard time making it fast on their bow bitts.

If anyone has ever had a line in their wheel, they know how I felt when this happened to us. The wind was still blowing hard enough that the two boats were separating before they were made fast. I backed towards their bow to give them the needed slack in the line, that was when one of those big vacuum cleaners I had underneath the boat sucked the line into the port drive. I wasn't able to get the line freed, and was now drifting out of the channel, so I had to make a decision, and quick.

I decided to tow on the little tug with the line in my wheel. I had also hoped the strain from towing would even free the line from the surge the tug was doing. That decision to tow the tug with the line in my wheel would be questioned later. With no way to anchor, and the rough seas making the whole job unsafe, I still think I made the right decision, regardless of what others had said. As we passed the Egmont Key light-house, I called dispatch, and asked for the instructions for this nightmare we had been on.

I was told, "Tug *Tampa* will meet you on the "B" cut flats and take her from you, he'll then take her on to Bay Boro Harbor, in St. Petersburg." That was just peachy, providing it wasn't too rough in "B" cut where the transfer would take place. Arriving to the flats we were still at idle speed, when the *Tampa* came alongside the little tug, Captain Harold said he couldn't make up to it. The quarter bitts were bending, and the bulwarks looked like they were about to pull over from the swell of the waves, this was not looking pretty.

Now what, the only option I could come up with was to go into Port Manatee to make the transfer alongside a dock. After advising the Manatee County Port Authority of our dilemma, we were given permission to make the exchange in their harbor. As I entered the slip, the *Tampa* put a bow line on the stern of the little tug to act as a brake. As I approached the dock we grabbed the first bitt we came to, and were finally secure to a dock at 04:50. All the while, tug *Tampa* was maneuvering the little fellow alongside the *Hawk*, securing her alongside us. We were now able to release the little tug by taking their tow line onto the *Hawk*, since it was still hung up in my port drive. Captain Harold was now able to put a towline on our two-day project and head back out the channel with her, goodbye and good riddance.

We could do nothing now but wait on the diver we had ordered to come cut this line out of our wheel. The wind was still blowing and it was freezing cold too. I thought to myself, whenever the diver gets here he had better use the head before he jumps in that water, or it'll be hours before he'll be able to. He came right on time and did what they do so well, within an hour the line was free and coiled up on our deck. If the dollar signs had not blinded the decision makers, this was a job the tug *Hawk* would not have done, or any other tug as well, at least until the weather had permitted.

Aluminum Gambling

Boat Rescue

While I'm on the subject of jobs that a six and a half million dollar tug-boat should not have been sent on, please read on. I was back in Port Manatee one day when I was dispatched on another rescue mission. I was told that there was a small gambling boat adrift off Bradenton beach, and was requesting tow assistance. Their steering had gone hard over one way and wouldn't move.

My first reply was, "Yeah, and you want me to do what?" "Here is her location, go tow her in," was the response. After plotting where the gambler was located, I told the people that were sitting behind their desks, "It appears that boat is in some shallow water of around sixteen to eighteen feet." I said, "Our draft right now is just over sixteen feet, are you sure you want us to take the chance of damaging these 1.8 million dollar drives hanging underneath this boat?" After questioning this move several more times, I was told each time, just go do what you can do, at least we'll be on the clock; this wasn't a good move I thought.

What puzzled me was that we had smaller tugboats to do this very job. I also knew the company at the time was going through bankruptcy. When it came to using common sense, sending the tug *Hawk* for that job was just like Elvis after a concert, it had left the building. I ran out the main ship channel to buoy eleven Egmont before turning south. Keeping a very close eye on my fathometer I didn't want any surprises, like finding the bottom of the bay.

I continued towards this little form in a distance that we had suspected was our broken down boat. Yes it was, sizing her up as we eased alongside; she was only 100 feet long, where the *Hawk* was 110. The seas were only a slight chop as we made up with two lines; I thought this fellow sure looks tender. After our lines came tight, my Mate Eddie Rollins starts yelling over the radio to stop, I asked him, "What's wrong?" He said, "I think this thing is aluminum," when the line had come tight their bitt broke right off the deck. I asked the Captain if his boat was aluminum, where he affirmed, "Yes it is, why?" I told him, "We just snapped your stern bitt off, that's why."

I told Eddie, "Turn us loose before we cause any more damage to this beer can." We turned our lines loose and got away from this aluminum boat. At this point, I relayed to the office what I had known all along, big boat plus little boat is no good. They said, "Okay, at least you tried, bring her back and we'll send a smaller boat." I could hardly get this image out of my head of some hands being around a throat as we headed back into the dock.

The gamblers Captain called me and said they had freed up their rudder, having it locked in midship position. I thought about the old Kenny Rogers song, "You picked a fine time to tell me Lucille." He was going to try to head in using her engines to steer with, I thought cool; he took off and appeared to be steering fairly well. I had to run the main ship channel again, while the little fellow ran the southwest pass channel; after all, she only had about five feet of draft. As we were turning into Mullet Key channel, I seen the gambler almost abeam of us, and he was strolling. I told Eddie, "Look over there, he's going to beat us to the bridge." Well look here, as we were going under the Sunshine Skyway Bridge, the little tug *Ray Hebert* was heading towards the gambler.

She was a leased tug and was only about sixty-five feet long with 1,600 hp, just the right size tug for this job. Since the gambling boat was doing so good steering with her engines, the tug *Ray Hebert* just ran along with her until they made it up to Tampa. We heard later from their crew that when they were making up to the gambler, she too bent the fragile aluminum boat, and this was done inside the harbor with a smaller tug, and with the waters calm as a duck pond too.

THE BIRTH OF LILIANA MARIE

On Thursday morning October 24 2002, we were working a job at the Port of Tampa. I knew my daughter Mary was expecting to deliver my very first grandchild at any time. When I received a phone call letting me know that the stork was on the way, I was ecstatic, and knew I had to get off the boat and go to the hospital. I had made arrangements for my relief to come in for me while I went for the big event, which was also something I had been waiting on for a long time.

Uncle Will, Aunt Lisa, and Grandma-Author photo

At the hospital there was a sense of tension, since this was Mary's first little person, and things didn't seem to be going like it should be. Regardless, she was at the place where problems were an everyday occurrence, and would be taken care of professionally. When I arrived at the hospital around 13:00, Mary was in the beginning stages of labor. The nurses had told us this might take a while. My wife and daughter-in law were suited up and setting on go, if, or when they were permitted to go into the delivery room during this blessed event. Since this was something I had not done for over twenty years, which was waiting on a baby to come into the world, I wondered how long it would take. I knew it was in Gods hands now, and prayed for his Devine Intervention to make sure both baby and Mom did well. Mary had one of those sonograms done which showed this little angel was going to be a girl. I had already bought her two tea sets months before she was born, knowing that her Paw Paw was going to be playing with her in the years to come.

You talk about someone that was going to spoil his grandchild, yep, that would be me, and loving every minute that I was doing it. Throughout the day it was discussed what to do because the soon to be Mom wasn't dilating like she was supposed to. So, late in the evening a decision was made to do a caesarian section on her. Finally, on October 24 2002 at 22:12, Liliana Marie came into the world as a gift from God. She weighed five pounds ten ounces and was eighteen inches long, definitely a site for sore eyes. I sure was glad this was over, and thanked the Lord for bringing us all through it okay. Our new Mama and baby both did good enough to be sent home in just a couple of days. When I started writing

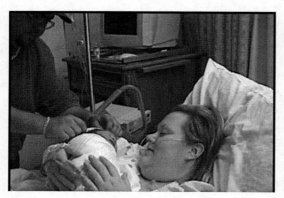

Mother Mary with a new Liliana-Author photo

My granddaughter Liliana Marie
Author photo

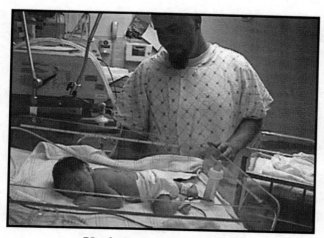

Uncle Josh and Liliana an hour old-Author Photo

this book, Liliana was almost three years old. She is the apple of my eye, and can do no wrong. When she was very small I fed her the inside of a fried potato, her first real food. We didn't tell Mary about it for probably six months, you know how new Mothers are; besides, it's a Grandpa thing anyway. This is a picture of Liliana in her dedication dress for the church; don't you think she looks like a little angel. I had been told by lots of people that you really have more fun playing with grandchildren than you do with your own. I still have fun with my children even today, but it does seem the grand's are allowed to get away with more things and are more mischievous with us Grandparents. I had injured my knee on the boat in early December 2002, and was off work from December 5 until December 31, while it had time to heal. With baby girl being brand new and feedings were at all hours, I do believe we bonded during the long hours that I held her for her early morning feedings. Just the thought of coming home and having her call my name, that would help bring me through some bad times in the near future. Let's go back to tug boating for a while; this next one is a memorable one.

THE LONGEST WEEK
OF THE YEAR

I went back to work on January 1 2003 with my crew being Eddie Rollins as Mate, Scoot Tyoe as engineer, and James Fehrenbach as deckhand. We ended up doing twenty-eight jobs that week; I had worked as many as thirty-five for the week, so that was no big deal. However, the hours we had worked that week was not normal. We worked more hours that week in the harbor than any other week, for the whole year of 2003, that many hours was the factor that wore us down, all ninety-six of them. After being off for the past four weeks, that was a real test for my first week back.

The first four days were spent doing jobs with dockings, sailings, and escorts up and down the bay. Sunday morning we were dispatched to the Tampa sea buoy with a boarding crew of men. These fellows worked as line handlers aboard the ships whenever a dead ship was towed in from sea. They were usually transported to the ship aboard a tugboat; there were eight men that rode out with us that day. We had departed Port Manatee at 05:00 on January 5 2003 to meet the *Cape Ducato* being towed by tug *Eagle II*; he was at idle speed when we arrived.

I went alongside the starboard side of the ship out at the sea buoy; the Jacobs ladder was already hanging over the side ready for the boarding party. Some of the Navy ships that were being brought into Tampa for shipyard work were very high-sided ships. The *Cape Ducato* happened to be one of those type ships, with probably forty feet of freeboard; it looked like a drive-in movie screen.

This boarding process was going to take a while, since the first fellow took almost five minutes to make that vertical climb, and he was one of the smaller men. The second guy started the climb and within six rungs up, he started running out of gas. He inched his way up taking a rest in between rungs, after just clearing the height of my wheelhouse he stopped. Eddie was standing on the bridge wing with the door open letting me know of their progress, since I couldn't see them after a certain point.

Just then, he said, "I don't think he's going to make it, he's starting to shake, oh no, he let go of the ladder." About that time, I saw him pass the window horizontally, not knowing if he went into the water I pulled the drives out of gear. Eddie said, "He landed on the boat; he's on the tires and is just lying there." This fellow even wanted to tie a cooler to his belt to take his drinks and water up with him. Scoot and James was on deck helping these guys get started up the ladder, so when the fall occurred they shifted gears, and went into a first-aid rescue mode. It appeared that he had passed out from exhaustion, and had just fallen back. The minute after we seen he was back conscience and talking with reasonable coherency, I was heading towards the lighthouse to meet up with the Coast Guard boat sooner.

I had already called the Coast Guard to get them coming my way, and to make sure there were EMS personnel aboard when we met up with them. As this tumble was witnessed by the rest of the men, it sparked a resistance to boarding the ship with an "I'm not climbing that ladder" attitude among the remainder of the crew. With just one man making it up on the ship, I now had to find another way to get the rest of these guys aboard.

After we had dropped off the injured man to the Coast Guard boat, we headed back to the ship. I had asked Captain Richard Borden who was aboard the *Eagle II*, "Is there another way to get these men aboard?" He told me, "I don't know, you'll have to look on the stern to see if there's another access."

Whenever we returned to where Richard had been circling with the ship, I went to the stern as he had suggested and checked to see if there was another way to get these fellows aboard. Lo and behold, where the ramp drops down from the stern of the ship, there on the backside of the ramp was a ladder hidden from view. With the *Hawks* bow being fifteen feet off the water line, we were able to have the rest of these line handlers climb right off of our bow and onto the stern ledge. Then scoot up the hard ladder mounted on the ramp which was a much easier climb.

If we would have known this ladder was there, it could have saved this one fellow from getting hurt. Regardless of what had happened to this one man, all of the company safety policies were adhered to without any compromise whatsoever. However, I do think that the physical fitness of someone climbing up the side of a ship should be looked at a lot closer, before their employer sends them to attempt what has to be a challenge to do, even for someone in good shape.

With all of the other workers finally aboard safely, they were now able to help the one fellow that made it up the Jacobs ladder to handle the lines from the assist tugs for the transit up the channel. This man falling only added about two hours to the whole job, the accident was just an unfortunate thing to happen. However, those two hours were also used to go over what could have been done different. When something like this happens that might have been prevented, soon after the incident was the right time to review it. Nobody enjoys seeing a body falling past their window the way I did, and I feel that the Lord helped that man from falling onto the bulwarks and possibly being killed. We heard later that after a short stay in the hospital, he was back at work.

This Navy vessel was one of many that were brought into Tampa Ship Repair for upgrading and routine shipyard maintenance. Others included the *Cape Kennedy* later that year in August, and the *Cape Lobos* in September, and later that year the *Cape St. Johns*, all in 2003. We finished this job at 15:00 that day, despite of the incident with the fallen man.

ANOTHER KEY WEST TRIP

With Eddie still as my Mate, and Scoot running as engineer, we once again headed south to Key West for a job that the tug *Hawk* was suited to do, November 24th, 2002. We were once again going to dock a tanker at the Coast Guard station, spend the night, and well, you know the routine by now. The one difference this time was I now had a scooter of my own, and although it was now after 9/11, I hoped there wouldn't be a problem touring the town this time as we had before. After the docking procedure of the tanker was completed in paradise, it was scooter time.

With Scoot having been to Key West numerous times before, he knew how to get around the area very well; he took me places down there I had

Me with my hair hat and real beard-Author photo

no idea even existed. We went by and seen the marker that is the most southern point of the United States, it's painted red, white, and blue, the appropriate colors. It seemed every place we went, people were asking us where they could rent the little scooters we were riding around on. We would just tell them, "You can't, we brought these from Tampa aboard a tugboat." You could rent bicycles, and little motor cycles, but we had the only skateboards powered by weed eater engines that we knew of. With wheels in my head turning, I wondered if you could rent enough of these things to make a living down here in paradise. Then a picture shot across my mind, me fixing broke scooters that had been abused by the tourists, no, I'll stay on the tug. Later that night, Scoot, Eddie, and myself were just hanging out, this time we had our bicycles, checking out the street scene. I don't think you can stand in one place anywhere in Florida and see so many different types of people that walked past us.

Of course Scoot hadn't had a haircut in six years, and me with my long-hair hat on, we fit in with the rest of the street people. There was this old couple that had came out of one of the shops there on the strip, this old gentleman walked right up to me and looked me right square in the face, and then said, "Man, that's a lot of hair, how long did it take you to get like that?" I said, "I don't know, maybe five years." He stared at me for a

Scoot with his real hair
Author photo

minute, just shook his head and said, "You fellows have a good evening," they then turned and walked away. Although my beard was real, with the addition of my hair hat and funny glasses, I have to admit, I was one wooly bugger looking fellow. I wore this get up when I went to Daytona Beach for the Turkey Rod Run every year in my old 1939 Ford street rod. A man can get a few raised eyebrows walking around looking like this, but being in Key West, it was just like being in on the nightly street party. You've seen my picture, the last one is Scoot in the wheelhouse with his hair combed forward, he looks like cousin "It."

A street person came up while we were standing there and stood with us. He asked if we wanted a drink of whatever it was he had in his hand, we said no thanks. He then asked us, "Where are you guys going to stay tonight?" We all three looked at each other and laughed, I said, "We're probably going to stay down by the water tonight." He says, "Not me, I've got me a new shirt, and I don't want to get it dirty on the first night, I think I'll go get me a room." He said, "For twenty bucks, I can get a room with AC and a TV, this will at least keep me out of the rain that's coming tonight."

After a few minutes he says to us, "You cats take it easy and be careful," he then strolled on down the street. We looked at each other in amazement, I said, "Twenty bucks for a motel room here in Key West, that had to be some real thick cardboard right?" I sure had a good time with my Key West get up; it was always fun to just blend in with the locals. When my wife first seen Scoot on the dock one day, she asked me, "Who is that big woman out there on the dock, is she a new crewmember?" I laughed and said, "That's Scoot," just about that time he turned around towards us. She says, "I'm jealous; he has prettier hair than I do." You know who couldn't wait to tell that one, right.

As they say, all good things must come to an end, well so did our night out on the town. Earlier when we had went to town the gate was open, as we went back through the Naval Base gate that night, it now had some guards posted. They told us, "Since 9/11, without helmets and lights you cannot ride your bikes to your boat, you will have to push them." We only had about a half a mile to go to the boat, no big deal. All because a bunch of Arabs didn't like the American way of life, of which they had enjoyed for several years. With the belief those people have they better get used to being in a fire pit, because that is where they're heading.

Frankie's

Paranormal Experience

We had made several trips to Key West, where this one in particular comes to mind. The next picture was after we had sailed the tanker *Paul Buck*, and were following her out of the Key West channel. Frankie was renamed by his Cuban wife, his given name is Armelio. He told us that when he had came from Cuba, his wife started calling him Frank and it just stuck with him. We usually sailed these tankers midmorning, this job time was no different. Frankie was always on the Captains watch with me and had worked with him for quite a while; I could always expect something strange to come out of him at any time. Later that night when we were on the 18:00 to midnight watch, here we go.

We had departed that Wednesday morning July 10 2002, much more aware of our surroundings than we were used to being, since 9/11. We had been heading north for several hours when we both saw something in the sky several miles away, out towards the west. It actually looked like it was just hovering instead of moving like an airplane does crossing the sky.

At first, we both thought it might be a helicopter, with an enormously bright searchlight mounted underneath it. We were running about forty miles offshore, with the object in question maybe another ten miles farther out. When all of a sudden, this light that we had been looking at for a good ten minutes left its hovering stationary position, and just took off up into the sky. Neither one of us knew what to say until Frankie says, "Cappy, it's an alien, a flying saucer." I said, "No Frankie, it had to just be a fast helicopter with the way it took off, it was probably an optical illusion." He says, "No, it is paranormal." I had one radar on a twelve-mile range,

Chief Engineer "Frankie" Pavon
Author photo

and the other on a three mile range, with no targets on either one, I asked Frankie to keep a watch out for a couple minutes while I went downstairs to walk the dog, and to get something to drink.

When I came back to the wheel-house, I could hear Frankie giggling to himself. I said, "What's so funny Frankie?" He says, "I am sorry Cappy, I was going to joke you." I said, "Joke me, what are you talking about?" He said, "The flying saucer we just see, when you back, I am going to hide; maybe you think the aliens come and take me, yes?" I said, "Yep, that would've probably been my first thought Frankie, ET had came and took you away." We had a good laugh, knowing it had to have been man made. We made it back to Tampa and secured the *Hawk* at 11:45 the next day.

Key West Then on To Miami And Fort Lauderdale

Seven weeks later, the trip to paradise once again fell on our duty week. Although Scoot was running as a Mate on another boat, he loved going to Key West and would volunteer, even if he had to run as an engineer. For this trip, Buddy Watts ran as Mate, Frankie and Scoot ran as engineers, and James Fehrenbach was the deckhand. With having as much notice as we were given, a plan was made for the Jacque Cousteau twins.

Buddy and Scoot were both scuba divers, so before we had even left Tampa, they had reserved two spots on a dive boat for the afternoon of the docking. The trip down was once again beautiful, and uneventful. The docking went well and we were once again secure at the Navy dock, standing by. The Cousteau twins could hardly wait to go blow some bubbles, they took off like they were wearing red suits with lightning bolts on them. I watched the Key West TV channel, which is actually a commercial of some of the businesses that's on a loop, shown over, and over, and over again.

I suppose there aren't too many people that go to Key West to watch TV anyway. I was ready to go visit the Mel Fisher museum again; I had brought enough money for some more jewelry, and another one of those grouper fish sandwiches. As soon as the divers came back, spaceship Frankie and I took off walking. We didn't bring any transportation with us this time, because when we left Key West we would be going to Miami for a few days, from there we would go to Port Everglades for almost a month.

More on that later, but for now, Frankie and I were on a mission; he had broken his glasses and needed another pair. We decided to call a cab; he would know a place that sold reading glasses, and Walla, straight to a drug store. Only thing about it, after the glasses were bought and we were outside, neither of us knew which way to go. I said, "You know Frankie that cab ride wasn't bad, let's do it again."

This cab thing was a little pricy, but it sure saved a lot of walking down the wrong streets. Key West isn't that big until you start looking for a certain place. The second cabby took us right where we wanted to go, to another seafood street café. After our meal, we strolled down to the docks where the street performers really put on a show for you. There were probably a hundred little booths set up with all kinds of artists selling their wares; people were doing tumbling acts too. That was how many of these people made a living, selling their crafts or receiving donations for their performances.

The next day, we sailed the tanker *Paul Buck* and then off to Miami. The tugboat that has helped us each time in Key West was the *Dorothy Moran*, who came from Miami. While we were there this time, I finally asked them about a piece of rubber fendering mounted on their wheelhouse. The Captain told me, "When you get to Miami, you'll see some of the flairs we have to work around; you will see why this fender is where it is." I'd never been to the Miami harbor before, and was really looking forward to seeing some of the big container ships I had heard about.

Coastal Towing was one of the tug companies that provided harbor tug service in Miami, we had been asked to swing in there to help them out for a few days. Coastal Towing also had a Tractor tug that was down for some repairs, they still had contractual obligations to their customers, so you know who was contacted. You know how it is, their people talks to our people, favors are done, and where money is still the bottom line, plus, the Mighty *Hawk* just happened to be passing Miami on her way to Port Everglades.

We had already been served the potatoes by going to Key West, this little stop over was the gravy. We pulled into the dock where we had been told to and met up with one of the Coastal tugs to get the layout of the berths. Their Captain also gave me their procedure for dispatching the tugs. I had also put my hair hat on when he had come aboard with the papers for me. After a few minutes of him looking at me out of the corner of his eyes, I pulled my hat off, and said, "Man it's hot." He liked to have fell out, he says, "Man, I was thinking, you are one hairy looking Dude." I said, "Yeah, I know, I get the same response everywhere I go." He then went on with his briefing, but now could look me square in the face when he talked, I guess I shouldn't do that to people, oh well.

For departures in the Port of Tampa, a minimum of two hours is required for a tug order; mainly because of the geographical area the boats have to travel. The Port of Miami is nowhere close to having the distance a tug has to go between job berths. In Miami, the tugs aren't ordered until the Harbor Pilot gets aboard the ship, minutes before they sail. Also in Miami, after you finish a job, you just secure your boat to a dock that is clear.

Sometimes you were given less than ten minutes to start the boat and get to the job before they started dropping lines from the ship. I thought, surely a fellow ought to know if a tug would be needed to sail a ship before getting to it. I figured I was just visiting anyway, and could deal with it for the few days we'd be there. The port was fairly busy with the *Hawkster* having several jobs already logged. About the second day there, the manager for Coastal gave us a visit to the boat. With the normal small talk out of the way, I now hear a request that is hard for me to do.

Mr. Coastal man says to me, "I know you have quite a bit of horse-power; I just don't need you to flex your muscle while you're down here." I said, "Excuse me, flex my muscle?" He says, "Yeah, if you show these pilots what kind of power you've got, I'll have to start upgrading my equipment." He says, "I've already told my people if asked about your horsepower, tell them you have 3,000 hp."

I said, "3,000, I have more than that with just one engine." I said, "If one of these pilots tells me to come full ahead to push a ship around, I'm going to spin him like a top." I can tell you this, of all the ships that we assisted while we were in Miami, there was no complaints about not having enough power. The Pilots in Miami were also a pleasure to work with

Seabulk's main office in Port Everglades-Author photo

where we showed mutual respect. Our tour in Miami had also had our crew lightened by one crewmember, Scoot had been taken off the boat to go back to Tampa and work on the *Eagle II*. When we were released from the Miami vise, we headed for the Seabulk docks in Port Everglades. It took us less time to run up the coast there, than it does from Port Manatee to Tampa. The tug *Broward* is Seabulk's pride and joy, and was going to the shipyard for repairs, the tug *Hawk* would now be used as her replacement. Her Captain would be riding with us as a guide; we would also be able to meet some of the people that worked in the so-called Crystal Palace, the cooperate office for all of the Seabulk's divisions.

You always want to make a good first impression; this was one of those times. The first day I told the Captain that was riding with us, "I'm going to meet some of the folks in the office." He said, "You're not going up there like that are you, some of these people here aren't as liberal as maybe you're used to." I said, "I'll bet when they get dressed in the morning, they put one leg at a time in their pants, it'll be okay." I didn't think just because I had my hair hat, and funny glasses on, that I should not go

Me and Carroll with our fake hair-Author photo

in and meet everyone. I couldn't get Captain John to go with me, so I struck out on my own. As I stepped into the elevator with some of the folks that was coming back from lunch, I did get some looks. The elevators walls are all mirrors, I can see through the glasses but you can't see my eyes.

There were some of these proper looking folks giving me the once over too. I would be facing straight forward, but looking towards them with my eyes, when one of them looked towards me, I would jerk my head in their direction. They didn't want to get caught looking at me, and would immediately look the other way. I was definitely making that first impression that I was looking for. As the door opened, and while the first bunch made a fast get away, there were others waiting to go down.

I just eased off the elevator and introduced myself as the Captain off the tug *Hawk*. I said, "This is my first time here to the main office, I just wanted to take a tour, if it was possible." One fellow threw his hand in the air, like getting permission, and said, "I'll take him." I thought, cool, I got me a guide. We lit out with him giving me the VIP tour, we were about fifteen minutes into it when a lady turns a corner and comes towards us.

She points right at me and says, "You must be the Captain off the *Hawk*." I asked her, "Why, is the word out?" She said, "It is now, your presence is known." I thought, well good, mission accomplished. I had already pulled my glasses off and showed them both they were just funny glasses. When I jerked my hat off, and said again, "Man it's hot in here," they both started laughing. They said, "We thought your hair was real, quick, put it back on before someone sees you," they thought it was funnier than if it was real hair.

I spent a little while longer on tour and headed back to the boat to give my report to Captain John. When I got back to the boat, one of the welders was coming out of the engine room with Frankie. I introduced my self to him, and he says, "What happened to your eyes?" I pulled my glasses out of my pocket, and said, "You mean these, oh they're not real?" He says, "Man, when you walked by a while ago I told my Buddy, come here man quick, look at this guys eyes; they are screwed up." I said, "Well, my hair ain't real either, and pulled my hat off." He absolutely laughed so hard until tears come in his eyes. I said to him, "Y'all must not have anyone do stuff like this around here."

He said, "I think everyone is scared to try anything like that." I told him, "I will certainly see what I could do to bring a smile on people's faces for the time I was there." Mr. Kenny Rogers who was our Big Boss, came down to the boat one day for a welcome visit. I told him of my visit to the office, he laughed and said, "Yes, he heard." He said, "You were seen walking around on the dock the other day, and I was asked, who is that big longhaired guy?" I replied, "That's the Captain off the *Hawk*." He then asked me, "What've you got on that tug, a rock group?" He then told us of the hair hat that he himself had one time, and the fun he had with it.

We had a good talk with Mr. Rogers, with him telling us about the jobs that were being looked at for the big boats, most sounded intriguing. The harbor jobs went well for the week with all parties being well pleased. We were relieved on the next Wednesday by a fresh crew, and drove back to Tampa in a rental van. The trip home would also be another adventure with UFO Frankie.

Buddy, James, Frankie, and I were given petty cash for tolls and our dinner meal. We drove across the Alligator Alley being the chosen route home. We pulled into a Cracker Barrel restaurant to eat supper, a good choice I thought. Buddy and James were smokers and set away from me and Frankie. This particular meal ordering process should have been recorded.

After looking at the menu, I ordered, no problem. Frankie tried to order, problem, he wanted to order chicken fried steak. I told him what it was, but he kept saying, "No, I no want meat, I want chicken." I'd say, "But it's beef Frankie, it's just called chicken fried." He'd say, "Why they say chicken fried, if is no chicken, I no understand." I said, "I don't know Frankie, I didn't come up with the name, order you some chicken." But I want chicken fried steak, but no beef." This was going nowhere fast; I finally told the waiter, "Just bring him some cooked chicken, and to fry it."

Sometimes it was hard to get things across to my man Frankie; it was also funny to see his expressions when he realized the meaning, or translation of a long exhaustive explanation. We finally made it home okay, with a good bet of where Frankie, James, and I would be heading the next Wednesday.

SECOND TOUR IN
PORT EVERGLADES

Just like clockwork, next Wednesday came, and we were heading for the east coast. I didn't mind running the interstate, but driving through the woods and going through the little towns just made the four hour drive more enjoyable. We could also stop and eat lunch at a little Cuban restaurant Frankie had told us about.

One thing about crew changing in Fort Lauderdale it took the whole day, between the crew coming on duty, and the crew going home. It was always good to get to the boat and get settled in, and didn't matter if there were any jobs to do or not. With the many years I had been running the boats at this point, I felt completely at ease, and was comfortable doing any job that came my way.

The Port Everglades gig was a tug boater's dream job. I could idle the *Hawk* to anywhere in that port in less than twelve minutes. In Tampa Bay, sometimes it could take two hours running time, just to get to a job. After being there at the Seabulk docks for a few days, I could also see a big difference between the Tampa Bay Towing tugs, and the Port Everglades Towing tugs. These guys even had satellite dishes on the docks for their TV's, at each of their tie up spots. I thought to myself, maybe this is equality as they see it, besides, the other divisions really shouldn't expect to have all the little perks as the Crystal Palace boats had, we were all just stepchildren anyway. Most divisions were only part of this huge Maritime Corporation from the acquisitions of companies that were already established within the marine industry.

Some of the fellows that were working in Port Everglades had actually worked for the founder of Hvide Marine, which is the original company's name, they really did deserve it. Their name had been changed after filing bankruptcy. This would probably be our last trip down south anyway, unless another rescue job came up, which was very likely since the *Hawk* class boats were used as multi-purpose tugboats.

What Direction Are We Heading at Seabulk?

Throughout the Seabulk years, there were decisions made by the management in Fort Lauderdale that to the working man, made no sense. One comes to mind that made me as a concerned employee, write a letter to Mr. Kenny M. Rogers, President of Seabulk Towing Inc., and ask some inquisitive questions. We had some visitors come down to the docks one day in Tampa back in the latter months of 2003, which always got the rumor mill going.

It seemed if someone came down to inspect the boats, they were for sale, automatically. These fellows turned out to be representatives of Sea River/ Exxon from California. They had their eyes on a *Hawk* class boat for a long-term bareboat charter, as the *Condor's* charter had been which was ending soon. I just couldn't see how a company could just come in and bareboat charter another one of our boats, no matter how big they were. After hearing that the tug *Hawk* was probably on her way to the West Coast, I then sat down, collected my thoughts, and wrote the following answer searching letter, sending it to the main office in Port Everglades.

Kenny,

You once told us in the crew room, okay fellows here it is, we are a **TEAM**, and I will be truthful with you when I talk to you. Bareboat chartering the *Condor* was a mistake, and we *will not* bareboat anymore of our boats. I will always be straightforward with you guys, and will always answer any questions I am asked, to the best of my ability. I am always a telephone call away, and if you have a concern you wish to discuss, my door is always open. Ever since Seabulk bought the company from Bay Transportation Corporation, Seabulk has done a remarkable job of dismantling what was once the most up to date technological state of the art harbor tug company in the Gulf of Mexico, and maybe even the country. After the acquisition of Bay Transportation, the number of vessels sailing under the Seabulk, or Hvide flags, was around 287, and today the number is around 184. We understand the sale of some of the vessels had to be done in order for the company to come out of bankruptcy. It just seems in all of towing's division of 30 tugs, Tampa is the port that has had more boats cut from their fleet than any other port, despite the volume of traffic into the port, and the extra running time to and jobs because of the geographical area the Tampa tugs have to travel. I have worked in Port Everglades with the tug *Hawk*, and can idle to the farthermost berth in about 12 minutes. We as employees of Seabulk Towing of Tampa just want to know, when will it end, and will there be a job to come to in the future?

Although we are asked to keep doing the professional job of ship docking assistance, we are having our tools, the tugboats, taken from us. We as employees in Tampa, wonder why the other ports aren't getting the same treatment? Why after years of building up the strongest tugboat fleet in the Gulf, which must have been what drew Hvide Marine's interest into buying the company, is allowed to be torn apart? We realize that towing is a small percentage of the company overall, but *it is 100%* of our world, and somewhere downsizing has to stop before there are no more tugboats to send away in Tampa. It would also build moral instead of what seems to be a continuing effort in the company of not keeping the men informed in what direction the company is going. If we had more meetings, and let us as Seabulk employees know what is going on with the company, instead of noninformitive speculation, which does no one any good, after all, we are part of the **TEAM**.

Signed—*Captain William C. Alligood*

A couple of days after I had mailed the letter Mr. Rogers called me, where we then had a good talk about my concerns. He told me, "Sea

River/ Exxon puts a very large amount of money into our account every month, we have to do what we can to keep certain wheels in motion." Although Mr. Rogers was the President of the entire towing division, he said his hands were also tied.

It appeared to me it really doesn't matter what position you hold, there will always be someone with an agenda, seemingly known only to that person. I was commended for the letter and my interest as an employee. I come away with that old saying ringing in my head; *money talks, and bull stuff walks.* As it turned out, the *Eagle II* was chosen over the *Hawk*, probably because of the lifting crane mounted on her stern.

They say money will bring you happiness, which might be true with the money holder. However, when the almighty dollar is used to obtain something that someone else holds dear, as I did with our tugs; money then becomes the source of that persons sorrow. It seems Big Business does, as Big Business wants, no matter who is affected or who is hurt in the process.

THE RESCUE OF THE

Chemical Explorer

I like to watch football on TV, especially the pinnacle of football, the Super Bowl. The year of 2004 was not starting out good for the home team. At 22:00 on Saturday night January 31, just twenty hours away from kickoff of the biggest football game of the year, we were told to load some gear for a rescue tow. The chemical tanker *Chemical Explorer* had broken down and had requested tug assistance; Rescue-R-Us was off again.

Some could, some could not, the tug *Hawk* could, and did. We departed at 00:01 on February 1 and headed south for the location of this ship. Plotted miles were almost 200 miles, with an estimated ETA of around 18:00. Figuring this ship was close to the Gulf Stream, which would be causing the ship to drift towards the east, I altered my course about mid afternoon to compensate for that. Good move, we arrived to her present location, almost 30 miles east of the position we had been given twenty hours earlier.

The tanker was dead in the water and didn't even have the use of her bow winches to pull my towing gear up onto her bow. This one required some creative thinking on my part, since the ships crew was unable to lift my towing gear even a foot off the deck. I positioned the *Hawk* on the bow of the tanker facing towards her stern. I then ran a line from my bow winch up through a chock on their starboard bow, and had their crew send it back down through the chock that I would be towing the ship from.

My crew had then shackled the two lines together; this allowed me to pull my towing gear up using the line from my bow winch. When I had pulled the line far enough up onto the ship, the crew tied it off with a stop line and made the towline fast on a bitt. Releasing my bow line, I could now retrieve it back aboard, we were made up to the ship and ready to head for the Tampa sea buoy. We were underway at 20:00 with our latest mission, we still didn't have TV reception, but at least the Super Bowl was on for the dock people.

I had called our office with our ETA for the Tampa sea buoy, and was told that the transit would be daylight only. With me knowing that I couldn't arrive any earlier, and before the cutoff time of entering the channel, I adjusted my speed. I now had just over thirty-three hours to make it to the sea buoy, at that amount of time we only had to make a speed of just over six knots. This ship was towing like another ship I had towed in the past,

Towing the *Dolsie* into Tampa-Author photo

the freighter *Dolsie*. The only difference between the *Chemical Explorer*, and the *Dolsie*, was the *Dolsie* stayed just on our port side.

The *Chemical Explorer* did her name proud; she explored both sides of our track line. Just like in this picture, but all the way to the starboard side as well. I had called the people on the ship during the daylight and asked if they were steering the ship. He said, "No, why do you ask?" I said, "Well, all night and all day so far, your ship seems to be going back and forth for some reason, I just can't quite put my finger on it." I told him, "It looked like a man that's walking his dog down a sidewalk, and the dog can't decide which side to squat on." He laughed at that one and said, "Yes, they had noticed it too." He then said, "We'll back you with any change you want to make; we'll be right behind you all the way." I told him, "Okay, and by the way, that was a good play on words too." I figured that since the seas were almost calm, and we were already running at a reduced speed, there was nothing else we could do anyway.

I kept adjusting my speed to arrive at the sea buoy for a 06:00 start in. Upon arriving I shortened up my towline and was told to proceed in. Two more harbor tugs met us out at the sea buoy for the transit up the channel, especially after the way she had been towing. We towed the ship all the way up the channel to just off their dock in East Bay. At the appropriate time, we retrieved our tow gear and were then released from this job completely; the other two tugs would only have to push her into the dock while their lines were secured.

Although we didn't have to, we all agreed to undock another ship before going home. Anytime a boat came back from an offshore trip, they had a twelve hour time period that allowed them to go home after securing their tug. We were told if we did this job, we could stay home for the remainder of the shift. That offer was like a no-brainer, so I said yes for the whole crew and done the job.

Mad Dog Spar in

Pascagoula, Mississippi

The title to this next story might sound like a rabid canine in the Deep South. It is actually the tow out of the base of an offshore spar drill rig. These oilrigs which come in several assorted sizes with all different types of designs are really distinguished by their names. This particular spar was called *Mad Dog*, and another offshore job just eight short days after we had towed the *Chemical Explorer* into Tampa.

My crew was David Storch as Mate, Frank Pavon, and Doug Bogard

***Mad Dog* spar in Pascagoula**
Author photo

were the engineers, with Juan Rosario, and Guthrie Crouch as deckhands. We departed 09:10 on February 11 2004, three days before my 35th wedding anniversary. We arrived 18:50 on the 12th, secured the tug and were told to standby. It was fairly cool and raining with a brisk breeze blowing out of the north, not ideal conditions for a tow out. We were told it might be a few

days before the spar could leave due to weather. This didn't surprise me at all, I had never seen one go on time yet, weather related or not. Eating, cards, and TV are consumers of time; we had an abundance of all three. The weather didn't really allow us to do any deck maintenance, but didn't slow the activity that went on in the galley, and eat we did.

It was always good to get a job started that you were sent to do. The tugs *Kelly Candies*, and *Devin Candies* both had 10,000 hp, and would be towing the spar out the channel, and then on to her drilling location. During our operations meeting, we were told we would be the picket boat until the spar had cleared the south end of the safety fairway. Three and a half days of standing by, and this operation was now getting started.

At 10:00 on February 16, this *Mad Dog* was pulled off the dock and departed Mississippi. The *Hawk* was made up to the spar right in the middle of the stern to push while the other harbor tugs pushed on either side of us. We even had some smaller tugs that just seemed to run along with us for moral support. There seemed to always be plenty of horsepower lined up for these types of jobs. It also seemed the farther out the channel we went, the more boats we lost. One after the other was released, until it was just the two big tugs towing this dog, and the Mighty *Hawk*. When our line was released just before dark, I was told to ease along with them until probably daylight. Somebody had it figured pretty close because at 06:30 the next morning, the *Hawk* was released from picket duty and told to go back into Pascagoula.

They needed to remove the positioning electronics that were installed when we had arrived, before heading to Tampa. The trips in for removing these same electronics would be a nightmare, a few months later. Around 08:00 I had called the electronics technician by satellite phone; this very expensive equipment owned by his company was originally installed by them, and would also be removed by them. That stuff looked like it went on the space shuttle; I was certainly not going to mess with it. We were secure by 12:20; but there was no sign of the fellows that we were going to unload this stuff on. Me and Doug had been on enough of these offshore trips by now that just one more day to us, meant one more day of pay.

The extra days added to your check really looked good, and that was the main reason that I didn't mind making these trips. On the other hand, there were those among us that seemed to go into withdrawals when we didn't leave on the planned date. It was somewhat funny to watch these younger guys, with some of the excuses they would come up with as to why they needed to be at home. I need to take my dog to the vet, my cousin's getting married, and my all time favorite, well they said we'd only be gone for X amount of time, "Never listen to what they," I'd say.

I would tell them, "Go to the Highway Patrol station and get a drivers handbook and study for a CDL, then go drive a truck, that way you could be at home." I had learned to never count on being back when you were told you would be. Things would change at the drop of a hat; I saw the hat drop on this one. Old sparky and his helper were almost six hours late, and didn't show up until 18:00 (6 pm).

They took less than thirty minutes to get their toys off the boat, and were gone. While the techs were doing their thing I had Frankie start the main engines, so when they were gone, we would be too. Thirty-two hours later we had once again done our job, we'd gone offshore and made the company some money. After all, without us fellows on the tugboats doing the jobs we did, there wouldn't be a company for them to work at. Admittedly, every company needs someone to sit behind a desk and hold a chair down, our company had that covered with some real chair-holding experts. I also think that the working employees are the real moneymakers anyway. The offshore crews should be commended when they complete a job safely and professionally that most shied away from doing. We were back home and secured at 02:40 on February 18 2004, what would be next on the agenda for the Mighty tug *Hawk*.

Towing The *Cape St. John* to Beaumont, Texas

It didn't take long; just over a month later and the *Hawk* was elected for a Naval adventure, since the *Condor* was still being restored from her New York charter. We were going to tow a dead Navy ship from Tampa, Florida, through Port Arthur, Texas, to the Naval Readiness Fleet in Beaumont, Texas. This sounded like an interesting job; I had never been there before and would also get to see some more of the tugs owned by Seabulk that worked the Port Arthur harbor.

This trip also had a sense of urgency to it too. We had to have this ship towed across the Gulf of Mexico, secured in Beaumont, take on fuel, and have the tug in Corpus Christi, Texas before a certain date for a Heerema job. Departing on March 26 and having to be in Corpus by April 1 didn't give much leeway for any problems. We had heard that our arrival date to Corpus Christi was so critical; Heerema was paying for part of the fuel on the Navy tow.

We were rigged and ready to go on the morning of March 26. The weather was really my only concern and with favorable weather reports, it was evident my God was going to ride across with us. We departed at 09:40 towing with tug assistance from the tugs *Canaveral*, and *Tampa*. She seemed to be towing fairly straight behind us, so the Pilot Captain Timmel, released both tugs.

This trip across was just as you see in those Navy recruiting brochures. The smooth sailing was what I had ordered when I prayed, and smooth sailing was what we received. It took us eighty-four hours to reach the Sabine Pass sea buoy, and that was with me adjusting our speed to run slower and arrive later. Reason being, I was told this would be another daylight transit only, and after transiting the Sabine Pass channel I could see why. This order had been relayed to us a day earlier, and even with all the slowing down speed adjustments we had made, it wasn't slow enough.

We had still arrived at 21:00 on the March 29, so we just idled east to west in the safety fairway until the next morning. Even with a Navy ship over six hundred feet long, and having our towline to an acceptable length, we still had adequate room for maneuvering. A safety fairway is like a highway for all waterborne vessels. They are also two miles wide where there are no oilrigs or any other stationary structure being allowed inside their perimeters. With us having to be in Corpus for the Heerema job on April 1, I certainly didn't want to deal with any delays. At 06:00 when I came on watch, I heard the word fog.

The Seabulk tugs that were coming to assist us with transiting this snake of a channel were in zero visibility fog. They had reported that they were pushed up on a bank waiting on the fog to clear and safe to move. This reason for a delay I didn't want to hear, I had seen fog last for days, but had also seen the sun burn it off fairly fast.

If we had to wait just one day before being allowed to transit the channel, it would make me late for getting to Corpus Christi. Well that didn't happen, at 07:40, I was told to start heading towards the channel, the fog that was inland was lifting to where the tugs could navigate. Thirty-minutes later, two harbor Pilots climbed aboard the *Hawk*, and one Pilot went aboard the ship, with the two-assist tugs not far behind. There was no turning back now, you couldn't just stop with a ship under tow, at least not until the harbor tugs had a line up.

The Senior Pilot gave me a heading, and said, "Just keep her on the ranges." I said, "What ranges, I don't see them?" After he pointed them out to me, I said, "Are you kidding me?" The ranges are designed to keep a vessel in the middle of a channel, and should be easily seen. You had better know where to look; some of them looked just like a path had been cut out in the woods so the range towers were visible.

Right off the bat a shrimp boat was coming towards us, I asked the

Pilot, "Do you want me call this guy, or are you?" He says, "Maybe he'll move, we'll see." This shrimper was lining up to pass us on our starboard side, but then he changed his mind. He was within five-hundred feet of us and cut across my bow to now pass on our port side. I asked the Pilot in a loud voice, "Do you see what this idiot's doing?" He said, "Yeah I do, run over him if you can." He says, "I'm surprised he didn't go back to our starboard side." I told him, "I'm sorry Partner, but where I come from, that's a close call." He assured me, "That was nothing, most of these guys are from Viet Nam and don't even understand English." He says, "When you do try to get them on the radio, there's hardly ever a response from them."

He said, "They have been reported numerous times, I reckon that since our Government bought the shrimp boats for them, they just figure they can do as they please." He went on to tell me that it would be about six hours to transit the channel to where this ship was going, and we'd probably encounter a lot more shrimpers. I thought to myself, I guess I'll start worrying when he does. The farther we went inland, the more I could appreciate what these very skilled Harbor Pilots dealt with on a daily basis.

You could tell the Senior Pilot had been doing this for years with just the way he said things. He was a true Texan, and bragged about the tonnage of ships that came into Port Arthur. I asked him, "Is it mandatory for a Texan to brag?" He just laughed and said, "When you handle the size ships we do here, and do it with the older equipment instead of these high tech boats that are now being built, it ain't bragging son." He then asked me about several of the older Tampa Bay Pilots, saying he knew them from when he sailed on tankers into Tampa.

He asked me how they liked these high tech tugboats. I said, "Does the word spoiled mean anything?" I said, "There are some of the Pilots that are happy with whatever boats are sent them, and never complain. However, there are also some that act like being sent a single screw boat, or one too big, or one too small, is like a slap in the face." I said, "There was even one time that the tug *Tampa* was turned down on a job, and she has 6,000 hp, twin screw with flanking rudders," of course that was one of the Pilots that showed favoritism towards our competition. I said,

"There was never satisfying those particular Pilots, it was blatantly obvious at how they went out of their way to accommodate them." He said, "A sign of a true Pilot is someone that can do the job with whatever they have to work with." I could not agree more with that statement, he must have also been a carpenter because he hit the nail right on the head.

We were bound for the Naval Readiness Fleet in Beaumont, Texas. With two tugs finally made up to the ship, if need be, we could now stop. There were these little river boats everywhere, pushing all types of barges, inbound and outbound. I just hoped I could find my way out of there when nightfall came. Mr. Pilot was right about how long the transit would take, by the time we had followed this winding channel it was right at six hours. We entered to what looked like a huge basin where there were dozens of old Navy ships. Some were anchored alone, but most were breasted alongside one another in various groupings. It was an awesome site to see some of these ships; I just knew some had to have seen some war duty. The Pilot told us those ships could be ready to deploy in a matter of weeks, and that was getting crews aboard too.

I reeled all my tow cable in and just waited until the two harbor tugs had the *Cape St. Johns* pinned alongside the group of ships she would be moored alongside. This process was done fairly rapidly by a bunch of men the tugs had put aboard the ship earlier in the day. After we were released from the ship, Mr. Pilot asked if he could sit behind the controls, I said, "Sure, but let me get where you have plenty of room to maneuver." You know how sometimes when someone can hardly wait to play with a new toy, then find out they really didn't want it and can't wait to give it back?

Well this happened to be one of those times, after he started spinning those controls making the boat spin too, he said, "Here take this thing, there's just too many moving parts for me." We laughed, and I told him, "You're just used to the older tugboats." I told him, "The secret is to never forget how we all got here, and where we came from." I hopped into the seat and did a little showing off with some maneuvers that impressed him. He says, "Now that's impressive, but when it's all said and done we just dock ships, and you don't need technology for that."

It took us two hours to retrieve all our gear with the help of a crane barge, and another hour to get to the Seabulk dock to offload it. After we had secured the boat at the R&R dock, it was time to get all of the towing gear off the boat. We sure didn't want 270 feet of chain bridles, 600 feet of emergency line, and anything else we could leave on pallets for shipment by truck back to Tampa, left on the boat. With fuel already set up for us we now had to find the barge where we were to get our fuel. It was now dark time too, which made reading markers more difficult. While going out the channel with these little boats passing closer than I liked, I heard my name over the radio.

I said, "This is the *Hawk*, come back." Lo and behold, our Texas Pilot was on an outbound ship, he directed me right to the barge where our fueling fellows were waiting on us.

Thank you Lord, we were finally secure at 20:25 and hooking up the hoses. Fueling went on until 23:00, when we were through I was too tired to head for Corpus Christi and decided to wait until morning to head out. I had already figured it would take less than twenty hours to get there from our present location. A good night's sleep would not make anyone mad, and we were also okayed by the tankerman to stay as long as we needed.

March 31 at 06:30 sure came quick; I knew we were supposed to be at the *Holstein* location by 08:00 on April 1. Departing at this time of the morning gave us about five hours to play with. As I went out the Sabine Pass channel I created a route with our Nobletec plotter. I had figured that if we maintained our present speed, we would be tied up by 03:00 the next morning. We also ran to Corpus Christi following the Texas coast running in the safety fairways. With us passing the entrance to most of the major Texas seaports south of Port Arthur, we saw a tremendous amount of marine traffic.

It seemed like there would be a lot more accidents with as many tug/barge units, and ships passing so close to each other. However, with safety being first and more awareness of where your own vessel is, marine collisions were down from years past. I always stress that point to my crews, be vigilant of your present surroundings, you never know when it might pay off when a surprise pounces out at you.

THE *Holstein* SPAR
FROM CORPUS CHRISTI

I'm pretty sure the explorer Christopher Columbus would have liked to have had the electronics that we have to work with nowadays. We arrived at the Gulf Marine Fabricators yard and were secure at 03:15 on April 1, four hours and forty-five minutes ahead of our scheduled report time. I thought to myself, that's cutting it pretty close, but we had arrived there at least by the appointed time, I could also be put on the clock. We had received word from Tampa that the tug *Condor* had not even left yet. I ain't no genius, but I did know it takes three days to come across the Gulf. I also knew that at this point we had at least three days to standby, the tug *Harvey War Horse* was the lead tug for this project and had not arrived either. She was to be the lead tug towing alongside the Candies twins, the towing group for the entire trip.

Just looking at the size of this spar, I knew there was going to be an enormous amount of horsepower involved with this project. The four white fairleads shown in the picture are four of sixteen, and will have anchor chains fed through them that were installed a year earlier which were already fastened to the floor of the Gulf, awaiting the *Holstein's* arrival. These chains will be fed through them and then fastened to winches on top of the spar; this is done with the ROV (Remote Oper-

Top side of the *Holstein* spar-largest worldwide-Author photo

ated Vehicle). This project was like all others we had been on before; it had been in the stage of planning for quite a while to make sure everything went well. After a few days, all the tugboats had finally showed up, we could then have the project meeting that explains the tow out plan.

These meetings were mandatory, and were also a meeting of the minds. It lets everyone at all levels know what is expected of them during the tow out. During these meetings is also the time to ask questions, about any doubts you might have with any kinds of maneuvers you are expected to perform. It also covers all contingency plans, just in case one is needed. Sometimes that plan "B" is called upon, this has happened in the past with other offshore drill rig projects.

I was amazed at the combined horsepower from all of the tugs that had been assembled just for this one job.

Harvey War Horse————16,500 hp—Lead tug center towing
Devin Candies————10,000 hp—Starboard side towing
Kelly Candies————10,000 hp—Port side towing
Condor————6,700 hp—-Starboard side pushing
Hawk————6,700 hp—-Port side pushing

Total of the main tugs 49,900 hp

That was the list of the main tugs and their horsepower. There were also several smaller tugs that would be placed in different positions on the spar for just the undocking, ranging from 1,000 hp to 4,000 hp. All toll, well over 60,000 hp was going to be working in unison to get one goal accomplished, and that was to get this two-billion dollar hole puncher into deep water. I was also told during the mandatory meeting that the *Hawk* would be going with the spar to the Green Canyon 645 drill site.

A high-level company representative from BP-Shell had told us, "Fellows, we are intrusting this very expensive piece of equipment to you, take care of her." This spar at the time was said to be the largest in the world, and had a two-billion dollar price tag on it. That was for the construction and everything in between. Which also included the transporting of it to the location where this modern marvel would be secured. The *Holstein* spar was 750 feet long, by 150 feet wide, and had a draft of 34 feet, and that was lying on her side. She would be held in place by sixteen anchors and chains in 4,300 feet of water. That meant that from the bottom of the spar to the sea floor there would be about 3,600 feet of nothing but water, and the sixteen mooring chains securing her.

When the drill crews started punching holes in the ground, there would also be the drill stems. With me being told that the *Hawk* would be the picket boat, I now had to get charts for the Port of Fourchon. That was where we would go into so the electronics could be removed, but not until after the spar was on location and we were released from the offshore part of the job. One of my crewmembers had rented a car so he could go into town and run errands as needed, well we needed. I told him that a cab would have cost the company a fortune, and since we used his car to run around to locate the charts, groceries, and supplies for both boats, I would split the cost of his rented car with the *Condor*, which was also agreed on by the tug *Condors* Captain.

There were numerous times we needed a car for the six days that we stood by waiting on the big move. Remember the management that I had alluded to earlier, their thinking was that you should have everything you need before you depart on an offshore trip. We had already been away from Tampa for more than a week and the ETD (Estimated Time of Departure) had yet to be made. Some supplies do not last forever as some thought they do, go figure.

We had some beautiful weather towing the *Cape St. John* to Beaumont, which meant all six men were eating three meals a day, and had been for ten days now. I have always thought management should make at least one offshore trip, you know, just to experience the job, and see what we as seamen do on the boats. Some of the decisions made and the policies that were put in place were very questionable. It was evident during this period of my career that some of our management, not having worked aboard tugboats didn't even have a clue as to what goes on offshore, and never would. At any rate, we now had the needed charts for Port Fourchon and were ready to get this show on the road.

The big day had finally arrived, and with everyone on the same page the slow-moving operations commenced. Frankie had been relieved by Harold Perkins as the Chief Engineer for the remainder of this trip, getting off the boat in Corpus Christi was a good move for Frankie as it turned out, you'll see what I mean later during this particular venture.

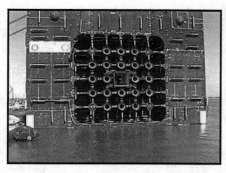

Bottom side of the *Holstein Spar*, 150 feet wide-Author photo

You can see the twenty holes that the drill stem will come through for each well drilled.

The white bars are zincs, and appear to be about six feet long. The machinery is grounded to the vessel and then through the water it has around it, so when the electrolysis in the water comes in contact with the spar, the zinc bars will deteriorate first before any damage can be done to the other metals. We were told there are enough zincs installed all over the spar that will last for the next seventy-five years, that's probably longer than the amount of oil that will

James, Dave, Me, and Mr. harbor Pilot-Author photo

be left in the ground by then. The two white painted areas at the water line on each outboard side of the spar was where the tugs *Condor* and *Hawk* were made up to push for the tow out. This would also be the view that we would have to look at for five full days. With all the tugs made up to their respective positions, and the Pilots aboard their respective tugs, we departed the berth with the spar at 10:40 on April 7 2004. Over six days after we had arrived, we were finally outbound Corpus Christi ship channel. The helicopters were flying and the cameras were rolling. Some of my crew had grown a little antsy and had already started with their homesick stories. Knowing this was going to be a long haul, I would just say, "CDL tests are given at the Highway Patrol stations everyday, go get one when we get back, but until then, roll with the flow boys." Mother Nature's outlook for the next few days was most favorable, so I said, "Let's enjoy it while we can, it will not last forever."

We had a Harbor Pilot aboard us, and one aboard one of the towing tugs. The distance between them and us was right at a thousand feet. I asked the Pilot if he knew how these spars could be set in such deep water, and drill holes in the ground with such accuracy. He said, "I guarantee there's as much technology that goes into offshore oil exploration as there is at NASA."

He says, "Think about it, this spar will be secured in 4,300 feet of water and drill twenty wells, most going in at different angles to hit the targeted pockets of oil or natural gas." "Yep, that's some high tech work alright, and done by some awfully smart folks," I told him. This project was not for beginners in offshore drilling either, from just the cost of the rigs alone, not including the operating costs. The maximum speed that this spar could be towed was pre set by the owner and the insurance carrier, and would be a blistering four knots per hour. A nautical mile is 6,080 feet, where a statute mile is 5,280 feet. No matter how you sliced it, thin or thick, this was definitely going to be several long days of monotonous trailing we had to look forward to.

The *Holstein spar* outbound Corpus Christi ship channel
Courtesy of Willem van Woercom

All along the route there were people trying to get a look at this very large object that was coming down the channel; they had their cameras working overtime. With these sightseers probably living in the Corpus Christi area, they knew that these big rigs went out, and usually never came back. If they were going to have pictures to look back on this event, now was the time. Although our speed limit was four knots, it wasn't fast enough for the *Hawks* idle speed of six and a half knots. After our release, I would have to figure the best way to tame the *Hawk* down to run that slow. Mr. Pilot disembarked the *Hawk* right at 14:00 and was released from the spar at 14:30. The *Condor* was released from the job completely and was told to head for Tampa.

I was told what we already knew, run along as the picket boat. The Lord blessed us with the best weather I had seen in a long time. I had said before, "If everyday was calm like it was those days in the Gulf of Mexico, there would a lot more people going on these offshore trips." The mere thought of rough seas made a lot of the men start squirming, especially when the office would just mention their names for an offshore job, it was always interesting to see their reactions. My last few years working; there were only a few people that made the majority of the offshore trips.

I had never gotten seasick on one, but I had been where I didn't want to eat. Not wanting to press my luck I would just eat fruit and crackers, more or less the foods that set easy on your stomach. At the present time we were eating anything we wanted. We even used the charcoal grill out on the back deck, and the deck was dry. Usually when you were offshore,

Common site of *Hawk's* deck offshore-Author photo

the deck looked like it does in the wet deck picture. You can now see why I said, "And the deck was dry," that didn't happen on every trip. Even though it was calm, and the salt mist wasn't coming on our decks, I still couldn't have the crew do any deck work like chipping or painting due to always having three men off watch and trying to sleep. I had been on trips before when we would burn well over forty-five hundred gallons of fuel per day. Just before midnight we would be called to give Willem our fuel reports, this was done every night. Willem was aboard the tug *Devin Candies*, and was also the tow master for this entire project. The *Hawk* had a fuel capacity of 95,000 gallons, but I had never taken on more than 85,000 for any job.

When the tug *Harvey War Horse* called in his fuel report, he gave his fuel usage for the day, and then said, "We have 210,425 gallons left aboard."

My chin like to have hit the floor, I looked at my engineer who had big eyes too. I said, "Now that's a lot of fuel, I thought we carried a lot." The three tugs that were towing this spar were designed and built to do what they were doing, towing anything large. The *Hawk* on the other hand, was designed for escort service on hazardous cargo vessels transiting in narrow areas. However, the very first time that Heerema used the *Hawk* class boats for one of these tow outs, they were called on for repeat work on almost every Heerema oilrig job after that.

Willem just loved the way the *Hawk* class boats maneuvered; they also had plenty of power to boot. I had been on several big projects with Willem as the tow master; he is also the man that tells everyone what to do and is responsible for the entire project. I'm sure his stress level was high enough at times to be orbiting with the space station.

This was definitely going to be a slow go with this picket boat duty, we were really there just in case we were needed. If one of the towing tugs would have a mechanical problem, we would take their place. We would run all around the spar several times a day, looking for anything out of the ordinary.

With us having been on the *Mad Dog* spar, we had been the picket

A most glorious sun rise on the *Holstein* tow-Author photo

boat for just one night. With this large unit, we would have plenty of time to eyeball this modern marvel over the next few days. The morning of April the 8th was the middle of spring, and was the beginning of what would turn out to be some of the most beautiful sunrises we would see. This picture was on the very first morning of the tow. I can only thank the Lord for a view that will not soon be forgotten. The only way to appreciate Nature in all her glory is to be in the right place when the scenery presented itself. Being in the middle of the Gulf of Mexico seemed to be that place, on this morning anyway. The electronics that were installed aboard the *Hawk* showed where all of the tugs were at all times in relation to the spar.

The *Holstein* had electronics mounted on her top side too; they were also capable of telling how many degrees the spar was leaning, one way or the other. We were observing the maximum speed limit quite well, and every time we obtained the speed of four knots, we thought we were cutting up. Our average speed was 2.5 to 4.0 knots per hour, and for the land lovers that aren't used to going at this snails pace except on a grid-locked highway, you should really try it sometime. We weren't knocking any fish out of the water at this speed but we were heading east, and that was at least slow progress. I took pictures of the spar and this towing trio of the Big Boys. This next picture shows what is done in order to get one of

Kelly Candies, Harvey War Horse, Devin Candies-Author photo

these very large offshore drill rigs to their location. With the combined horsepower of over 36,000, it was an awesome sight to see. The Candies twins were sister boats with identical machinery, and were also equipped with Azimuthing drives like the *Hawk* had. But they also had a center engine with a fixed propeller, made just for long straight tows like we were on. Mr. *War Horse* on the other hand, was just pure brute power, with a crew of Cajuns aboard; I would have loved to sit at their table for a meal.

I had eaten many a meal prepared with the Cajun style, south Louisiana cuisine is like no other in the country, which can also has some heat in it too. Whenever I cooked a meal on the boat, I couldn't add the heat spices to the cook pot because of certain babies complaining of the pepper. They sure would've missed out on some good eating if they were aboard the Harvey tug. Of course, you could tell we hadn't missed any meals, and wouldn't as long as the weather stayed this pretty.

Having been where the weather could turn on you like an uncaged lion. With it being springtime, what happened in the next couple of days was no surprise and would also be winter like. We had already passed a lot of offshore drill rigs that were working. The deeper the water, the more complex the drill rigs had became. They have evolved to these deep-water spars like shown here. This is also what the *Holstein* spar would look like after the drilling module was installed and operational.

A working offshore spar drill rig-Author photo

These rigs were the latest in technology that the offshore industry had to offer, I couldn't imagine what was to follow. The deep-water rigs were also designed to take everything that Mother Nature would throw at them, within reason. Of course, that's when they were up righted, and secured to their mooring pilings on the bottom of the ocean floor. In the eight short years that I had been going offshore in the oil patch, the different oilrigs had changed dramatically.

The very first offshore jacket project that I was involved in, was set in around 900 feet of water. We were now heading to a location where 4,300 feet was now a normal depth. When the *Holstein* is running at peak production, their production will be more than an amazing 100,000 barrels of oil, and 90 million standard cubit feet of natural gas daily.

After three and a half days we now heard of some foul weather heading our way. Willem told all the boats we would be slowing down because they didn't want to get to the *Holstein* site too soon. The *DCV Baldor* was already there, and would play a big part in the setting up operations on the spar. On Sunday morning, the freak front was hitting us pretty hard. Coincidently, the rain was coming down so hard just about the time the *Kelly Candies* lost one of her generators. Willem called, and said for us to come over quickly, get in front of them in case we were needed. Their electrical system has an automatic switchover, and was set up that when a generator shut down abnormally, the other generator would automatically start up, which it did.

They were back on line before we could even get close to them, I thought man that's cool, I want one of those systems too. I still hung close to them just in case, running just off their port side, at least until the rain had let up some. Some of my Indians had grown restless the previous day, and suddenly had things back home to do. I told them, "Yes, you do, but not at home, we are following this spar." I would tell them, "You guys need to find another line of work if a few days offshore can get you out of sync this bad."

I said, "What about being on one of the tugs towing this rig, long after we're released, they'll be out here until the whole operation is finished." I'd say, "Just think about it boys, we're only three plus days out with a bunch of days to go," that'd light 'em up just like a shuttle taking

Drilling module after being set by *Heerema's Thialf*
Courtesy of Heerema Marine Contractors

off from the launch pad. After the rain had passed I thought to myself;

that was a front very reminiscent to the winter cold fronts. It was also giving my little Indians something to do, holding on.

We had also slowed down to an average speed of 1.1 to 2.5 knots. The spar was being towed at that speed, but with seas building as time went on, I quit following it. I started to tack with the seas, trying to keep from getting thrown around like I knew would happen otherwise. We would run ahead of them a few miles, turn around and run the other direction right into the seas, just like we had done on my first trip with Brother Dave several years earlier. There are times throughout the years working in rough waters that you are glad to have them behind you, experiencing them again brought back bad memories. We had heard that Heerema was going to be bringing in the *DCV Thialf* all the way from Africa, just to set the drilling module atop of the *Holstein* spar. The *Thialf* was the bigger version of the *DCV Baldor*, and had been profiled on the Discovery Channel's TV program. The *Thialf* had the distention from all others with a world record lift of over 12,000 tons, done in the North Sea. I wouldn't mind seeing this large piece of machinery with a capacity of 14,200 mT, or 15,600 short tons. With nine lifts made, the lift of the North module was the one that broke the heaviest lift record for the Gulf region of 7,564 metric tons. As the lift was made, this picture was taken on the placement of the finished module. The alignment of the pieces is a very crucial time, and is done with the movement of mere inches at a time. We would be long gone, and probably back in Tampa docking ships when this operation commenced. She had accommodations for 736 workers with dimensions of 661 feet long, with a beam of 290 feet wide, just as I had remembered seeing on the Discovery Channel, she was truly a mechanical marvel.

We were now within a few miles of the location of the *Baldor*, where the actual drilling would take place. It was also now into our sixth day, and then the words we had been waiting to hear come across the radio from Willem. He said, "Okay *Hawk*, you're released; you need to head into Port Fourchon to have the electronics removed from your boat."

The Run into Port Fourchon

It was 23:05 on April 12 2004, I told Willem, "It's been fun, you fellows be careful, and we'll see you next time." He asked me, "About how long will it take you to reach Fourchon?" I said, "Just over a hundred miles, we should be there in ten hours." Little did I know, we would be getting some very nasty beam seas most of the way. Beam seas are the waves hitting the boat from the side, which are also the most uncomfortable to transit.

When David came up for the midnight watch, the seas were ten to twelve footers. During the night they had grown to be anywhere from fifteen to eighteen footers, no wonder I was being levitated off my bed all night. When morning came and it was now my watch, I wouldn't even take a chance trying to carry hot coffee, so bottled water was the ticket. On my way to the wheelhouse from the galley, a swell pitched the boat right out from under my feet; I ended up flat on my chest with my head up against the bulkhead. These were the type seas I would love to have some office riders with me, so they too could experience only what we tell them.

As I carefully made my way up the stairs, I could sense from the smell that David had been on vacation during the night. He must have driven his *Buick*, over in *Europe*, and had hit an outside toilet. The sickening smell was unmistaken; it definitely had seasick written all over it. If there was anything stacked on top of anything else, it was either down the stairwell, or scattered all over the floor of the wheelhouse.

I told David, "Take that waste paper basket that you've been hugging all night down stairs, and do it now." I told him, "Stay down stairs too; I'll take her all the way to the dock." He had slowed down quite a bit and really had to, just to keep the seas from beating the boat apart. I slowed down even more, this would make our ETA later than I had figured, and it was also something I couldn't help.

At this point I would have idled the *Hawk* to Fourchon; I thought to myself, my Daddy never whipped me as bad as these seas were beating us. We were finally getting closer to shore with the calmer waters. Having never been into Fourchon, I just followed the charts and went right to our destination. The weather-beaten *Hawk* was secured at 15:05 at the Heerema dock, the boat was still at last. Old Sparky was there on the dock waiting on us to get their very expensive toys. I had called our Marketing Manager Bartley Wilkins, and relayed to him of what our last twenty-four hours had been like.

I asked him that we be allowed to stay secure in Fourchon for the night, and get some rest before heading back to Tampa. He said, "Yes, by all means, we'll deduct the time from when you actually return and are secured in Tampa." I was looking forward to hitting the bed and not having it being jerked out from under me, so I made a call to the Heerema office and told their representative about our plans to stay the night. This Dutchman would hear nothing of the kind. He said, "No, you are to depart for Tampa as soon as the electronics were removed." Trying to explain to him what Bartley had said was a futile move on my part, so to the east we would head in a short while.

I told him, "We need to at least run to the store for some supplies for the trip back." He says "If you can go and get back within an hour, do it and depart," then he hung the phone up on me. This cat had to be an arsonist, because he built a fire inside of me that woke me up big time. I told Boyd, "When old Sparky takes you to the store, get there as fast as you can and get back." I had Dave start the main engines and was set on go when Boyd got back with our supplies. Maybe this fellow had one of those "Big Pictures" that I was not looking at.

We departed at 17:10 with just a short two hours in port. The timing could not have been worse too, I had gotten very little sleep if any in the last twenty-four hours. My watch started in less than an hour so I told

David, "Hit the bed now and I'll get you up a little early." After the way the Flying Dutchman had acted, I just hoped he didn't act this way with everyone. The one thing we did have in our favor was the seas would now be on our stern. The following seas could actually speed the boat up, which was what we all wanted now.

We had also just departed one of the busiest ports I had ever gone into. While going in and then back out, we had seen boats stacked three deep, jockeying around for their turn next to the different docks. Some were fueling, while others were taking on the many different supplies to be taken offshore. It seemed to be a hub for the oil patch, and had every size vessel you could imagine, going and coming. Maybe with us not staying overnight was a Godsend. I would have hated to be woken up just to let another boat to the dock that we were moored to.

The ole girl had taken a beating, but she was now heading towards the Tampa sea buoy. David knew what I had been through for the past twenty-four hours and came up early to relieve me. I can tell you right now, he didn't get an argument from me. As tired as I was, I could've probably went to sleep out on the deck. This trip was now like a trailer, it was behind us. The *Hawk* had made it back to the Seabulk docks in just over 35 hours. Finally secured at 04:15 on April 15, we were all also packed for the trip home too.

TUG *Seafarer* WITH BARGE *M 244* TO PASCAGOULA

It didn't take long for something to come up that would be another strange job. I had just gotten off from a week of harbor duty when I received a phone call that very afternoon. The oh so familiar voice was Dwayne Wheeler, he told me, "There's a possibility of towing the Maritrans barge *M 244* to Pascagoula, Mississippi." He then said, "Regardless if we tow the barge or not, since Larry Shelton doesn't have a Mate we still want you to go with him to Lake Charles, Louisiana leaving Saturday."

Tug *Seafarer* in 2005 in Tampa, Fl.-Author photo

We had heard rumors about some escort jobs coming up for the LNG tankers that were going in there now. LNG (Liquefied Natural Gas) was being imported into Lake Charles on some very large tankers. They were being required to have an escort tug tethered to the ship for the entire transit up the channel. These jobs would be reminiscent to those done in Charleston, several years ago.

Thirty-three hours off duty and I was back at it. I had reported back to the *Hawk* on Thursday afternoon at 18:00 May 13, and found we weren't even close to departing. The barge tow was still up in the air, so while a Maritrans decision was yet to be made, the *Hawk* worked a couple of harbor jobs. Just as we were finishing the second job we received word that the job was a go. That was when the fun began; it was also just after midnight, my watch. We had to get the tug *Seafarer* from the shipyard and take her to where the barge was anchored, half way out of the bay. This operation meant that we had to put the tug into the notch of the barge and towing both units together. We just wouldn't have the assistance of the *Seafarer's* propulsion; she was just going for the ride. Some of their engineers were going to be doing some engine work while we towed them across the Gulf. I thought; wow, that must be one tight schedule they have.

With their tug secure to the barge and the *Hawk* made up to tow, we headed outbound Tampa Bay at 04:00 May 15 2004. The *M244* was a pretty good size barge, and held 244,000 barrels of product. It was also the barge that replaced the barge *Ocean 255*, which was scrapped after burning up from the fiery collision with the *Balsa 37* back in August of 1993.

The tug *Seafarer* however had the damage that was done to her repaired and was given another barge. I had no idea of the speed we would tow this 600 foot barge. We were however expected to get this tug and barge to Pascagoula, Mississippi and then have the *Hawk* at the Calcasieu River sea buoy by daylight the next Tuesday. I had figured four days would give us plenty of time to complete our mission, providing we had no surprises. The weather that I have written so much about in the past wasn't an issue at all for this entire trip.

Since I was on the Mates watch, when I called the *Seafarer* to see how they were enjoying their ride, my old pal Marshall Ancar answered the radio. About the only time I had an opportunity to talk with him was when we assisted them with their barge to the different docks back in Tampa Bay.

He calls me one morning and asks, "Do you see this ship coming up behind us?" I said, "Yes I do, she must be running twice our speed." This ship passed us on our port side by maybe a half mile, then about a mile past us, she crossed in front of us to be on our starboard side. Marshall says, "Can you believe that, all this water out here and this idiot has to come this close to us?" I told him, "That's how accidents happen, they were probably asleep."

Saturday afternoon, we were told that this channel run too would be a daylight transit only. We had made pretty good speed so far and would now be pulling the throttles back, just to kill some time. Larry and I both would make adjustments during our watches, trying to time our arrival for daylight. Well, we must have done it right, because we arrived at the Pascagoula sea buoy at 08:30. The harbor Pilot called and said to proceed in with the barge. Larry had got concerned about this little delay, and had told the *Seafarers* Captain he would appreciate a quick release.

There were two harbor tugs that had met up with us in the channel, and as soon as they were made fast to the barge, we took in our tow gear while still underway. We were released at 10:20 Sunday morning, May 16 2004; this gave us almost two full days to get to our next assignment. Larry told the *Seafarers* crew, "Thanks, we'll see you back in Tampa."

M/V Tenaga Dua IN

LAKE CHARLES, LOUISIANA

I had calculated a ten knot average would get us there well ahead of time. Larry however had a different view; he built a bonfire in the main engines. I questioned him about how hard we were running, but Larry said he had been on a lot of offshore trips, and he wanted to cover as much ground as he could as fast as he could, so with him running the show, I did as he said. The *Hawk* was scooting across the water faster than we needed to, and by the next afternoon the throttles had been pulled back so we could once again, murder the clock and kill some time.

Even after slowing down as much as we had, our arrival to the sea buoy was half past midnight Monday night. My watch was spent running up and down the channel at idle speed, all night long, who'd a thunk it. During the many passes that I made by the anchorage, I saw the LNG tanker *M/V Tenaga Dua*. She was definitely a big girl and appeared to be the size of the oil tankers I had worked when I was in Mexico.

Larry was up by 06:00, the *Hawk* was tethered to the ships stern by 08:15. I was up for part of the transit just looking at this operation; this was going to be a dream. We had the ship secured to the LNG berth and was released by 13:05, that was just under five hours for the entire transit.

We also had fuel set up, since the so-called urgency of our trip; it hadn't been taken on before our departure from Tampa. Our fueling was done off a barge, after we had taken on 40,000 gallons of the liquid gold, it was time to light the grill. We secured the boat across from the LNG dock where the grill master Larry whipped us up a tugboat meal. Next on the agenda was a good night's sleep before departing the next day.

That night shot by like Larry was on the throttles again, very fast. Exactly twenty-two hours had passed and we were once again made up to the *Tenaga Dua*. But now it was for the undocking operation, by 11:05 she was outbound for sea to get another load of gas. Larry did the sailing, at 12:00 I came up for my watch which meant I would be there for the entire transit. At 16:40 we were released right near a berth called the AB dock at the mouth of the Calcasieu River.

This also happened to be where my Buddy, Dave Scarborough was standing on the bow of his boat, the OSV *Howard H. Hughes*. OSV (Off-shore Support Vessel) were the vessels like this one, which was a multi use workboat. They supplied the offshore drill rigs with everything from drill mud, drill stems, drill bits, water, fuel for their power plants, and even groceries. The offshore drilling platforms are dependent on these boats for most of their operational supplies.

I went over towards their bow to talk for a couple of minutes. It turned out to be a good move, I asked him about the berth they were at, and got some good info. He said, this dock is known as the AB dock, and appeared to be just what we needed for future trips. He gave me some phone numbers of contact to receive permission to moor the tug to their dock when we returned, I told him, thanks Buddy, and we were gone. Just over 660 miles to go, fifty-six hours later we were once again, you guessed it, secure to the Seabulk dock in Tampa, at 00:30 May 22, 2004.

Phoning my Wife, I could only think of one thing to say, "Lucy, I'm home." Our principle job was assisting ships in and out of the berths that they moored to within the harbor in Tampa, Florida. That is also why I was back aboard the next afternoon, to finish out my work week. My twelve hours off was now history, and we were sailing a ship at 17:00 that afternoon. This LNG tanker duty was supposed to be split between the tugs *Condor*, and *Hawk*.

M/V Ramdane Abane

BACK TO LAKE CHARLES

With normal harbor duty taking place for the *Hawk*, the *Condor* made their presence known for a week or so in beautiful Lake Charles, Louisiana. Our turn came again on July 27 2004; we departed for the LNG tour to assist the *M/V Ramdane Abane* up the channel. I left at 17:45 with a familiar crew, my Mate David Storch, Dave Costa and Heath Scott as engineers, and Carlos Collins as the deckhand, all of whom I have had prior voyages with. With me being on the *Hawk's* last trip, I remembered that it took us fifty-six hours to transit back home to Tampa; this one should be pretty close to the same amount of time. The summer months also allowed us to figure the times of the ETA's closer than when we would be bucking the winter seas. With our prayers said and a beautiful sunset to look at, we were happy to be assigned to this trip, and said goodbye to Tampa Bay. Our report date was daylight on July 30, this was not a problem. As time went on and a few more short cuts made than we

Gods' easel for his sunsets
Author photo

had taken last trip, it was evident we were going to be well ahead of time. Summer time in the Gulf just could not be any prettier, and was just the opposite of what winter brings. I called the AB dock by sat phone when we passed the sea buoy, and obtained permission for us to tie up at their facility. After that call, I then called the Pilots office to let them know we were back in town, and ready for some action.

Their dispatcher said, "Welcome back," and then told me that the ship would start in around 10:30 the next morning, and the Pilot wanted us to meet him at buoy #34. I told her we would be at the AB dock for the night and would be at #34 at the appropriate time for the ship. We had everything going for us on this trip, and even broke the record by one and a half hours, big deal right? We were secured to the AB dock by 00:30; this was just what we needed too.

With this dock, and us being allowed to tie the boat there, it saved us a lot of just running up and down the channel, thanks Brother Dave. The next morning after breakfast we got a good look at several different boats. Crew boats, supply boats, and even some more tugboats, they were all curious about the words, "Tractor Tug" painted on the side of our bulwarks. I figured we could leave at 10:00 and be at buoy #34 with time to spare. When it came time to depart the dock to go meet the ship, and with so many eyes gazing our way, it was also time for some trick maneuvers. I came off the dock sideways, backed out the channel about 1,000 feet, and spun a couple of circles. I then idled out the channel, knowing those fellows were doing some talking about what they had just seen, and it was impressive.

As it turns out, we could have stayed secure for another hour. Our alongside time was 12:20, and as with most escort modes, we were tethered to the ships stern running along. Having been on the last LNG job, I told David to come on in and get comfortable, this transit would take five to six hours to the dock.

There are some beautiful houses along the banks of the Calcasieu River, most looked to be some very expensive fishing camps. The wake from the ship would wash far into some of the little waterways that went off from the channel. Since the channel was deep, and the little creeks and many tributaries were much shallower, it was obvious that since we weren't moving that fast, the sheer displacement of the water from the ships movement was the culprit.

On this trip, we also had a couple of riders from the Coast Guard part of the way. Just like the Anhydrous Ammonia tankers in Tampa, these

LNG tankers also had a Coast Guard escort. A rainsquall was coming our way with a lot of lightning in it. They asked me if could they secure their boat to the *Hawk* and come aboard until the light show was over. I told them, "Sure, come on up to the wheelhouse." I was always happy to show off the console of the "Star Ship Enterprise."

They were happy to get aboard, and were amazed at our home away from home. We asked them questions about the LNG tankers and how often did they expect their frequency into Lake Charles. That was something not known to them, so we'd have to ask someone else. We would be in a position to find the answers to our questions, within the next few days. When I was told the particulars of this job, as usual, a wrinkle was also thrown into the mix. After the *Ramdane Abane* LNG job was docked, and then sailed, then after being released from the escort, the *Hawk* with a partial crew was going to be staying for a few days.

This inbound transit and the docking took just over six hours to complete. This time we needed no fuel, and were secured to the same dock as before. We would also have one of the Lake Charles Seabulk tugs keep us company for the night. Maybe these fellows could enlighten us as to what the LNG ship schedule looked like. They did, and what we heard was not what we wanted to hear either.

With the cargo discharged, the LNG tanker was ready to depart their berth at 16:20. I had also been assigned one of the Captains from the Lake Charles fleet to show us the different docks. When Mr. Pilot, Captain Mowbray, started saying his commands, I looked at our rider and asked him, "What did he say?" I asked him, "Can you repeat please?" He says, "Do you not understand the commands that I'm giving you?" I replied, "No sir, you're saying things I'm not familiar with."

He them informed me that he had been to some simulator up North, and that they had learned the proper terminology for working Tractor tugs. I said, "Well sir, this ain't my first rodeo, I've been on Tractor tugs for eight years now, and have always been given commands like we were a conventional tugboat." I said, "If you want to go towards the dock, tell me to come ahead and at what power, if you want to come away from the dock, tell me to back and I'll pull you off the dock." He says, "Tell you

what, I'll give them to you the way I learned them, you see if you can figure them out." I said, "You got it Partner, lets get the show on the road."

During my exchange with Mr. Pilot, the Seabulk chaperone was turning all different shades of colors. He says, "These guys aren't used to
someone talking to them like that." I said, "I can't do my job if I don't
understand what he wants, your point is what?" He just sat down and
said, "Man, this is going to be a long job." Whenever the Pilot gave me
a command, I would answer him the way I interpreted it. He would say
things like, "Back the *Hawk*, idle speed, in line, with a tight line." I'd say,
"Back *Hawk* dead slow, straight back." I asked Captain Rider, "If I back,
ain't my line going to be tight?" I told him, "Mr. Pilot had better go back
to school, and unlearn this new fangled terminology."

We made it through the entire job this way, commands said his way,
answered my way. He tells me during the job that he would like to meet
with me to discuss what he had learned when he went to the simulator
school. I told him, "I'll be working here in Lake Charles at least until
Wednesday, I would then be going back to Tampa, set it up, and I'd be
there." After our release, I told him, "Take care, that was a good job, and
I look forward to our meeting."

It was 22:50 on July 31 2004, being released at that time meant the
Hawk was now on the Lake Charles divisions payroll. After our transit
back and securing close to the dock, my Mate David Storch and engineer
Heath Scott departed the boat at 04:30. They would go back to Tampa
to work on other boats. The office figured that a three-man crew, along
with our Lake Charles rider would be sufficient for this harbor duty.

My Tampa bound crew had only been gone a few hours when Virginia Rozas, their dispatcher called telling me, "Come around to the City
Dock where our boats use as a home berth." It took more than an hour to
get around there, and on the way; we saw some of the oil refineries with
some very big tankers at their docks.

As we approached the dock, there Virginia was to meet us where she
had a box of doughnuts and a newspaper for each boat. This little gesture
which does wonders in moral building never happened in Tampa, at least
not in the past few years, and a Sunday morning to boot. After securing
the boat, we were introduced to her where she said, "Anything you need,

just let her know, she would do what she could to make it happen." It was obvious that she had paid attention during her management classes.

We were sent on several jobs during the next few days, I found out my verbal exchange had spread like wildfire. Some of the Pilots told me they had heard about my first meeting with Captain Simulator. Some said they thought it would be too confusing with changing the way the tugs have worked for so many years, the best thing he could do is to forget about the changes he was trying to make, and just dock ships. I told them, "In Tampa, the Pilots give their commands to every tugboat the same way, and there is no confusion what so ever." They themselves gave me commands that weren't foreign to my ears. The big bad Mighty *Hawk* also impressed these Pilots with her trick maneuvers.

On our last night we were dispatched for a job at midnight. Just minutes after we had departed the dock for that job, Virginia called and switched jobs on us. We were sent down close to the AB dock for a 05:00 job, called the *Swan*. When we arrived to the *Swan's* location, it turned out to be one of those heavy lift ships. It was like the one that had hauled the Navy ship *USS Cole* from the Republic of Yemen, after those idiot terrorists had blown a hole in her side.

The *Swan* had a three-legged jack up drill rig setting on her deck. The Candies twins, *Kelly* and *Devin* along with another one of their company tugs, the *Grant Candies*, were stretched out on tow lines, and all three boats had different headings. They were holding the *Swan* in place, but with her facing inbound while she pumped out her ballast tanks.

When the pumping was done, the tugs *Samson* and *Hawk* made up to her with a line, and then one by one the other tugs were released. I could not believe that we had been sent almost three hours down the channel just to turn this ship around. There were three tugs already there with close to 30,000-combined hp. Maybe it was some contractual agreement that I didn't know about, who knows.

I suppose you could say, I just didn't see the big picture, oh no, now they've got me saying it. By having almost five hours to get there, I had just idled to the job, and still had arrived at 04:00. We didn't start the job until 05:00 and was not released until 07:05. Our Louisiana tugboat tour was coming to a close, we were secured back at the City Dock by 09:05 August 4 2004.

Larry and his crew were on the way to relieve me, Dave, and Carlos. After they had finally arrived, we still had roughly five hours before our flight. Whenever we had departed Tampa eight days earlier, I never put getting to fly on an airplane again into the equation. I told Larry about the simulator Pilot, and also told him he might be visited by him. We loaded our gear into the rental van, and departed the boat at 13:00; we then took a tour of beautiful downtown Lake Charles, Louisiana.

My Chief Engineer collects Harley Davidson shot glasses, yes, we had to find the Lake Charles Harley shop. We rode around for a while, but made sure we got to the airport early. Our flight time finally arrived, when we were called to go through the metal detectors, Homeland Security was on top of it. We all three had to take off our shoes, socks, and our belts to be checked.

At that very moment, the charge of racial profiling that some of the visitors, or Arab speaking people living in our great nation were making, had very little credence in my mind. We jumped on a shuttle plane and were off to Houston, Texas where we then boarded one of the bigger planes headed to Tampa. By the time we had changed planes and arrived in Tampa, it was almost midnight.

A comedian/taxi driver took us to the office where our personal vehicles were. With the last two days sort of blending together, I had no problem going to sleep after getting home. I even told my Wife, "I'll get with you tomorrow on that." I was glad to be home and like to have kissed my granddaughters face off the next afternoon, because afternoon was when I finally rolled out of bed. I was like a racing engine with headers on it, thoroughly exhausted. The next few of days would be like none I had ever experienced.

Diagnosed As

A Heart Attack

I had been back home for a day and a half, where just hours earlier I had returned from town with my Mother. I thought I'd mow the yard since it was Friday, that way the weekend would be spent with my family. It was the hottest part of the day 13:00, in the hottest month of the year, August. Which is why after feeling so weak during my lawn mowing, I attributed the sensation of a complete power drain, to the heat.

The date was August 6 2004; it seemed like someone had turned a switch and cut my power source. My decision to go inside the house instead of falling off the mower was the best choice. So I went inside, took a shower, and went to bed. This was unlike any feeling that I had ever felt before. Thinking back on the past week I had, I just figured between the heat and having been up for almost two days, it must be fatigue.

Not wanting to eat anything and just wanting to sleep was not my normal routine. Sunday at dinner was my first meal, definitely not normal for me. My Wife checked on me quite often throughout the entire weekend with great concern. With things not being normal, she convinced on Monday morning that I was going to the Doctors office, just to see what he thought.

Monday afternoon was the earliest time that I could get in to see him. After my primary Doctor had seen me, the electrocardiogram must have showed something he didn't like, because I was sent to a heart specialist the next day with the EKG strip. It was now four days since my initial bad feeling, I was feeling better so whatever had happened, had evidently passed. .

Dr. Sanchez was the heart man, and after looking at the EKG that I had brought from my primaries office, he said, "You've had an MI." I asked him, "What does MI stand for?" He says, "Oh excuse me, that's a Mila Cardio Infarction, you've had a heart attack." When the heart Doctor did his own EKG, he told his nurse to get me scheduled into the hospital immediately for some exploratory surgery. He said, "We need to go in there and see what's going on." I said, "Can't we schedule this for next week, I'm flying to Lake Charles, Louisiana in the morning, I have to go to work." He said, "We had better do this now, I don't think you'll be going anywhere for a little while." So, off to Blake Memorial Hospital I went and had some ticker work done.

August 10 2004, I had two stents put into my left descending artery. I had just become a member of statistics, like millions of other Americans who were already members of this distinct fraternity. After my surgery, I was put into the cardiac intensive care unit for my recovery. My Dad had also started his heart problems when he was in his early fifties, and my Grand Father had also died from a heart attack. I guess the word hereditary now had a larger meaning to me than it did a week ago.

Wednesday morning and in the hospital, this was not where I expected to be. I had also called the office the previous day to let them know about the surgery, and I probably wasn't going to make my flight. I had always been job conscience throughout my life, and my job at that point seemed more important than exploratory surgery. I guess that's why the Doctors make the big bucks, his decision to stent me probably saved my life.

My stay in the Hospital was also when Hurricane Charley visited the state of Florida, this made me feel helpless. I came home the next Saturday afternoon, four days after stent day. The next week brought on several phone calls, from me to the office in Tampa. I was concerned about the possibility of not receiving a paycheck, and was told by more than one person that nothing could be done. I was told, "September first was coming up, you will be eligible to collect for sick days then." I had not worked since August 4, and did not return to work until September

8, where I received a one-day paycheck for a six-week period; this also let me know just how vulnerable we are at any given moment.

Mr. Kenny Rogers is the only member of all of the Seabulk Management that called me at home during my five weeks of heart rehab time, just to see how I was doing and to give me encouragement; he has my utmost respect for doing that. In 1998, I was out for three months with shoulder surgery; I also didn't miss one paycheck for the entire period that I was off work. Of course, the other team was in charge back then during that period, where I also received weekly phone calls.

I got through it okay with the help of family members, and my belief in God, who makes all things possible. I would also have to draw on my faith for the month of December 2004, when the Murphy's Law principle came along with us on the trip of the year for my crew and me. I'll have to write about that one in my next book, *My Lifetime on the Water II*.

THE MIGHTY *Hawk* IS CUT FROM THE FLEET

On the morning of August 22 2005, almost six months after my last off-shore trip, I received a phone call from Dwayne Wheeler with some news I did not want to hear. He was letting me know that when I came into work Wednesday, I would be delivering the tug *Hawk* to Lake Charles, Louisiana for at least a year or maybe even longer.

Some people working with our company thought that they were the US Government, which we all know does not like to share information between their branches. Some even thought that certain things that were going on within the company, was too sensitive for the working people to comprehend. Although, we had heard rumors of losing one, or maybe even both of the big boats to the Lake Charles Division of Seabulk Towing, due to an impending contract with British Gas. This move was no surprise when the decision to relocate yet another Tampa tug elsewhere was made, it was just bad timing.

We were told about most decisions made after the

A rare sight of calm waters in the Gulf of Mexico-Author photo

fact, instead of when we should have been told, to at least brace us for the upcoming changes. The relocation of tugs from the Tampa Division had been going on since the company was sold to Hvide Marine, so why change now I thought. My Mate for this boat delivery was James Fehrenbach, Dave Costa and Frankie Pavon as engineers, and a new man, Scott Whittemore was the deckhand.

Scott asked me, "Are we going to be able to see land on the way across," after I had explained the formula for the height of eye, it shed a light on that question for this greenhorn. He also couldn't believe the flying fish we seen skimming just off the water that are so prevalent, especially when the waters were as calm as they were for this trip. We had departed at 11:00 on August 24 2005, which was one day after my Mothers seventy-ninth birthday, I was also able to be at home and celebrate it with her.

There was also a hurricane named Katrina that was still several hundred miles east of the Florida coast when we departed on this crossing. She was the storm of all storms that would become this nation's most costly, and the deadliest, biggest most destructive natural disaster ever. I have heard the term "Lull before the Storm"

Oilrig at night with a supply boat alongside-Author photo

used many times, and knowing this category-one hurricane was nowhere close, I just figured that the good Lord was blessing me with calm waters, which would probably also be my last Gulf of Mexico crossing aboard a tugboat. At this particular point in my career, I had 29 years of credited service towards my awaited retirement. Losing what I would consider my boat to another division was probably going to be the straw that broke the camels back for me; at the time, it just seemed that retirement might be the most viable option for me. It took us all fifty-six hours to get across the smoothest waters I had ever seen. Knowing now what would happen in just two days, was completely unthinkable at the destruction heading our way. Early the next day, the Mighty *Hawk's* presence was made known. She was put into the normal harbor operations of docking and sailing some pretty big ships.

We were requested on several jobs right off the bat, and even got to work with Captain Mowbray. He was the same Pilot that had went to the simulator up north and had whipped that foreign sounding simulator terminology on me a year earlier. He welcomed me to Lake Charles, and said, "I look forward to using the *Hawk*." I told him, "Thank you, and we're also ready to be used, I was on the *Hawk* last year and remember working with you on an LNG tanker." He said, "Yes, I remember your voice."

I thought Oh Boy, here we go again. His job went better than I had expected, every command was given to me as if I were back in Tampa, and was a very welcomed surprise to me. I had Captain Bill Neal off the tug *Samson* training with me, and would be one of their Captains that would be at the helm of the *Hawk* when the training was completed. His name was also Bill, but his stature was in no comparison to mine, we dubbed him Little Bill. He told me he had worked in Lake Charles since 1992, and was ready for this new Tractor tug technology. He too had gone up north to the simulator school to learn all about the Tractor tugs and their operations. Little Bill seemed to already have a handle on how the boat reacted when the drives were turned a certain angle; that was definitely a plus for him. Scoot and I had been told that the company wanted us to work two weeks on and two weeks off during the training process of these Louisiana boys.

During the first few days it was obvious from the tanker traffic that came into the Port of Lake Charles; this was definitely a busy oil Port. The oil refineries that made the gasoline we all need so much for our everyday operations was stretched out for as far as the eye could see. The weekend of August 28 2005 had an apocalyptic event that changed millions of lives, when hurricane Katrina hit the Gulf Coast. We had been keeping an eye of the impending storm and was wondering exactly how we would be affected. We were also thinking of a secure berth we could tie the boat and weather the storm, so to speak.

After the Port had been closed on Saturday afternoon, and the last ships that were inbound were secured to their berths, we were told to secure the *Hawk* at the City Dock. We were only 161 miles as the crow flies from New Orleans, where Katrina was expected to come ashore just south of this heavily populated metropolis, with their below sea level elevation. We had heard of fifty-five foot waves offshore, there were reported twenty-two foot seas just outside the jetties where the ship Pilots boarded the many vessels that frequented the Port. I wondered what would happen to the many oilrigs we had passed on our transit to Lake Charles. With the weight of water being eight pounds per gallon, the sheer weight of a 30–40 foot wave could be disastrous, which is what happened to numerous rigs.

It seemed that Lake Charles would be spared from this monster storm, but would definitely be affected in days to come by what had just happened. On crew change day my crew and I were to fly out of New Orleans when we flew back to Tampa; this was not going to happen. Other arrangements had to be made to bring our reliefs to the boat and for our flight home too. Well, Houston, Texas was now the chosen airport, there was just one little hitch with that very bad plan.

After being up from 05:30 on Tuesday morning working jobs, all day and night, we now had to drive for three hours to return the rental car to the airport, so we could make a 08:05 flight. That of course was not done, until Scoot and his boys had arrived to the boat around 02:30 on Wednesday morning. I knew flight plans had to be changed because of the hurricane; I was just not impressed with whoever came up with this airport location, when a twenty-minute ride to Lake Charles airport was more preferred. We just figured that the five days prior to the storm-making landfall evidentially wasn't enough time for the proper changes to be made.

I suppose the cynicalness of my writings is more evident than when I first started this book. Living through the latter years of my career just seemed to breed mistrust with the actions of certain members of man-

agement. My Doctor told me that on the job stress is one of the leading causes of heart attacks, there was definitely stress on this job. Oh well, I once again looked forward to my airplane ride; this was to me the highlight of the

View from Houston to Tampa-Author photo

whole trip. Although we had crossed the Gulf of Mexico by tug, and had seen the many oilrigs working out there, this was the view for the trip home, which only took hours instead of the days it had taken to get there. Lord willing and the creek don't rise all things would work out for the best, and life goes on. I had strange mixed feelings within me, knowing that when these Louisiana Captains were trained, and we had departed Lake Charles for the last time, I would probably never see the tug *Hawk* again.

I know the *Hawk* is just a piece of metal with working parts throughout, but to me, the departure from what I had called my home away from home for so many years, was also heartbreaking. Although there were other boats to work on; there just wasn't any that could perform as the *Hawk* class boats did on an everyday basis. With years of running different type boats throughout my Maritime career, I can appreciate the many advances of technology that has been made within the industry. I can't imagine what the on going developmental stages within the Marine industry will bring for the new breed of tug boaters; it'll be interesting to see.

THE RETURN TO LAKE
CHARLES ON THE *Hawk*

I returned to Lake Charles on September 14 2005, for a two week on, two week off schedule, during the training period of the two Captains that would be operating the *Hawk*. Scott Whittemore also went back with me because there was still no deckhand assigned to the tug *Hawk* since her arrival into the Lake Charles Division, does foot dragging come to mind, it did to me.

We were aboard by 10:00 and soon departed the dock for an inbound LNG tanker, *Methane Kari*, which was the main reason for having the *Hawk* change her address, to work these large ships. Captain Bill Neal was also back aboard, he was looking forward to being one of the *Hawk-ster's* main men. Little Bill did the job and seemed to have most of the operational procedures down fairly well, and just as a tugboat textbook scenario is played out, the job docking went as well.

After the tanker had been discharged of its valuable cargo, the next day tugs *Samson* and *Hawk* put her to sea, reversing the docking process. Most jobs went well, and with the thousands of jobs that I have done throughout the years, the Harbor Pilot is ultimately in control of the end result. That week with Little Bill was uneventful and without any fancy maneuvering to be done.

However, the second week with Captain John Maxey was different, and also most memorable. John wasn't as far along as Little Bill was, although he had done every job so far, up come a job that was not for either trainee to do, it was a Timex moment, time to watch. We were sailing a ship where the Pilot had asked us to work bow to bow, I suggested to John that I might better do this one, and there was no argument from him on that account. This was a maneuver I had done many times before, even with the single screw boats of past years. Having my line through the chock on the very bow of the ship, I had total control of the pointed end. Facing the ships bow, I would put the *Hawk* in a walk mode in the direction that the Pilot needed to go towards.

During the job, John says, "It'll be a long time before they can expect me to do that maneuver with this boat." I told him, "Not to worry; no one jumps on a strange boat and can run it to its potential, right off the bat." I told him, "That's what I'm here for, to show you fellows what the *Hawk* can do, she'll get you out of trouble fast, but can also get you into trouble just as fast if you do something wrong." This particular job could have been done different with just changing the placement of the tugboats, but since the *Hawk* was the new boat in town, several of the Pilots just wanted to see what she could do, and yes, he was impressed with the job we did.

The first training tour that I was in Lake Charles, hurricane Katrina made her devastating presence known. The second of these training tours was no different when it came to hurricanes visiting south Louisiana. Hurricane Rita had showed up during this fourteen-day tour and seemed to try and out do the total devastation that Katrina had already done. Along with well over a hundred other boats, we hunkered down once again in a place called the Contraband Bayou to wait for Rita to pass. There were boats of all types seeking shelter from the category

Boats stacked five deep for weather-Author photo

three-force winds that hit the Gulf Coast area for the second time in less than four weeks. The *Hawk* had five Vietnamese shrimp boats tied outboard of her during the storm. These fellows were some hungry people, after looking at their boats and the condition that they were in, I wouldn't have left shore on any of them.

During that stormy period, we went on six-hour watches for the duration. I was glad to be on a boat that I knew could withstand the winds and rain which fell during landfall of hurricane Rita. After the storm had passed that early Saturday morning of September 24, the Lake Charles Port Authority Harbor Master, Captain Jim Robinson, United States Coast Guard Retired, came aboard the tug *Hawk*. He had asked me, "Would it be possible to use her as the Flag Ship so he could coordinate the Port operations from aboard us?" I had told him, "It would certainly be possible for that to happen, and it would be a pleasure to help out."

He told me that he had heard of the *Hawks* coming into the Port, and had looked forward to riding her for some jobs, this was just happenstance. I told him, "Different circumstances would have definitely been more preferable on my part too." While it's all part of the job, going through a hurricane aboard a tugboat just wasn't how I wanted to spend my tour. Just as my past fifty-four years had been, the Lord had once again kept me safe from any harm, and had built a hedge of protection around me.

Watching the TV and listening to the radio, revealed just how devastating Rita had shown her ferocity towards the Louisiana landscape. The reporters referred to hurricane Rita as the storm that just would not quit, two recent trips to Lake Charles with two hurricanes back to back, that'll make a fellow sort of reluctant of a third trip. While I was writing the latter chapters of this book, it also happened to be during the training tours on the *Hawk*. It seemed the training was only taking place in between hurricanes, and not much training going on without the needed ship traffic.

I keep thinking of what Captain Harold Dale used to say, "I believe the end times are so close I don't even buy green bananas, they won't have time to ripen before the Lord comes back." With the events that were happening, and so close together, it sure makes a fellow think, especially when you are being hit with hurricane force winds head on. I had kept in touch with my family the best I could; they also had no idea as to our status until I periodically called them with updates. Hearing their voices was very comforting, especially after Mother Nature has spanked you for several continuous nail-biting hours. With so many power lines down and most roads impassable because of downed trees, it really seemed that a tugboat was the best place to be.

It wasn't until Sunday morning that the Port tried to get back to a normalcy. Although the Calcasieu River channel had yet to be surveyed by NOAA and the Army Corp of Engineers, there were many boats departing the safety of the harbor. Captain Robinson had put out a warning message over several of the VHF radio frequencies, advising them that they were leaving at their on risk, because the channel in fact had not been surveyed yet. There were reports of sunken barges, shrimp boats, pleasure craft, even hundreds of refrigerators that had washed up on

Port warehouse sign
Author photo

the bank just off the inner channel close to Clifton Ridge. There was all kind of debris floating by where we were tied up at the City Dock in Contraband Bayou, with a name like that; it makes you wonder what that bayou was used for in the past. That question was answered from a book that Doug Bogard was reading at the time, *"The Pirates Laffite."* It seemed that Jean and Pierre Laffite used the very waterway that we were in. They brought in the contraband goods that they sold in New Orleans in the early 1800's, using the intercostal waterways to escape detection. The history of New Orleans had been felt throughout the coast of Louisiana for more than two centuries; I was also in a history-making event with hurricane Rita.

I knew with what we were looking at floating on top of the water was trouble for somebody, all I needed to do was to get something submerged just under the water to go through one of my drive units and cause some damage.

I had escaped from any storm damage so far, and really wanted to keep it that way. Right around lunchtime the Port Director, Mr. R. Adam McBride came to the boat to take a damage assessment tour of the Port; this tour was definitely cleared with the bosses. While riding around into the lake area, it showed extensive damage everywhere you looked on the shore. There were some very expensive boats tossed about as if they were nothing, stacked up like cordwood. With the sites that we were seeing I thought to myself, the two months of August and September were not good months to invest your money with any insurance companies.

Our tour came to an end with me maneuvering the *Hawk* right back to where we had left from earlier. Captain Robinson and Mr. McBride were both amazed at how graceful a 110-foot tugboat could slip into a hole of no more than 115 feet, and expressed it with their comments. I just smiled, and said, "Yes sir, she's a dandy, y'all come back when you can stay longer." Mr. McBride visited us periodically, looking for status changes in regards to the shipping channel opening, and with no office, the Harbor Master had stayed aboard the *Hawk* for several more days with his operations.

Finally, on September 27 2005, the Coast Guard opened the channel for transit to shallow draft vessels only, at least until the Army Corp of Engineers and NOAA had completed their surveys. It had already revealed some spots that would need some dredge work; Captain Robinson was not pleased with that report. With me being in the so-called eye of the storm that followed Rita, the real storm, I was also privy to the behind the scenes that takes place trying to get back to an orderly run major Sea Port.

We had several Coast Guard officials that came aboard that morning, things also seemed to happen more rapidly after their arrival. Do P's and Q's come to mind, it did ours, whenever visitors come aboard your vessel it is time for professionalism to shine. Your actions are always a reflection of you and your crew, we made the company proud.

The presence of those uniforms also made you feel proud, with the dangerous jobs that are undertaken in the time of crisis situations. There were so many things going on around me, I thought I was on a merry-go-round. The local press reported on the real storm damage that had occurred in the Calcasieu River area and Lake Charles, while the national media covered other events, such as the pats on the back, and the blame game press conferences. After seeing the TV coverage, I can attest to the lack of an education that some of these supposed learned professional press people claim to have. Just from my John Q. Public observation, I think they should go to the disaster areas and report the news, instead of trying to make it.

Captain Robinson departed the *Hawk* after a large generator was supposed to be tied into their Port office facility. He thanked me for the hospitality that we had showed him for his two-day visit, I told him, "We were more than glad to do our part, come again when it's not such turbulent times." Several members of the Coast Guard hung out with us for the remainder of that day, at least until their trailers were set up for their temporary housing.

Later that same day Captain Robinson showed back up to spend the night aboard Motel *Hawk*; the power had yet to be hooked into their office, so A/C was nonexistent. The hurricane had caused devastating damage to their power grid, and since electricity runs air conditioners, it seemed more boarders were on the way. We were limited with the six bunks that we had aboard the *Hawk*, so when Albert DuPlantis who was also the manager for Seabulk Lake Charles showed up, he was put in the bunk that Captain Robinson's had been using, what else could I do. There was a fold out sofa that had been aboard the boat for years; Captain Robinson said he had slept on a lot worse, so he slept on it up in the wheelhouse, close to the radios. I was glad to be there for them, although the accommodations were cramped at times, all parties were appreciative.

Chef Albert treated us to some authentic Cajun cooking while he was there waiting on power to be restored at his house. He whipped us up some chicken and sausage gumbo the first night, pan-fried blackened fish with crawfish etouffée on white rice the second night. I thought if they don't get that channel open for shipping, we were all going to explode from the meals that were gracing our table from Albert's recipes.

I hadn't pulled any pranks on anyone in a while, so one night while several of us were watching Albert cook, one came to me. Scott was watching TV, so I told Little Bill, "Go ask Scott if we had any black beans," I then stepped into the pantry where we kept our canned goods. When he came into the galley to look, I heard him looking in the cabinets over the counters; I just hoped he didn't find a bag of dried black beans, all I needed him to do was open the pantry door so I could jump out at him.

He kept saying, "I know I saw some in here somewhere," I wanted to say, "Look in the pantry, they're in here with me." Finally, he flipped the pantry light on and opened the door having no idea what was about to happen, and just knowing his bean mission was coming to a close." When that door flung open, I came strolling out of there with my arms flailing around and saying, "I've already looked in there for black beans and can't find any."

Poor ole Scott came full astern backing away from me, then going into a defensive stance almost all the way across the galley. With him never expecting to see someone come bouncing out of the closed-door pantry, after he had composed himself from that little scare, he said, "You can bet I'll open that door very slowly from now on." We all had a good laugh at Scotts expense, one of them said, "You need to put that in your book," well here it is. I tried to keep up with the events as they happened during the latter writings of my book, these two hurricanes had given me enough material to finish it, or so I thought. Oh well, let's deal with some water problems.

With the extra showers that were taken with our newly acquired boarders, some city workers, and our normal crew, it was time to replenish our water tanks. Albert had lined up for us to take on water at the Talen's fuel dock, which was close to where the LNG docks were. That was where we had heard there was an enormous amount of debris in the water. After we had topped off with water we eased into the TMT slip about a quarter mile down stream, just to see what had floated in from the storm surge.

The reports were right, along with the six sunken boats and all. The dry foliage from the swamps were mixed in with everything from dead cows, furniture, trees of all sizes, wood from ripped apart houses, and hundreds of refrigerators. Worst of all, the thought of peoples belongings from a lifelong of accumulation, gone in a matter of hours. It was absolutely heart breaking to look at, knowing there were people that had lost everything they had in the world. You don't have to work aboard a tugboat to see what a big hurricane can do; you can however feel the aftermath within the Marine Industry, up close and personal.

A full seven days after Rita had turned the Port of Lake Charles upside down; Captain Robinson told us the channel had been cleared for thirty-five foot draft ships to transit. There was also smoke coming out of some of the refineries that were sorely needed to be up and running for the fuel products that they produced. The Port of Lake Charles refineries relied on the crude oil that were brought in by tankers, they were also needing the shipping channel open for deep draft vessels. Although Captain Robinson was back in the Port office running the operations in daylight, he still called the *Hawk* home at night. We were also kept up on the progress that was taking place in regards to the Port having ships to dock, my sole purpose of being there.

Floating debris in the TMT Basin at the LNG Docks
Author photo

Finally, on October 3, ten full days since our last job, we were sent out past Cameron to escort the LNG tanker *Berge Arzew* up the channel to their designated berth. Cameron was also the epicenter of hurricane Rita coming ashore, of which we had only seen on TV. Passing by out there was a real eye-opener, as it's been said before, TV can not show what actually being there, and seeing for yourself visually can do, that site will make an everlasting impression on me. The amount of debris that was suspected to have come from the Cameron area and the adjacent communities

Four working boats washed onto the Calcasieu River Banks
Author photo

was absolutely staggering to look at. It was a sad site knowing that literally days earlier there were seamen working on these boats, trying to make a living for their families. This particular strip of river was north of Cameron, and was really only the tip of the proverbial iceberg. We saw dozens of shrimp boats, large fishing boats, and even a small ship high and dry, some as far as a quarter-mile away from the water. Where houses and commercial buildings once stood, there was nothing but rubble and debris as far as you could see. We still had a job to do, and knew that the Maritime community would bounce back as it has many times before. After all, hurricanes are just a part of living on the Gulf Coast, and have been for centuries; you just hope and pray that one like the last two visitors never hits you.

The day went without incident, having helped this 908-foot long LNG tanker to the dock. Since there were so many of the navigational aids blown away, there had been a daylight transit only rule put in place, at least until sufficient buoys were put back on station at crucial points of the channel such as the turns. That meant we wouldn't sail this LNG tanker until crew change day Wednesday morning, two days later. That is exactly what happened, at 06:00 October 5 2005 we put a line up to sail this big girl from this recently storm torn part of the world.

We actually thought we would be escorting her to the jetties down past Cameron, but to our surprise, the *Hawk* was cut loose just past marker "88." We thought this is better for us, since we didn't have the three hour ride down, and then three hour ride back, we would be at the dock when our relief's got there. Does anyone see it coming; we all figured that since the office had an extra week to set things up, it would go off without a hitch.

Around noon, Doug talked to Scoot by cell phone, he said the confirmation number that he was given for a rental car was no good. He went to three other car rental businesses, and still no car was available to bring them to Lake Charles. Finally, at 13:00, a shuttle van was found to bring them to the boat and take us back to the airport in Houston. Scoot calls and tells me, "The driver said it was going to take four hours to get to Lake Charles, which would put them to the boat at 17:00."

That wouldn't be a problem, except our flight was departing at 19:05, I did the math and it didn't add up. So we had to come up with plan "C," "A" and "B" were already a bust. I asked Captain Maxey, one of the trainees, "Could you take us to Houston, then you could pick up Scoot and Frankie, and bring them back to the boat." He said, "No problem; that would simplify things, just clear it with Albert." Well, that little idea was shot out of the air, since they didn't want to leave the boat unattended, the engineer trainee would be there to watch the boat, so let's go I thought.

I had remembered that Captain Robinson told me if he could help us with anything just ask. Ask I did, I called him and relayed to him our dilemma, where he said, "I will be glad to take y'all, let me clear it with my boss." I then had to clear plan "D" with Albert, and Jeff Williams, who was Albert's boss in Port Arthur, Texas.

And all this finagling was just trying to get us to the airport for a 19:00 airplane ride. After this plan was finally okayed, I called Albert to come take us to the Port office to be ready when Captain Robinson was finished with his afternoon conference call. I knew it's hard to get on a tugboat, but I never knew it would be this tough getting off one.

The ride to Houston took almost three hours getting Doug, Scott, and me there about an hour before our flight time. I called Scoot to see when they had actually arrived to the boat; 16:40 was the magical time, which would have not given us enough time for the return trip. This little adventure wasn't over yet either, when we went to the Airtrans Airline counter to check in, the attendant told us that our plane was late, and would not get us to Atlanta for our connecting flight to Tampa. That flight was part of plan "A" too, so now, plan "E" was going to another airline to see if we could get a flight. Delta Airlines was the transportation savior of the day, for two of us any way.

After getting the okay from Dwayne Wheeler to change airlines, there was one catch, we would have to pay for the tickets ourselves. Doug was going to put all three tickets on his credit card for reimbursement later; it would be better that way. Doug and I had our ID's out for the purchase of the tickets, which everyone knows is mandatory. Poor ole Scott was searching frantically for a little bag that he carried his billfold in instead of his pants. He looked up at us, and said with a sad puppy dog look, "I think I left my bag in the back of Albert's truck," which was back in Lake Charles three hours away.

Doug and I looked at each other and turned to the counter attendant, we both said at the same time, "It appears we're only going to need two tickets, one of us ain't going to make this flight either." Scott called Albert and told him what he had done, he had no ID, no money, no credit card, and as soon as Doug and I had our tickets, no one to sit with. We both gave him a few dollars for sodas and eats, and bid him farewell. We left this puppy on the porch with his sad eyes, knowing we were about to catch the last flight to Tampa for the night. I suppose when events happen as they had since around noon, it had to end with laughter, it was about to.

As we went through the metal detectors, a man approached us and said, "The computer has randomly selected you two for a total screening, follow me." With me in my socks, we were led to an area where my laptop bag was searched, and a wand was scanned over my body, along with a body pat down. I was told to put my shoes on, and that everything was okay to proceed to the boarding area.

I hadn't noticed what one of the screeners was doing while I tied my shoelaces. Doug says, "You're not going to like this." When I looked up; the screener had his arm about half-way inside one of those gloves that's used in the artificial insemination of livestock. He says, "The first finger isn't bad, but that second one might get tight." I said, "Doouugg, don't leave me, get back here." That man says, "Hold on Buddy, it's a joke, I'm not really going to do it." He tells the other screener, "You should have seen the look on his face when he seen this glove." All I knew was that Doug could have got a refund on my ticket, it that cavity search had of been real, I was not flying Delta that night.

After I seen it was a joke, we all laughed, but at my expense this time, I thought this is one for the book. We made the flight to Atlanta on time, and even made the connecting flight to Tampa. The next day at my home I called the office to check on Scott's status, and was told he had caught a 08:00 flight home. I then asked Dwayne Wheeler if the company had done anything about replacement boats for the *Hawk* and *Condor* since those two boats would now be in the Lake Charles fleet.

He says, "No not yet," I replied to him, "Nothing ever changes does it Dwayne, it's Seabulk Procrastination Incorporated as usual?" The busiest seaport that Seabulk has harbor tugs working in was still having its tug fleet torn apart. I was also told that I would be on the tug Canaveral when I returned on my next duty day, I began my career on a single screw boat, seems I would end it on one too.

I had been on the boats long enough to see the many changes that had taken place within the past few years. You would expect to see progression within a company, instead of what was taking place in the Tampa Division. Although certain members of our management would reassure me that things were going as planned, I couldn't help but notice that our competition in the Tampa market was steadily replacing their tugs with newer and up to date tugboats.

I knew that at some point, like Carroll had done just a year earlier, I too would throw in the towel and retire. I had not turned fifty-five years old yet and really wanted to stay around for a few more years. I also knew that the longer I stayed working in the business that I loved so well for so many years; I'd miss the excitement of it once I had retired.

I made another trip back to Lake Charles, Louisiana for one last training session aboard the tug *Condor*. During the last days that I was there, some of the harbor pilots told me of how they appreciated me bringing the two *Hawk* class tugs there to Lake Charles. I told them, "I can guarantee I had nothing to do with it, if I had; they would still be in Tampa." I was still unsure of what tugboat that the company would have for me to operate when all the shuffling was done and over with.

The tug *Escambia* had been brought over from Mobile, Alabama as one of the big boats replacement. There was talk of leasing a boat as the other replacement, now that made a lot of since, send boats to another port, and then go out and lease a boat. Can someone turn on the light; I'm still in the dark on that move.

I prayed to God almighty as to what my next move should be. Not knowing what the future would bring after Seacor acquiring Seabulk, and with that company not being Union, I thought it best to go join Carroll in the ranks of retirement. Maybe it was time to take it easy for a while, and maybe even write a book about my little granddaughter Liliana, sounds good right.

Carroll's Retired and Things Just Ain't the Same

You will never know how much you miss someone that you have spent over twenty-eight years working with, until they retire and leave the workplace. With Carroll being the first Captain I had the privilege to work under, we had a lifetime of good times together. He was with me at the hospital the day that our twins were born. We probably spent more time on the job together than we did with our real families. Those were the times I would not trade with anyone, and really miss the most. We have kept in touch with each other since his retirement, where he has urged me to retire with him. He says to me, "I haven't been stressed the least little bit since I've left the boats," that's something I cannot say with any sincerity.

Carroll holding Liliana at Port Manatee-Author photo

After I had made Captain, we were not on the same boat, but had always been on the same shift. Running down the bay and getting a call from Carroll in the middle of the night seemed to always be like taking a vitamin, a little perk me up. As with any job, there are those times when things seem to just not be going right, or you didn't feel good. After we had talked for a few minutes, he could change my mood, that was another talent he had besides running a tugboat, both left the company when he did.

Sometimes we reflect back on some of the many events we've shared throughout the years, remembering well the ones that make the memories so cherished. Carroll went with me the day I went to Wauchula, Florida to pick up my 1939 Ford back in March of 1993. The next year after I had put hundreds of hours putting my first street rod together, it was the beginning of a ritual with us. We have spent every year since 1993 together in Daytona Beach for the Turkey Rod Run with our wives. The closeness of a true friend that can be counted on during hard times is something everyone should have.

Bill, Lois, Shelly, and Carroll
Author photo

**Carroll holding Gulf
Golden crabs**-Author photo

My wife and I have been to Pigeon Forge, Tennessee to spend some vacations with Carroll and his family, where there were more memories made. We also went on our first cruise together to Key West, and then to Cozumel, Mexico. When I do finally decide to retire, it'll be a sure bet that Carroll and I will be spending time together. I hope the events of the past few years don't prohibit us from sharing times like shown here on top of a mountain in Tennessee. We had both collected a lot of tugboat memorabilia throughout the years, and had even discussed maybe opening a restaurant or café to display it.

We also figured that since it would have a tugboat theme, we would serve meals like those that we had prepared on the tugs so many times before. We had seen many things come and go throughout the years; one that comes to mind was the two years that crab fishermen brought their catch into Port Manatee.

During the slower days we would get some crabs from these crabbers, and then have a feast with both crews chowing down on some of the most delicious crustaceans we had ever eaten, butter wasn't even needed. This was just one of the many times we shared, which made it a pleasure to work with Carroll, especially in the early years. I do believe the tugboats were the catalyst that brought Carroll and I together as seamen, but our lifelong friendship has been a gift from God, and I thank him for it from the very bottom of my heart.

When it's all said and done, Carroll was the first Captain to start teaching me how to run the tugs, and was an intricate part in helping me with the career that I chose to fill my life with. There were many other people that gave me guidance and help with the different decisions that I made throughout the years, and I thank them all for it. However, Carroll was just one of the people that I worked closest with, and is probably the one man I hated to see leave the company the most, Good Luck Zeke, I wish you all the best.

I hope you have enjoyed my first book, where I have shared a light on the world of tugboats, or at least the way mine was. I have enjoyed writing it and believe I'll start another one. There have been tugboats for well over a century doing all kinds of jobs, mainly doing ship assistance, of what they are best known for doing. The true mystiques they possess have long been alluring to all ages. Most of the years for me were enjoyable doing many different types of jobs, with some being easy, some were not. They are all dangerous if due care is not taken into consideration with safety being first.

Although, there were the accidents that I wrote about, safety is always first; I suppose that's why they're called accidents instead of on purposes. With so many stories to tell, there were many other events that I did not write about, but I did try to cover most things that were the most memorable, and were the real highlights of *My Lifetime on the Water*.

Glossary

This is just a small section of nautical words with the different terminologies used aboard tugboats that I have written about in this book. With literally hundreds of words used in the Marine Industry I just highlighted the ones used in the everyday workings, I probably missed a few, sorry.

- Bow–is the front of a boat
- Stern–is the back of a boat
- Port–is the left side
- Starboard–is the right side
- Fore–the forward section
- Aft–the back section
- A wheel is also known as a propeller, as is the wheel used to steer some of the older tugboats, the only similarity is that they are both round, but have different functions.
- The single-screw tugboats have one propeller for their propulsion.
- The twin-screw tugboats have two propellers, which creates more propulsion with better overall maneuverability.
- The original styles of Tractor tugs have their drive-units forward of midship, and work their lines off their stern.
- The stern drive Tractor tugs have their drive-units aft, and work their lines off their bow.
- The SDM is short for the "Ship Docking Module," a style of tugboat with a drive-unit on each end of the tugboat, eleven feet off their

centerline, they also work their line off the stern of the tug, actually facing backwards.

- The wheelhouse is where the vessels is operated from, and has all the pertinent equipment needed for navigating, winch controls, radar, radio communication, the total operation of any boat.

- The decks are the floors of a boat, whether inside or outside, the outside decks are usually painted with a non-skid material applied when a deck is freshly painted to prevent a seaman form slipping when wet with water.

Tug *Florida*-Author photo

- A hatch is the access door from the outside deck, usually with individual dawgs or a mechanism that makes it watertight.

- The porthole is a tugboats window, usually with four tightening dawgs, making them watertight also. They also come in various sizes and have the all familiar shape of a circle.

- The engine room is where all of the vessels machinery is usually installed, such as the main engines, generators, HPU's (Hydraulic Power Units, such as tow-winch engines), however, most are operated from the wheel-house and are maintained below deck.

- The keel is the bottom structure of a boat, and is the centerline of larger vessels.

- A bulk barrel is measured at 42 gallons per barrel.

- A DCV is known as a (Deepwater Construction Vessel) such as Heerema's *Baldor* and *Thialf,* which primarily works with offshore oilrigs.

- The letters LNG is short for (Liquefied Natural Gas).

- The letters SPM is short for (Single Point Mooring), also known as a (Mono Buoy), the type used in the Mexico operations.

- The letters OSV is short for (Offshore Support Vessel), which are the different type boats that work the offshore oilrigs.
- The bulwarks of a tugboat are like a short metal wall on the outboard side of the lower deck that acts as a safety-rail.
- The bitt is where a line is made fast to secure it, usually placed on the bow and stern, also with smaller bitts placed on the quarter positions of the tugs in the bulwarks.
- A towline is the line used in the towing of ships, barges, oilrigs, or anything on the water needing a tow. The larger tugboats tow from winches with wire cables.
- A beam-sea is the waves hitting a vessel from the side, and is the most uncomfortable seas to transit.
- A monkey-fist is a weighted ball made of a small line and metal, which is used in the transfer of lines from one vessel to another.
- A sea-buoy is the first buoy marking the safe entrance to the shipping channel into a seaport when coming from sea.
- A flood tide is the current with an inbound tidal flow.
- An ebb tide is the current with an outbound tidal flow.
- Slack water is referred to as the period of time that the tide is at the highest point, or the lowest point, before changing directional flow.